THE EVERYTHING
EASY MEXICAN
COOKBOOK

Dear Reader,

Of all the foods in the world, I truly believe Mexican cooking is the most exciting, and sometimes even the easiest. More than any other cooking style, Mexican cooking takes the wonderful ingredients of many different countries and puts them together in one meal. It is, in cooking terms, the true melting pot of the world.

In many ways, Mexican cooking symbolizes our shrinking world. There are few barriers. If you like it, and the ingredients are either grown in Mexico or can be obtained from one of the many different countries using Mexico as a stop on their trade routes, it's fair game to throw in the pot.

The result is sometimes very interesting. After all, where else can you mix hot peppers with mangoes or put cayenne pepper in your chocolate candy? What other culture would unabashedly combine Greek olives with Spanish wine and Mexican fruits? Where else would you put peanuts and lettuce in a holiday drink?

Mexican meals also have no pretensions. They are meals of necessity. You use what is on hand to make the most wonderful tastes you can make in no time flat. And then you enjoy what you have created, surrounded by your family and friends.

I hope these recipes provide the opportunity for you to experience the variety and unique tastes—but most importantly the excitement—that Mexican cooking has to offer.

Margaret Kaeter and Linda Larsen

Welcome to the EVERYTHING® Series!

These handy, accessible books give you all you need to tackle a difficult project, gain a new hobby, comprehend a fascinating topic, prepare for an exam, or even brush up on something you learned back in school but have since forgotten.

You can choose to read an Everything® book from cover to cover or just pick out the information you want from our four useful boxes: e-questions, e-facts, e-alerts, and e-ssentials.

We give you everything you need to know on the subject, but throw in a lot of fun stuff along the way, too.

We now have more than 400 Everything® books in print, spanning such wide-ranging categories as weddings, pregnancy, cooking, music instruction, foreign language, crafts, pets, New Age, and so much more. When you're done reading them all, you can finally say you know Everything®!

QUESTION
Answers to
common questions

FACT
Important snippets
of information

ALERT
Urgent
warnings

ESSENTIAL
Quick
handy tips

PUBLISHER Karen Cooper

MANAGING EDITOR, EVERYTHING® SERIES Lisa Laing

COPY CHIEF Casey Ebert

ASSISTANT PRODUCTION EDITOR Alex Guarco

ACQUISITIONS EDITOR Lisa Laing

ASSOCIATE DEVELOPMENT EDITOR Eileen Mullan

EVERYTHING® SERIES COVER DESIGNER Erin Alexander

Visit the entire Everything® series at www.everything.com

THE
EVERYTHING®
EASY MEXICAN
COOKBOOK

Margaret Kaeter and Linda Larsen

Aadamsmedia

Avon, Massachusetts

An Everything® Series Book.
Everything® and everything.com® are registered trademarks of F+W Media, Inc.

Published by
Adams Media, a division of F+W Media, Inc.
57 Littlefield Street, Avon, MA 02322. U.S.A.
www.adamsmedia.com

Contains material adapted and abridged from *The Everything® Mexican Cookbook* by Margaret Kaeter, copyright
© 2004 by F+W Media, Inc., ISBN 10:1-58062-967-9, ISBN 13: 978-1-58062-967-6; *The Everything® Tex-Mex Cookbook*
by Linda Larsen, copyright © 2006 by F+W Media, Inc., ISBN 10: 1-59337-580-8, ISBN 13: 978-1-59337-580-5.

ISBN 10: 1-4405-8716-7
ISBN 13: 978-1-4405-8716-0
eISBN 10: 1-4405-8717-5
eISBN 13: 978-1-4405-8717-7

Printed in the United States of America.

10 9 8 7 6 5 4 3 2 1

Library of Congress Cataloging-in-Publication Data
Kaeter, Margaret, author.
 The everything easy Mexican cookbook / Margaret Kaeter and Linda Larsen.
     pages cm. – (Everything series)
Includes index.
 ISBN 978-1-4405-8716-0 (pb) – ISBN 1-4405-8716-7 (pb) – ISBN 978-1-4405-8717-7 (ebook) – ISBN 1-4405-8717-5
(ebook)
1. Cooking, Mexican. I. Larsen, Linda. II. Title.
 TX716.M4K339 2015
 641.5972–dc23

                    2014038758

Many of the designations used by manufacturers and sellers to distinguish their products are claimed as
trademarks. Where those designations appear in this book and F+W Media, Inc. was aware of a trademark claim,
the designations have been printed with initial capital letters.

Always follow safety and commonsense cooking protocol while using kitchen utensils, operating ovens and
stoves, and handling uncooked food. If children are assisting in the preparation of any recipe, they should always
be supervised by an adult.

Cover images © StockFood/Maximilian Stock Ltd; © StockFood/Giblin, Sheri; © StockFood/Cooke, Colin;
© StockFood/Jon Edwards Photography. Interior images © iStockphoto.com.

This book is available at quantity discounts for bulk purchases.
For information, please call 1-800-289-0963.

Contents

Introduction

MEXICAN COOKING HAS A rich heritage that begins at the dawn of civilization. More than 7,000 years ago, at the same time the Aztec people were designing intricate calendar systems and building astounding pyramids, they also were holding festivals accompanied by flavorful dishes. Dine on lush tropical fruits, bean-stuffed chili peppers, spicy tomato sauces, grilled corn, honeyed sweet potatoes, and cocoa-crusted turkey, and you find yourself in the land of the Aztecs.

Yes, the ancient Mexican diet was both flavorful and varied. For centuries, Mexican cooking endured and even thrived on a rich array of fruits and vegetables, always accompanied by some type of beans, corn, and hot peppers. In fact, many of the foods we take for granted today were first used as food by the Aztec cultures. Turkey, mangoes, corn, pineapples, peanuts, beans, squash, avocados, cocoa, vanilla, chilies, and sweet potatoes, for example, were all common elements in Aztec dishes. Even foods we identify with European countries—such as Italy and tomatoes—were first cultivated by the Aztecs. But then came an even more exciting time for the Mexican table. When the Spanish conquistadors first landed in Mexico in the early 1500s, they brought with them a multitude of new foods. Most important were the animals that could provide milk and meat—cattle, pigs, sheep, and goats.

Don't forget the addition of rice to the Mexican diet. While the native peoples of Central America had cultivated corn for more than 7,000 years, they quickly adopted the versatile, white grain that had been introduced to Europe centuries earlier. Throw in a bit of European wine and you have the makings of modern Mexican cooking.

This merger of cooking styles has continued over the years. While many people usually credit the Spaniards with bringing foods to Mexico, they forget that the country is on the Pacific Rim. Polynesian and East Asian food also influenced Mexican cooking as trade routes grew. As a result, varied seafood dishes, spices, and flavorings such as soy sauce frequently pop up in Mexican dishes.

Still, the result is always uniquely Mexican. While the country adapted—and continues to adapt—to new ingredients, the people have never forgotten what makes their cooking unique. New fruits, vegetables, cheeses, red meats, fish, and poultry may be added to the diet as trade relations change and grocery stores gain greater variety, but the Mexican meal will always revolve around corn, beans, and chilies in at least one dish.

In fact, many of the dishes that were served to the first conquistadors are still served in the same style today. Tamales filled with beans, turkey, or fruit and cooked in open pit fires are mentioned in historical documents, along with drinks made with cornmeal and cocoa. Chili sauces, stuffed chilies, tomato moles, and eggs with mashed pinto beans were also served to the travelers of 500 years ago.

Mexican cooking is also known for its combinations. It's a rare dish that uses just one or two ingredients. Meats, for example, are marinated then drenched in sauces containing dozens of ingredients. Fish may be broiled or baked, but it is always topped with a unique sauce. Even something as simple as a salad of melon balls will have a tart sauce draped over it.

And, to the dismay of many a traveler, the ingredients often don't seem to make sense to anyone but a Mexican. A favorite candy, for example, combines sweetened milk, cocoa, pistachio nuts, and chili powder. Fruits will be marinated in vinegar with chili peppers. Beef steaks will be cooked with sweet fruits, and even drinks will contain cornmeal, peanuts, and chopped vegetables. Poultry will be marinated in a cocoa sauce.

Don't be dismayed by a list of ingredients you haven't heard of. While Mexican cooking may seem difficult and complicated, it is not. So get your taste buds ready, and have a great time in the kitchen cooking these fabulous Mexican recipes for your own family.

CHAPTER 1

Getting Started

For many people living north of Mexico, Mexican food has gotten a tainted reputation. Many people think that it has to be hot, that it must have tons of chili peppers in it, and that everything has to be slopped onto one plate so that the beans, red rice, and tortillas all mush together. And they also think that is has to be complicated, but that couldn't be farther from the truth. Mexican cooking is flavorful, easy, and fun.

Myths and Misconceptions

Unfortunately, overeager restaurateurs striving to bring some small bit of Mexican cuisine into our lives perpetuate some common misconceptions about Mexican food. In their efforts to create meals that appeal to a palate not accustomed to spicy foods, they have eliminated the subtle blending of flavors and the wonderful textures in Mexican meals.

Blend, Blend, Blend

Mexican cuisine has actually changed very little over the several thousand years that the country has been settled. Europeans brought new varieties of meats, vegetables, and cheeses, but the basic tenets of Mexican cooking are the same today as in the days of sun goddesses and tall pyramids.

Mexicans blend everything. There is absolutely no mixture of foods and spices they won't try. While Europeans and people in the United States tend to remain firm in their beliefs about what foods go together, Mexicans like to throw those ideas back at us. Separate flavors are good, but when they are combined, they create something so unusual, so mouthwateringly wonderful, that you just have to try adding another combination of ingredients. Marinate the steak in garlic and olive oil? Sure, but can't we add just a little oregano, a few peppers, and some green tomatoes?

At first, the tastes might seem odd, but you will quickly get used to the idea of appreciating the melded flavor as something new in and of itself. Don't ask, "What's in this sauce?" but instead appreciate it for the complete flavor that it offers.

ESSENTIAL

Never fill a blender more than halfway. Cover the top with a towel to prevent spills while blending. A combination of half liquids and half solids is the best mix. Begin blending by pulsing a few times to make sure the blades are clear. If something gets stuck in the blades, use a wooden spoon to loosen it. Never put your hand inside the blender.

Don't worry that you find mussels and lobster tidbits alongside pork hocks and chicken cubes. It's Mexican. Don't fret when you find chocolate in your meat sauce or wine in your eggs. It's Mexican. And don't cringe when you see specks of chili powder in your candy or peanuts and beets floating in your water. The blend of flavors is tantalizingly, uniquely Mexican.

As a result, you will quickly find that Mexican cooking uses just a few basic main ingredients—meat, beans, tortillas, and vegetables—but combines them in a multitude of different ways:

- **Soups:** These may be blended together or they can be European-style with larger chunks of meat.
- **Dry soups:** These are more like casseroles. They start with a soup consistency but use tortillas or white bread to soak up the ingredients.
- **Stews:** These are exactly like their European counterparts, mixing large chunks of meats, fruits, and vegetables.
- **Moles:** These slightly chunky, heavy gravies can be eaten as is or they can be used as stuffing for tamales. They can also be used as toppings for whole pieces of meat such as chicken breasts.
- **Salsas:** *Salsa* literally means "sauce" and can be used to describe anything from a watery salad dressing to a thick mixture of tomatoes, onions, and spices.

Common Spanish Cooking Terms

You'll find many terms in this cookbook, some that you've heard before, and probably some that you haven't. But don't worry. Just because you haven't heard it before doesn't mean it is a complicated ingredient. Here's a list of definitions to keep in mind as you cook:

- Verde: green, usually meaning the recipe uses green tomatoes or tomatillos
- Picadillo: shredded meat, vegetable, and/or fruit filling
- Salsa: sauce
- Relleno: stuffed
- Arroz: rice
- Pollo: chicken

- Nopale: cactus paddle
- Carne: meat, usually beef
- Raja: roasted chili strip
- Lomo: pork

You can also refer to the glossary (see Appendix) for more listings.

Tortillas

Of course, the more you blend your ingredients, the more you need something to put them in. Enter the tortilla. Be it rolled, folded, fried, baked, or soaked, it's still a tortilla.

History of the Tortilla

The corn tortilla is distinctly associated with Mexico. The ancient people of Mexico made tortillas by letting the corn kernels dry on the ears in the fields. The kernels were soaked in lime water until the skins could be rubbed off. The wet corn then was ground on a flat stone until it was a fine powder that could be used to make dough. The dough was made into thin patties, then baked over open fires.

Today, true Mexican food aficionados will still make their tortillas this way. However, the Mexican homemaker is more likely to buy masa harina, dehydrated masa flour. Although some people substitute cornmeal, masa harina is actually made from white corn, as opposed to the yellow corn more popular in the northern climates.

Healthy Tortillas

Health-conscious people have also altered the traditional Mexican tortilla. Today, it is just as common to use baked tortillas made from wheat flour as it is to use corn tortillas. Some people will also add ingredients such as tomatoes, spinach, or spices to the masa flour to create a more flavorful tortilla.

As with any culture's cuisine, Mexican food is always changing. Most Mexican cooks now use flour tortillas for some dishes and many are experimenting by adding spices or other flavors. Relax. If you like sun-dried tomato tortillas, it's OK. You will still be eating authentic Mexican cuisine. You won't be eating it in the style of ancient civilizations, but you will be eating it as the people of Mexico eat it today.

Chili Peppers

After the tortilla, probably the one food most often associated with Mexican cooking is the hot chili pepper. Unfortunately, most people assume this means that the dish must be hot, when the opposite is often true. The chili peppers are added for flavor and sometimes for spice, but even a large dish will often contain only a couple chili peppers, along with a similar amount of onion.

Capsaicin, the chemical combination that gives chili peppers their "heat," is the ingredient in many commercial cold medicines that is used to make people cough so that they don't stay congested. Peppers also contain vitamins C, A, and E, while being good sources of potassium and folic acid. Some people eat hot peppers to clear their sinuses when they have a cold.

In ancient times, the chilies were added partly to help preserve food, but also to add unique tastes to the ubiquitous turkey meat they ate. As a result, one common cooking technique is to change the type of chili peppers added to a sauce. By doing this, you can create a completely different dish.

And it's not hard to do. There are nearly seventy varieties of chilies, ranging in size from large peas to nearly a foot long. They come in every color from red, purple, and green to yellow. As a general rule, color has no effect on flavor, but size does: The smaller the chili, the hotter it tends to be.

If you don't like the spice chili peppers add to your foods, don't leave them out completely. Just add fewer. Or, instead of chopping the pepper into small pieces, add it whole and remove it before serving the meal. That will provide some of the flavor without adding any unwelcome bits to the dish.

Seven Chilies You Need to Know

1. **Jalapeños:** These chilies are very popular. Either red or green, they reach about three inches and have a medium heat.
2. **Poblanos:** These are dark green, medium-sized peppers that are often used for roasting or stuffing. They are relatively hot.
3. **Chiles de árbol:** These dried red chilies are long and thin with a papery skin. They are very hot.
4. **Chipotles:** These are dried, smoked red jalapeños. They are usually dark reddish brown and add a smoky flavor to dishes. They are relatively mild.
5. **Moritas:** These are a variety of dried, smoked jalapeños. They are small and brown with a spicy taste. They are not as smoky as chipotles but are hotter.
6. **Habaneros:** These are the hottest of the chilies. They are lantern-shaped and can be orange, red, or green.
7. **Serranos:** These are small, thin chilies that taste similar to jalapeños but are a little hotter. The red ones are a little sweeter than the green.

Spices

Mexican cooking uses a number of spices that are unique to the cuisine. However, it's more common to see a combination of more common spices working together with chili peppers to create the unique Mexican flavor. There is very little that you can't find in a well-stocked grocery store. And, if you really want to try a dish that calls for something unique, it's likely you can find it at a specialty store such as a food co-op.

Mexicans take their flavorings seriously. Many recipes call for you to roast the spices first. Some will have you using only fresh spices because the dried variety will either lose its flavor or create a totally different flavor. Some recipes will call for specific types of a spice, such as Mexican oregano or Mexican cinnamon. The tastes in most cases are not that different from the American versions, but they are noticeable. However, if you can't find the Mexican variety, don't worry. The food will still taste great.

Following are spices you should know how to obtain before you start any Mexican recipe:

1. **Cinnamon sticks:** Look for the rough-edged variety from Sri Lanka as opposed to the tightly wound variety used in the United States.
2. **Cilantro:** Also known as coriander, it has a unique, strong flavor. Fresh is always better-tasting, but dried can be substituted.
3. **Oregano:** More than a dozen different varieties grow in Mexico, and it's the most common spice in the Mexican kitchen. You will need both fresh and dried, as they are used in different ways.
4. **Cumin:** This lends a distinctly Mexican flavor to many dishes. Buy the seeds whole and grind them as needed. Some people add whole seeds to a dish to get a burst of flavor when they're bitten into.
5. **Epazote:** This herb's strong, bitter flavor can dominate any dish, and for this reason, it is the one herb most often used alone in Mexican cooking. It actually is treated as a weed in North America but can be hard to find in a grocery store. Use fresh whenever possible because it loses much of the flavor when dried.
6. **Anise:** This is used in many dishes. The leaves are used to wrap food in, but dried, ground anise can flavor anything from candy to stews.
7. **Cocoa:** This is not sweetened. The sweetened variety is never used, not even semisweet chocolate. Traditionally, Mexicans used ground cocoa beans.
8. **Cloves:** These are often used as part of a spice mixture for moles and sauces.
9. **Nutmeg:** This also is used as part of a spice mixture.
10. **Corn husks:** Dried corn husks are most often used to make tamales. They are first soaked in water. They are actually considered a spice because the flavor is transferred to the corn flour when steamed.
11. **Annatto seeds:** Also called achiote, these are the seeds from a tropical tree. They have a musky, earthy flavor. They are used as a commercial dye to add orange tints to cheeses and other foodstuffs.
12. **Tamarind:** This is a tough, brown seedpod that produces a sticky paste. It is the main ingredient in Worcestershire sauce.
13. **Chili powder:** There are as many different types of chili powder as there are chilies. Most are simply dried, ground versions of chili peppers, although some contain mixtures of different chili peppers It's best to experiment to find your favorite. Note that chili powder is usually added for its flavor, not to make the dish hotter-tasting.

Nuts

Nuts are used as both a spice and a thickening agent in many Mexican dishes. Among the most common you will find in Mexican recipes are:

1. **Pepitas:** pumpkin seeds
2. **Pistachios:** wrinkly, green nuts (Do not use the white- or red-dyed types.)
3. **Cashews:** use unsalted, freshly roasted when possible
4. **Peanuts:** skinless, unsalted are the best, if available

Beans

In ancient times, when the only source of meat protein came from turkeys, Mexicans turned to beans both for variety and to provide other proteins. As a result, beans were a staple of the Mexican diet long before the Spanish arrived. And they continue to be popular today.

Most people associate either black beans or the pinkish pinto beans with Mexican cooking. However, there are more than twenty different varieties of beans that are commonly used in Mexican dishes. A Mexican kitchen has as many different types of beans as the Italian kitchen has pasta shapes.

There is no one right bean for any recipe. In the countryside, the Mexican cook will have her own garden and plant the varieties her family likes. In the city, people will buy what they like or what the grocery store has in stock that day.

However, the various beans do taste different, so it's worth experimenting. The milk lima bean, for example, will give a totally different flavor to a refried bean dish than the heartier black bean. In the end, though, if you like it, that's all that counts.

No one really knows why the Mexicans started creating refried beans. Perhaps it was a way to make a quick dish out of their staple food. They could prepare the beans days and even weeks beforehand, then just recook them as needed.

Chances are you will want to make your refried beans fresh. Resist the urge to serve them right out of the pot, though. Letting them sit in the refrigerator for a day or two before mashing them with spices and reheating them lets the true flavor of the beans emerge.

Cheese

Cheese didn't exist in Mexico until the Spanish conquistadors brought milk animals to the land. In nearly 500 years, though, Mexican cooks have embraced both the flavor and nutrition in cheese by adding it to many of their dishes. They have also developed some of their own unique cheeses that have yet to be exported from the country in large amounts.

However, most Mexican cheeses have either a similar European counterpart or they don't play a crucial role in the dish. As a result, many Mexican cooks will substitute a common European cheese from time to time. Also remember that Mexican cooking is known for being able to adapt to the ingredients available. If you can't find an authentic cheese, don't be concerned. A transplanted Mexican would just use what was available!

Cheese Substitutes

Following are some of the common cheeses in Mexican recipes along with their European substitutes. Note that in this book we did the work for you and just list the substitute in the ingredients.

1. **Queso añejo:** This means "aged cheese." Parmesan and Romano are good substitutes.
2. **Queso panela:** This is a semisoft cheese that looks like mozzarella but does not melt well. Cottage cheese and ricotta are good substitutes.
3. **Queso fresco:** This means "fresh cheese." Fresh ricotta or a mild fresh goat cheese is a good substitute. Cottage cheese also works well.
4. **Queso manchego:** This is a semisoft cheese that melts easily. Monterey jack is usually substituted for it.
5. **Queso Chihuahua and queso menonita:** These are hard, aged cheeses that have a mild flavor. Mild or medium-sharp Cheddar is a good substitute. Colby also works well.
6. **Queso de bola, quesillo Oaxaca, and asadero:** These are made by cooking the curds and pulling them into long strings. Although they have a unique flavor, mozzarella is a good substitute.

Meats

Poultry, red meat, fish, and seafood are important ingredients in Mexican cooking, but they are more often on the receiving end of the spicy sauces. As a result, they don't get a great deal of attention in most Mexican recipes. In fact, a typical recipe will call for "carne," or simply beef. Even when making seafood meals, the authentic recipes usually don't specify what main ingredient to use.

FACT

As in most poor cultures, when red meat is used, the entire animal is used. As a result, tripe (intestines), heads, tongues, and hocks (feet) are common ingredients in many Mexican meat dishes. If you've never tried any of these food items, it's worth the venture. The unique textures and interesting flavors can be delightful, and they are rarely as unusual as you might expect.

Still, there are things to keep in mind. Mexico is a large exporter of beef, so it is readily available in Mexico. However, many people don't have refrigerators and beef is still relatively expensive. As a result, it is often reserved for special meals. Pork is more common than beef in daily meals, but lamb is actually the most common red meat. Poultry is still the protein of choice for most Mexicans.

ESSENTIAL

With a subtropical climate, there are no shortages of fresh vegetables and fruits in the Mexican diet. Perhaps the only truly unique item in this arena is cactus. Mexicans put nopales, or cactus paddles, in a number of different recipes, treating them almost as those in the United States treat string beans or broccoli. Nopales aren't difficult to cook, but, unless you live in the southwest, it can be very difficult to find fresh ones.

For people who live on the coasts, seafood is a common meal. Interestingly, it has as many variations as the red and white meats in terms of sauces and mixtures, but fish is actually grilled more often than meat. It's common to serve a grilled lobster tail with absolutely no sauce, while beef or pork is never served "naked."

It's important to know your fish when using it in cooked meals, especially the moles or picadillos. You need a fish that will keep its consistency, not turn rubbery, or, worse yet, disintegrate into the mix. Most recipes do well with bass or flounder. If you have a wide variety of fish available in your area, it's best to ask the fish seller how the fish holds up to long cooking before you try it.

While many people will substitute green or unripe tomatoes in recipes that call for tomatillos, the two are not the same. Tomatillos are actually a member of the gooseberry family. However, green tomatoes give a very similar flavor when substituted in cooked dishes.

Today, it's very easy to find fresh tropical fruits in even the northernmost grocery stores. It can take a little bit of time to learn how to peel or deseed these fruits, but it can be well worth the effort to gain a taste of the real thing. Canned fruits virtually never taste the same as the fresh variety.

Putting It All Together

Mexicans like to eat. In fact, they eat more meals than most of the rest of the world. If you're putting together a true Mexican feast, it might be fun to devote an entire day to the Mexican style of eating. Here's what you would do:

1. **Desayuno** is served early in the morning and usually consists of coffee with milk and tortillas.
2. **Almuerzo** is served in midmorning and includes eggs, beans, tortillas, chili sauce, and coffee.
3. **Comida** is served in midafternoon during the siesta period, when the sun is at its peak. Many businesses close so people can go home for this meal. It begins with appetizers and is followed by soup. The next course

is a dry soup, followed by fish or meat with a salad and vegetables. The dessert is a sweet or fruit.

4. **Merienda** is served in the early evening. It is usually a cup of hot chocolate or coffee with tortillas.

5. **Cena**, or supper, is served any time after 8 P.M. If comida was a large meal, this will be a light meal. However, if it is a fiesta, the meal will start as late as midnight and rarely before 10 P.M. In this case it might be served more as a buffet or, in the case of a formal gathering, it will have even more courses than the comida.

CHAPTER 2

The Basics

Tomato Salsa

This basic recipe can be altered to your taste by adding more and different chilies, or by adding beans and vegetables.

INGREDIENTS | SERVES 8

4 medium tomatoes
1 medium red onion
1 (4-ounce) can green chilies or 2 fresh green chilies
¼ cup fresh cilantro
1 small green or red bell pepper

What Makes a Salsa?

Salsa means "sauce." It can be hot, cold, chunky, or runny. Except when you use it as a dip, salsa is used as a topping for a dish or as a basic ingredient to complement the other ingredients in a recipe.

1. Dice the tomatoes into ¼" pieces. Remove the skin from the onion and cut into ¼" pieces.

2. If using fresh chilies, remove the stems and seeds and cut into ¼" pieces. Chop the cilantro into ¼" pieces.

3. Remove the stem and seeds from the bell pepper and chop the pepper into ¼" pieces.

4. Combine all the ingredients and let sit overnight in a covered container in the refrigerator.

Green Tomato Salsa

This is excellent served with tacos or as a dip for tostada chips.

INGREDIENTS | YIELDS ABOUT 2 CUPS

1 large white onion
2 habanero or jalapeño peppers
8 medium green tomatoes
1 bunch fresh cilantro
2 teaspoons salt
1 teaspoon ground black pepper

1. Remove the skin from the onion and chop into ¼" pieces. Remove the stems from the peppers and chop into ¼" pieces.

2. Remove the stems from the green tomatoes and place the tomatoes in a food processor or blender; blend on medium setting for 30 seconds.

3. Remove stems from the cilantro and roughly chop the leaves so the pieces are about ½" long.

4. Combine all the ingredients; mix well.

5. Refrigerate for at least 12 hours before using.

Chile con Queso

This is the perfect dip for tortilla chips. It also makes an excellent sauce to pour over enchiladas.

INGREDIENTS | SERVES 16

1 medium yellow onion
2 garlic cloves
5 chipotle chili peppers
2 jalapeño peppers
2 medium tomatoes
½ pound Monterey jack cheese
½ pound Colby cheese
2 tablespoons vegetable oil
1 cup sour cream

1. Remove the skin from onion and garlic; chop into ¼" pieces.

2. Remove the stems and seeds from the peppers; chop into ¼" pieces.

3. Chop the tomatoes into ¼" pieces. Grate the cheeses.

4. Heat the oil at medium temperature in a large skillet. Sauté the onion and garlic until tender, but not brown, about 8–10 minutes. Add the peppers and tomatoes; cook for 3 minutes, stirring constantly.

5. Turn the heat to medium-low. Add the cheeses to the pan and cook, stirring constantly, until the cheese melts. Stir in the sour cream.

Corn Tortillas

As tortillas are the basic ingredient in Mexican cooking, you may want to make large batches of these ahead of time and freeze them.

INGREDIENTS | MAKES 8–20

2 cups cornmeal or masa harina
1½ cups warm water
1 teaspoon salt

1. In a bowl, mix the ingredients to form a soft dough. The dough should not stick to your hands. If it is sticky, add cornmeal 1 teaspoon at a time until it doesn't stick any longer.

2. Divide the dough and roll it into balls about the size of golf balls.

3. Flatten the balls between 2 sheets of wax paper. If they stick, scrape them off, add more cornmeal, and start over. Flatten to about ¼" thick.

4. Place each tortilla separately in an ungreased frying pan and cook over medium heat until slightly brown, usually 1–2 minutes. Flip and cook on the other side until slightly brown.

Flour Tortillas

*For a different taste, grind up jalapeño peppers and
add them to the dough or use whole-wheat flour.*

INGREDIENTS | MAKES 8–20

2 cups flour
1 teaspoon salt
1 teaspoon baking soda
1 tablespoon lard or margarine
½ cup cold water

1. Preheat oven to 350°F.

2. Mix together all the ingredients well. If the dough sticks to your hands, add more flour, 1 teaspoon at a time, until it doesn't stick.

3. Divide the dough and roll into balls about the size of golf balls.

4. Flatten the balls between 2 sheets of wax paper. If they stick, scrape them off, add more flour, and start over. Flatten to about ¼" thick.

5. Place the tortillas on an ungreased baking sheet and bake in the oven for about 2 minutes. Flip and bake for 2 more minutes, or until lightly browned.

Refried Beans

Use refried beans instead of ground beef, pulled beef, or pulled chicken in any recipe.

INGREDIENTS | SERVES 8

2 cups dried pinto beans
8 cups water, divided
1 large white onion
½ cup lard
2 teaspoons salt
1 teaspoon ground black pepper

1. Soak the beans overnight in 4 cups water.

2. Drain off the water and rinse the beans. Bring 4 cups water to a boil in a medium saucepan. Add the beans and cover; boil for 5 minutes. Lower heat to medium and simmer for 2 hours.

3. Remove the skin from the onion and chop into ¼" pieces.

4. Melt the lard in a large frying pan over medium heat. Add the onion, salt, and pepper; sauté on medium heat for about 10 minutes or until the onion is tender.

5. Mash the beans with a potato masher. Add the mashed beans to the lard and onion; stir lightly to combine.

6. Cook on medium heat until the liquid evaporates, about 3–5 minutes.

Tostadas

For taco chips, simply break the tostadas into chip-sized pieces. For a unique taste, sprinkle with dry ranch dressing mix.

INGREDIENTS | MAKES 8

½ cup vegetable oil
8 (6") corn tortillas
½ teaspoon salt

1. Spread the oil evenly over the bottom of a large frying pan. Preheat to medium-high temperature.

2. Place the tortillas in hot oil, one at a time, and fry until crisp, about 30 seconds–1 minute. Flip the tortillas when one side is brown to ensure even cooking.

3. Sprinkle with salt while cooking.

4. Place on paper towels to drain.

Basic Picante Sauce

For a less spicy sauce, keep the jalapeño whole and remove it after simmering the mixture.

INGREDIENTS | YIELDS ABOUT 3 CUPS

1 large white onion
1 fresh jalapeño pepper or ¼ cup canned jalapeños
6 medium ripe tomatoes
6 tablespoons vegetable oil
1 teaspoon salt
¼ teaspoon granulated sugar
1 tablespoon fresh, crushed cilantro or 1 teaspoon dried cilantro

1. Remove the skin from the onion and chop into ¼" pieces.

2. Remove the stems from the jalapeño (if using fresh) and tomatoes and chop into ¼" pieces.

3. Preheat the oil to medium temperature in a large frying pan. Add the onion and sauté for about 10 minutes or until tender, but not brown.

4. Add the remaining ingredients. Turn heat to medium-low and simmer for about 10 minutes.

Red Rice

*Add some spice to this recipe by including ¼ cup of your
favorite hot peppers chopped into small pieces.*

INGREDIENTS | SERVES 8

3 cups water

1 cup short-grain white rice

2 medium red tomatoes

1 bunch fresh green onions or scallions

1 tablespoon vegetable oil

1 teaspoon salt

1 teaspoon ground black pepper

1. Bring the water to a boil in a medium saucepan. Add the rice, cover, and boil for 5 minutes. Reduce heat to medium-low and simmer for 15 minutes or until the rice is tender. Drain off remaining water from the rice.

2. Remove and discard the stems from the tomatoes. Place the tomatoes in a food processor and blend on medium setting for about 30 seconds.

3. Remove the skins from the onions and chop into ¼" pieces.

4. Heat the oil to medium-high in a large frying pan. Add all the ingredients; stir well. Cover and simmer for 10 minutes.

Chicken Stock

*Add almost any mix of meats and vegetables to this basic broth to make a
healthy, hearty soup. You also can substitute turkey for the chicken.*

INGREDIENTS | YIELDS 3 QUARTS

1 medium yellow onion

2 large carrots

2 celery ribs

2–3 pounds chicken bones

2 teaspoons salt

1 teaspoon ground black pepper

1 tablespoon dried parsley

1 gallon water

1. Remove the skin from the onion and chop into 1" pieces.

2. Clean the carrots and chop into ½" rounds. Chop the celery into 1" pieces.

3. Add all the ingredients to a large stockpot; bring to a boil. Reduce heat, cover, and let simmer for 3 hours.

4. Strain the broth and discard the vegetables and bones.

Guacamole

This is a wonderful topping for potatoes and meat dishes, as well as a popular dip for tostadas and raw vegetables.

INGREDIENTS | SERVES 8

2 large, ripe avocados
1 medium red tomato
1 small yellow onion
½ cup canned jalapeño peppers
1 tablespoon lime juice
1 teaspoon salt
½ teaspoon ground black pepper
Lime wedges

1. Cut the avocados in half lengthwise and pry out the pits. Remove the peels and cut the avocados into 1" pieces. Mash with a fork.

2. Cut the tomato into ½" pieces. Remove the skin from the onion and cut into ¼" pieces. Drain off the liquid from the jalapeño peppers and cut the peppers into ¼" pieces.

3. Combine all the ingredients; mix well. Garnish with lime wedges.

Shredded Beef

Shredded beef can be used in enchiladas, tacos, and many other dishes that call for either beef chunks or ground beef.

INGREDIENTS | YIELDS 4–5 POUNDS

2 garlic cloves
4 medium tomatoes
3 fresh jalapeño chili peppers
1 bunch fresh cilantro
1 bay leaf
4 pounds top sirloin
2 teaspoons salt
2 teaspoons ground black pepper
1 (8-ounce) bottle Italian salad dressing

1. Peel and mince the garlic. Cut the tomatoes into 1" pieces, reserving the juice. Remove the stems and seeds from the chili peppers. Remove the stems from the cilantro.

2. Place all the ingredients in a heavy pot. Cover and cook over medium heat for about 5 hours.

3. Remove the meat from the broth, let cool, and cut into 2" cubes. Shred with forks or in a food processor. Discard broth.

Green Chili Sauce

Use as a green sauce for tacos, enchiladas, or any other dish.

INGREDIENTS | YIELDS 2 CUPS

1 cup fresh green chilies (the type of your choice), roasted
1 cup canned tomatillos with juice
¼ cup fresh parsley
¼ cup chopped onion
1 garlic clove
¼ cup canned jalapeño peppers, drained
1 teaspoon salt
½ teaspoon ground black pepper
¼ cup olive oil

1. Remove the skin, stems, and seeds from the green chilies.

2. Combine the chilies, tomatillos with their juice, parsley, onion, garlic, jalapeños, salt, and pepper in a blender or food processor; purée.

3. Heat the oil in a medium-sized frying pan over medium heat. Add the sauce and cook for about 5 minutes, stirring constantly.

Red Chili Sauce

This is the classic enchilada or burrito sauce. It can also be made with other chilies.

INGREDIENTS | YIELDS 2½ CUPS

12 dried red ancho chilies
1 small white onion
3 garlic cloves
3 large red tomatoes
4 cups water
¼ teaspoon salt
1 teaspoon granulated sugar

1. Preheat oven to 250°F. Toast chilies on a baking sheet in the oven for 8 minutes. Transfer the chilies to a bowl filled with cold water. Remove the stems and seeds.

2. Peel the onion and chop into ¼" pieces. Peel the garlic cloves. Chop the tomatoes into ¼" pieces.

3. Combine all the ingredients in a medium pot. Cover and simmer on medium heat for 30 minutes. Every 5 minutes, remove the cover and push the chilies back down into the liquid.

4. Add mixture to blender; purée. Strain to remove the skins.

5. Add mixture to a frying pan and heat on medium, simmering for 5 minutes.

Spicy Chicken

Spicy Chicken can be used in enchiladas, tacos, and many other dishes that call for either beef chunks or ground beef.

INGREDIENTS | YIELDS 4–5 POUNDS

2 garlic cloves

4 medium tomatoes

3 fresh jalapeño chili peppers

1 bunch fresh cilantro

1 bay leaf

2 teaspoons salt

2 teaspoons ground black pepper

1 (8-ounce) bottle Italian salad dressing

1 fryer chicken (about 2½ pounds)

1. Peel and mince the garlic. Cut the tomatoes into 1" pieces, reserving the juice. Remove the stems and seeds from the chili peppers. Remove the stems from the cilantro.

2. Combine all the ingredients in a heavy pot. Cover and cook over medium heat for about 5 hours.

3. Remove the meat from the broth and let cool. Remove and discard the skin and bones, and shred the meat with forks or in a food processor. Discard the broth.

What Makes a Pepper Hot?

The heat of a chili pepper is caused by the presence of a volatile oil called capsaicin, which can burn the skin and eyes. As a result, if you are handling a lot of chilies, such as picking them fresh from your garden, it's important to wear rubber gloves. Always wash your hands with lots of soap after handling even a small amount of chili pepper.

Plain Tamales

Plain tamales are a nice addition to any Mexican feast.

Substitution for Corn Husks

You can substitute parchment paper for the corn husks when you're making tamales, especially these plain ones. Cut the paper into 4" × 8" rectangles and spread the dough to within 1" of the edges. Fold the sides in toward the middle so they touch, fold the top down and the bottom up, tie with string, and steam until the paper comes away from the dough.

1. Cover corn husks with hot water and set aside to let soak. In large bowl, combine lard, sour cream, and water and beat on medium speed until light and fluffy.

2. Add masa harina, salt, and cayenne pepper and beat well. Add chicken broth as necessary to make the mixture spongy and fluffy (dough dropped into cold water should float).

3. Drain husks and spread tamale dough on husks to within 1" of edges. Fold sides of husks to the middle so edges meet, then fold up bottom and fold down top to enclose filling. Tie with kitchen string. Place in single layer in steaming basket, and steam over simmering water for 1 hour.

CHAPTER 3

Salsas

Citrus Salsa

For a change of taste, substitute orange juice for the lemon and lime juices.

INGREDIENTS | SERVES 12

2 large ripe tomatoes
1 medium white onion
3 garlic cloves
1 fresh or canned jalapeño pepper
¼ teaspoon fresh cilantro or ⅛ teaspoon dried cilantro
¼ cup lime juice
1 teaspoon lemon juice
1 tablespoon dry white cooking wine
1 teaspoon chili powder
½ teaspoon ground black pepper

1. Cut the tomatoes into ¼" pieces. Remove the skins from the onion and garlic, and mince. Remove the stem and seeds from the pepper and cut into ¼" pieces. Chop the cilantro into ⅛" pieces.

2. Combine all the ingredients in a medium-sized mixing bowl; stir until well mixed.

3. Cover and refrigerate overnight. Let stand at room temperature for 1 hour before serving.

Roasted Red Pepper Salsa

While salsas are always delicious with tortilla chips, try something different and serve dollops of salsa on toasted French bread or use garlic bagel chips for dipping.

INGREDIENTS | SERVES 12

2 large red bell peppers
12 scallions
3 tablespoons fresh cilantro
¼ cup black olives
⅓ cup grated Parmesan cheese
¼ cup olive oil
4 tablespoons lime juice
½ teaspoon salt
½ teaspoon ground black pepper

1. Preheat oven to 350°F.

2. Remove the cores and seeds from the red peppers. Slice into 1–2"-wide strips. Coat the insides with olive oil and bake for 1 hour or until lightly brown. Let cool, then chop into ¼" pieces.

3. Remove the skin from the scallions and discard all but 2" of the white and light-green part; chop into ¼" pieces. Chop the cilantro into ⅛" pieces. Remove the pits from the olives and slice into ¼" pieces.

4. Combine all the ingredients in a medium-sized mixing bowl. Cover and refrigerate for 12 hours. Let stand until mixture reaches room temperature before serving.

Pineapple, Mango, and Cucumber Salsa

Serve with Grilled Swordfish (see recipe in Chapter 10).

INGREDIENTS | SERVES 8

½ cup fresh pineapple
½ cup fresh mango
½ cup cucumber
⅓ cup red bell pepper
1 medium tomato
3 tablespoons green onions
1 fresh jalapeño chili pepper
3 tablespoons fresh cilantro
½ teaspoon salt

Green Onions and Scallions

Scallions are small, yellowish onions that have a relatively mild flavor. Green onions are elongated, white onions that grow no bigger than your index finger. It's common to eat the stems of green onions as you would chives.

1. Remove the top, core, and rind from the pineapple; cut the fruit into ½" pieces. Remove the skin and seeds from the mango; cut the fruit into ½" pieces. Peel the cucumber and cut into ½" pieces. Cut the tomato into ½" pieces. Reserve the juice from the pineapple, mango, cucumber, and tomato.

2. Remove the roots and cut the green onions into ½" pieces. Remove the stem and seeds from the red bell pepper and cut into ½" pieces. Remove the stem from the jalapeño and cut into ½" pieces. Remove the stems from the cilantro and cut the leaves into ½" pieces.

3. Combine all the ingredients, including the reserved juices; mix well.

4. Refrigerate for at least 4 hours before serving.

Cucumber and Lime Salsa

This is a wonderful salsa to serve with chicken or veal because its light flavors don't overpower the meat.

INGREDIENTS | YIELDS 2 CUPS

2 medium cucumbers
2 key limes
1 garlic clove
1 medium white onion
2 sprigs parsley
¼ cup lime juice
1 teaspoon salt
1 teaspoon granulated sugar
½ teaspoon ground black pepper

1. Peel the cucumbers and cut into ½" cubes. Peel the key limes and cut into ½" cubes. Peel and mince the garlic. Peel the onion and cut into ¼" pieces. Chop the parsley into ¼" pieces.

2. Combine all the ingredients in a medium-sized mixing bowl. Cover and refrigerate for 3–4 hours before using.

Dried Fruit Salsa

This makes an excellent sauce for chicken, but it also works well as a dessert when put into warm Flour Tortillas (see recipe in Chapter 2).

INGREDIENTS | YIELDS 2 CUPS

¼ cup golden raisins
¼ cup dried apples
¼ cup prunes
¼ cup dried apricots
¼ cup dried pears
¼ cup dried peaches
¼ cup pecans
1 small green onion
1 cup dry white wine

1. Cut all the fruits into ¼" pieces. Chop the pecans into ¼" pieces. Peel the green onion and remove the roots; chop the onion and stem into ¼" pieces.

2. Combine all the ingredients in a mixing bowl. Mix well so the wine covers everything.

3. Cover and refrigerate for 8–10 hours before serving.

Green Almond Salsa

This makes an excellent tostada chip dip, but also can be used as a sauce when cooking chicken or pork.

INGREDIENTS | YIELDS 1–1½ CUPS

3 tablespoons olive oil, divided

1 slice white bread

1 cup blanched almond slivers

3 green tomatoes

½ cup canned green serrano chilies (canned jalapeños can be substituted)

3 garlic cloves

½ cup fresh cilantro

½ cup diced fresh green bell pepper

½ teaspoon dried coriander seeds

½ teaspoon salt

½ teaspoon ground black pepper

What's Hot

The hottest parts of a chili pepper are the seeds and the pith, the fleshy interior that attaches to the seeds. The flesh contains less heat than the interior of the chili. Although chilies can be red, yellow, or green, the color is not an indication of how hot they are.

1. Heat 2 tablespoons of the olive oil in a frying pan on medium-high heat and fry the bread on both sides until it is medium brown, about 2–3 minutes. Set on paper towels to soak up the remaining oil. When the bread is dry and cool, chop it into ¼" pieces.

2. Add the remaining olive oil and the almond slivers to the frying pan. Reduce the heat to medium and sauté the almonds until they are medium brown. Drain off the grease.

3. Cut the tomatoes into quarters. Drain the chilies. Remove the skin from the garlic and cut each clove into quarters. Remove the stems from the cilantro.

4. Add all the ingredients to a blender or food processor. Blend on medium speed until all the ingredients are well melded. Small pieces may remain.

5. Pour the mixture into a medium-sized saucepan and simmer on low heat for 10 minutes.

6. Refrigerate for at least 4 hours before serving.

Chipotle Salsa

Use this as a unique enchilada or taco sauce. It also makes an excellent marinade for pork chops.

INGREDIENTS | YIELDS 2 CUPS

6 chipotle chili peppers
½ cup water
1 medium yellow onion
3 medium red tomatoes
3 garlic cloves
2 tablespoons olive oil
½ teaspoon dried oregano
½ teaspoon salt
½ teaspoon pepper
½ teaspoon granulated sugar
1 tablespoon lime juice

How to Ripen Tomatoes

Most tomatoes you buy at the store are not ripe. To ripen tomatoes, set them on a sunny windowsill until they give slightly when lightly pressed. Do not store tomatoes in the refrigerator, as their texture will quickly become soft and mealy.

1. Remove the stems from the chili peppers and place them in a small saucepan with the water. Turn the temperature to low and simmer for 15 minutes or until the chili peppers are puffy. Drain off the water and chop the chilies into ¼" pieces.

2. Peel the onion and chop into ¼" pieces. Cut the tomatoes into ¼" pieces. Peel and mince the garlic.

3. Heat the olive oil in a medium-sized frying pan at medium heat. Add the onion, garlic, and chili peppers. Sauté until the onion is clear and limp, not brown, about 4–6 minutes. Drain off excess olive oil.

4. Add the tomatoes, oregano, salt, pepper, and sugar to the frying pan; stir well. Cover and simmer on low heat for 20 minutes.

5. Remove from heat and let cool. Stir in the lime juice. Refrigerate for at least 4 hours before serving.

Crimson Prickly Pear Sauce

This is excellent as a basting sauce for swordfish or tuna steaks.

INGREDIENTS | YIELDS 2 CUPS

16 fresh prickly pears (avoid those with yellow-gray green rinds)

½ cup granulated sugar

1 tablespoon lime juice

1 tablespoon orange liqueur

What's a Prickly Pear?

This egg-shaped fruit comes from the same prickly-pear cactus that gives us the cactus paddles used as a vegetable. The flesh is very watery and tastes a bit like watermelon and strawberries, although one variety (with yellow-gray green rinds) tastes very sour. When ripe, the rind yields slightly to the touch.

1. Remove the rind from the prickly pears by cutting off both ends and running a slice down both sides. If ripe, the rind will pull off easily.

2. Chop the prickly pear fruit into approximately 1" pieces and place in a blender. Blend on medium-high until you have a purée. Strain through cheesecloth or a fine-meshed strainer. Reserve both the juice and purée. Remove the seeds from the purée.

3. Put 2 cups of the prickly pear juice in a medium-sized saucepan with the sugar. Cook over medium heat until the mixture is reduced by half.

4. Remove from heat. Add 1 cup of puréed prickly pear, the lime juice, and orange liqueur; stir well.

5. Refrigerate for at least 4 hours before serving.

Roasted Morita Cream Sauce

Serve warm over potatoes or fresh vegetables.

INGREDIENTS | MAKES 2 CUPS

½ cup whipping cream
½ cup plain yogurt
2 fresh morita chilies
1 cup whole milk
2 tablespoons olive oil
1½ tablespoons flour

1. Make thick cream by pouring the whipping cream into a small saucepan and cooking it on low heat until it is lukewarm. (It must not go above 100°F.)

2. Remove from heat and stir in the yogurt. Pour into a clear glass jar and cover with a loose cap or clear plastic food wrap. Place in a warm place (80°F to 90°F), such as the top of the refrigerator.

3. Let the cream develop for 12–24 hours. Stir gently and chill for 4–8 hours.

4. Remove the stems and seeds from the chilies and cut into 1" pieces.

5. Put the chilies and milk in a food processor or blender and blend on medium setting until smooth.

6. Heat the milk and chili mixture in a medium-sized saucepan over medium-low heat.

7. In another saucepan, blend the olive oil and flour. Cook over medium heat, stirring constantly for 2–3 minutes. After about 3 minutes, begin gently whisking in the heated milk and chili mixture. Continue to cook and stir until smooth and thickened.

8. Whisk in the thick cream.

Pumpkin Seed Salsa

This sauce can be used like this for dipping, or you can add 2 more cups of chicken broth and use it as a sauce when baking chicken.

INGREDIENTS | MAKES 2 CUPS

1 cup hulled pepitas (pumpkin seeds)
1 small white onion
2 garlic cloves
½ cup fresh cilantro leaves
2 large radish leaves
3 small romaine lettuce leaves
3 serrano chilies
1½ cups chicken broth
1 tablespoon olive oil

Roasting Nuts

Roasting nuts must be done slowly or else the nuts will taste bitter. After you have roasted any nuts, pick out those that have dark brown or even black places. If roasting them to eat, add a tablespoon of sugar to each cup of nuts to make your own pralines.

1. Place the pumpkin seeds in a large skillet over medium heat. Spread out the pumpkin seeds and toast them, stirring regularly, until nearly all have popped and turned golden. Spread on a plate to cool.

2. Peel the onion and cut into quarters. Peel the garlic. Remove the stems from the cilantro, radish, and romaine leaves. Tear the leaves into 2" pieces. Remove the stems and seeds from the serrano chilies and chop into 1" pieces.

3. Put all the ingredients except the olive oil in a blender or food processor. Blend on medium setting until you have a smooth purée.

4. Pour the olive oil into a large frying pan. Add the purée. Cook on medium setting, stirring constantly, until the sauce is very thick.

Jicama Salsa

This makes an excellent condiment for grilled fish or chicken.

INGREDIENTS | YIELDS 2 CUPS

1 medium carrot

1 small zucchini

4 fresh radishes

1 medium white onion

4 garlic cloves

2 tablespoons fresh cilantro leaves

1 medium jicama (about 2 pounds)

½ cup chopped fresh green beans

1 chipotle chili pepper

1 cup boiling water

1 teaspoon dried oregano

½ cup white vinegar

½ cup water

½ cup olive oil

1 tablespoon lime juice

A Word about Oregano

Oregano is one of the most common herbs found in the Mexican kitchen. It comes in many different varieties, although we usually see just one fresh variety in the United States. Unlike many spices, dried oregano is used by Mexicans even when fresh is available.

1. Peel the carrot and zucchini, and dice into ¼" pieces. Snap off the ends of the green beans and cut into ¼" pieces. Remove the roots and tops from the radishes and cut into ¼" pieces. Peel the onion and cut into ¼" pieces. Peel and mince the garlic. Remove the stems from the cilantro and dice the leaves finely. Remove the skin from the jicama and dice into ¼" pieces.

2. Place the carrot, zucchini, green beans, radishes, and chili pepper in a small pot containing the boiling water. Cook for 2–3 minutes, then drain. Remove the stem and seeds from the chili pepper; chop the pepper into ¼" pieces.

3. Mix together all the ingredients in a large mixing bowl. Cover and refrigerate for 4 hours.

4. Let warm to room temperature before serving.

Pear-Ginger Salsa

Use this delicious recipe as a sauce for chicken or other poultry dishes.

INGREDIENTS | MAKES 2 CUPS

1½ cups canned pears
½ red bell pepper
2 scallions
⅓ cup golden raisins
2 teaspoons fresh grated gingerroot
1 tablespoon canned jalapeño peppers
1 tablespoon white wine vinegar
1 teaspoon salt

1. Drain off the juice from the pears and cut into ¼" pieces. Remove the stem and seeds from the red bell pepper and cut into ¼" pieces. Remove the skins, roots, and stems from the scallions and mince. Mince the gingerroot. Drain off the juice from the jalapeño peppers and mince.

2. Combine all the ingredients in a medium-sized mixing bowl.

3. Cover and refrigerate for 8–12 hours.

Jalapeño Jelly

This is excellent served with lamb chops or simply spooned over a chunk of cream cheese on crackers as an appetizer.

INGREDIENTS | YIELDS 3 PINTS

6 fresh jalapeños
5½ cups granulated sugar
1½ cups cider vinegar
2 tablespoons fresh lemon juice
1 bottle pectin
Green food coloring

1. Remove the stems and seeds from the jalapeños and cut into ¼" pieces.

2. Combine the jalapeños, sugar, cider vinegar, and lemon juice in a large pot over medium-high heat; bring to a boil. Boil for 5 minutes, stirring occasionally.

3. Stir in the pectin and boil for 1 minute. Remove from heat and stir in 8 drops of green food coloring.

4. Pour into sterilized jars, seal, and place in a hot water bath for 5 minutes.

Garlic Salsa

*This is an excellent substitute for tomato salsa or even picante sauce,
especially for people who prefer lots of garlic in their recipes.*

INGREDIENTS | YIELDS 2 CUPS

20 garlic cloves
1 small white onion
2 medium red tomatoes
1 fresh serrano pepper
3 lemons
½ cup fresh parsley leaves
½ teaspoon salt
½ teaspoon ground black pepper
½ teaspoon paprika
1 tablespoon dried oregano
½ cup olive oil

1. Peel and mince the garlic and onion. Cut the tomatoes into ¼" pieces. Remove the stem and seeds from the serrano and cut into ¼" pieces. Juice the lemons. Mince the parsley leaves.

2. Combine all the ingredients; mix well.

3. Cover and refrigerate for 8–12 hours before using.

Pico de Gallo

Use as a sauce for tacos or as a side for your favorite meat dish.

INGREDIENTS | SERVES 4

1 medium jicama
1 large orange
1 small yellow onion
1 tablespoon lemon juice
1 teaspoon salt
1 teaspoon medium-hot red chili powder
½ teaspoon dried oregano

1. Wash, peel, and chop the jicama into ½" chunks. Peel and section the orange, reserving the juice. Peel the onion and cut into ⅛" pieces.

2. Combine the orange and jicama in a medium-sized bowl. Pour the orange juice over the mixture. Add the onion, lemon juice, and salt. Stir until evenly mixed.

3. Cover and refrigerate for at least 1 hour before serving.

4. Sprinkle with chili powder and oregano before serving.

Adobo Sauce

This is typically served over meat. If making a pork or beef dish, reserve some of the stock and replace the chicken broth with that.

INGREDIENTS | YIELDS 2½ CUPS

6 dried ancho chilies
1 large white onion
2 garlic cloves
1 cup canned tomatoes
½ teaspoon dried oregano
½ teaspoon ground cumin
2 tablespoons vegetable oil
1½ cups chicken broth
1 teaspoon salt
½ teaspoon ground black pepper

1. Remove the stems from the chilies and chop the chilies into ¼" pieces. Peel the onion and chop into ¼" pieces. Peel and mince the garlic. Drain the tomatoes.

2. Combine the chilies, onion, garlic, tomatoes, oregano, and cumin in a blender or food processor; blend to a thick purée.

3. Heat the oil in a medium-sized skillet to medium heat. Add the purée and cook for about 5 minutes. Stir in the broth, salt, and pepper, and then serve.

Nogada Sauce

Heat and serve over anything from pork chops to cheese-stuffed jalapeño peppers.

INGREDIENTS | YIELDS 1¼ CUPS

1 garlic clove
1 cup walnuts
5 peppercorns
¼ cup bread crumbs
2 tablespoons cider vinegar
2 tablespoons granulated sugar
½ teapsoon salt
6 tablespoons water

1. Peel the garlic.

2. Add the walnuts, garlic, peppercorns, and bread crumbs to a food processor or blender. Blend until finely ground.

3. Add the vinegar to the mixture; stir well. Stir in the sugar and salt. Add just enough water to make a thick sauce.

Mole Poblano

Use as a sauce for poultry or red meat. Use as a filling for tortillas or tamales by adding 3 cups of chopped, precooked chicken, beef, or turkey to the sauce and warming it thoroughly.

INGREDIENTS | SERVES 8

6 dried ancho chilies
1 large onion
1 garlic clove
1 (6") corn tortilla
2 cups canned tomatoes, with juice
½ cup salted peanuts
⅓ cup raisins
2 tablespoons sesame seeds
¼ cup oil
1 tablespoon granulated sugar
¼ teaspoon anise seeds
¼ teaspoon ground cinnamon
¼ teaspoon ground cloves
¼ teaspoon ground coriander seeds
¼ teaspoon ground cumin
1 cup chicken broth
1 ounce unsweetened chocolate
1 teaspoon salt
1 teaspoon ground black pepper

1. Remove the stems and seeds from the chilies. Peel and quarter the onion and garlic. Tear the tortilla into 1" pieces.

2. Combine the chilies, onion, garlic, tortilla, tomatoes with their juice, peanuts, raisins, and sesame seeds in a blender. Blend on medium speed until you have a thick purée.

3. Heat the oil to medium temperature in a large frying pan. Add the purée and cook, stirring constantly, for about 5 minutes. Stir in the sugar, anise, cinnamon, cloves, coriander, cumin, and broth; bring to a boil. Reduce heat to low and simmer uncovered for 10 minutes.

4. Add the chocolate and continue simmering, stirring constantly, until the chocolate melts and blends into the sauce. Add the salt and pepper.

Mole Poblano

Legend has it that the nuns of Santa Rosa received a surprise visit from their arch-bishop in the late 1500s. They had little time to prepare dinner for such an esteemed guest, so they added everything in their kitchen to their mole sauce. Today, this is one of the most famous—and most used—sauces in Mexican cooking.

CHAPTER 4

Appetizers

Brie and Papaya Quesadillas

Serve as an appetizer with Guacamole (see recipe in Chapter 2), sour cream, and Pico de Gallo (see recipe in Chapter 3). Or add some spicy chicken to the quesadillas to create an easy, one-dish meal.

INGREDIENTS | SERVES 6

½ medium yellow onion
2 large red chili peppers
1 ripe papaya
1 pound brie
½ cup water
12 (10") flour tortillas
4 tablespoons butter
4 tablespoons oil

1. Remove the peel from the onion and cut into ¼"-thick slices. Remove the stems from the chilies and dice the chilies into pieces about ⅛" square. Peel and deseed the papaya; dice into pieces about ⅛" square. Cut the brie into ¼" strips.

2. Heat the water on high in a medium-sized skillet until boiling. Remove from heat and add the onion; let stand for 10–15 minutes. Drain and set aside.

3. Warm the tortillas by placing them in the oven for 10 minutes at 250°F. Melt the butter in a small saucepan over low heat. Add the oil to the butter and stir until mixed. Remove the tortillas from the oven but leave the oven at 250°F.

4. Place a few strips of cheese on each tortilla. Add several onion slices, ¼ teaspoon of diced chili peppers, and 1 tablespoon of diced papaya. Add another tortilla to make a sandwich, then brush the top tortilla with the butter and oil mixture.

5. Place the quesadillas 1 at a time in a large skillet on medium heat. Brown both sides. Place the quesadillas on a baking sheet in the oven to keep warm while the others are being made.

6. Cut each quesadilla into 6 triangular wedges to serve.

Fried Plantains

If you can't find plantains, try this same technique with bananas. Use bananas that are just starting to ripen, as they hold up better during the cooking process.

INGREDIENTS | SERVES 4

12 plantains
¼ cup vegetable oil
¼ cup ground horseradish
½ teaspoon salt
¼ cup sour cream
¼ cup brown sugar
¼ cup honey

1. Remove the skins from the plantains and cut into 2" lengths. Using a heavy spatula, press down on each piece until it is ¼"–½" thick.

2. Pour the oil into a medium-sized skillet and turn to medium heat. Fry the plantain patties until they are lightly browned on each side.

3. Make a sauce by combining the horseradish, salt, and sour cream. Make another sauce by combining the brown sugar and honey. Use the sauces for dipping the hot plantain patties.

Spinach con Queso

Serve with broken, warm Tostadas (see recipe in Chapter 2) for dipping.

INGREDIENTS | SERVES 8

1 (10-ounce) package frozen, chopped spinach
1 small white onion
1 medium red tomato
1 pound Velveeta cheese with jalapeños
½ cup whole milk
1 (2-ounce) jar diced pimientos

1. Thaw the spinach and squeeze the water from it until the spinach is as dry as possible.

2. Remove skin from the onion and chop into ¼" pieces. Chop the tomato into ¼" pieces.

3. Combine the onion, cheese, milk, and pimientos in a medium-sized pot over low heat (or in a slow cooker set on the lowest temperature setting). Cook, stirring periodically, until the cheese melts. Stir in the spinach and tomato.

Queso Fundido

This is another recipe that is perfect for serving with warm Tostadas (see recipe in Chapter 2).

INGREDIENTS | SERVES 8

½ pound Cheddar cheese
½ pound Monterey jack cheese
3 medium eggs
½ cup salsa

1. Preheat oven to 350°F.

2. Grate the cheeses. Mix together and place in a large baking dish.

3. Beat together the eggs and salsa; pour over the cheeses.

4. Bake for 30 minutes.

Cauliflower Tortas

Serve with an assortment of salsas for a colorful snack.

INGREDIENTS | SERVES 8

1 head cauliflower
2 large eggs
2 tablespoons flour
1 teaspoon salt
½ teaspoon ground black pepper
4 cups vegetable oil

1. Rinse the cauliflower, remove the outer leaves, and separate into florets. Cook in boiling water until almost tender, about 8–10 minutes. Drain.

2. Separate the eggs. Beat the egg whites until they form rounded peaks. Beat the egg yolks until smooth. Pour the yolks into the whites gradually, beating lightly with a fork to combine.

3. In a separate small bowl, combine the flour, salt, and pepper. Roll the cooked cauliflower in the flour, then dip in the eggs, coating well.

4. Heat the oil to 375°F in a frying pan. Add a few cauliflower florets at a time and fry until brown on all sides.

Mexican Roll-Ups

Serve with an assortment of fresh salsas for an interesting treat.

INGREDIENTS | SERVES 6

2 fresh jalapeño chili peppers
1 bunch green onions
½ cup pitted black olives
16 ounces cream cheese
½ teaspoon garlic salt
½ teaspoon medium-hot red chili powder
6 (8") flour tortillas

1. Remove the stems and seeds from the jalapeño peppers and chop the peppers into ¼" pieces. Remove the roots from the green onions and chop the onions and stems into ¼" pieces. Chop the olives into ¼" pieces.

2. Combine all the ingredients and mix until well blended.

3. Spread on tortillas. Roll up and serve.

Tomato Empanadas

These can be made ahead of time and frozen. They can be reheated in a microwave.

INGREDIENTS | SERVES 6

½ pound butter
8 ounces cream cheese
2 cups flour
2 medium red tomatoes
1 small yellow onion

1. Mix together the butter and cream cheese until creamy. Add the flour and mix well. Roll into a ball, cover, and chill for at least 4 hours.

2. Preheat oven to 350°F.

3. Cut the tomatoes into ¼" pieces. Peel the onion and cut into ¼" pieces. Mix together the tomatoes and onion.

4. Roll out the dough to about ¼" thick. Cut into circles about 3" across.

5. Put 1 teaspoon of tomato and onion mixture in the center of each circle. Fold in half and seal the edges with a fork. Prick the top of each empanada with a fork. Place on a baking sheet and bake for 15–20 minutes.

Cabbage Tamales

Serve as an appetizer before any traditional Mexican meal, such as Mexican Pot Roast (see recipe in Chapter 12).

INGREDIENTS | MAKES 36

1 fresh cabbage
1 pound lean ground beef
1 pound ground sausage
1 cup condensed tomato soup
1 cup dry rice
4 tablespoons chili powder
½ teaspoon salt

1. Preheat oven to 300°F. Remove the core from the cabbage. Separate the leaves and place in a pan of warm water.

2. Combine the ground beef, sausage, soup, rice, chili powder, and salt. Mix well with your hands so that all the ingredients are blended.

3. Remove the cabbage leaves from the water and pat dry. Place about 2 tablespoons of the meat mixture in the middle of each cabbage leaf. Roll up and secure with a toothpick.

4. Place the rolls in a 9" × 12" baking dish. Bake with foil cover for 1½ hours.

Spinach Balls

In addition to being used as an appetizer, these often are added to a basic chicken stock to make an interesting soup.

INGREDIENTS | MAKES 24

½ cup cooked ham

3 large eggs

2 pounds fresh spinach

½ cup cubed Cheddar cheese

¼ cup flour

½ teaspoon salt

1 cup vegetable oil

1. Cut the ham into ½" cubes. Separate the egg yolks from the egg whites.

2. Wash the spinach and remove the hard stalks. Place the spinach in a medium-sized saucepan and add 1" of water. Cook on medium heat until the spinach is thoroughly cooked; drain. Let cool slightly, then form into balls about the size of golf balls.

3. Push a piece of ham or cheese into the center of each ball.

4. Beat the egg whites until stiff. Gradually beat in the yolks, flour, and salt. Coat the spinach balls with the egg batter.

5. Heat the oil to medium-high. Fry 1 layer of spinach balls at a time until lightly browned.

Totopos

Change the ingredients to suit your whims. Hot peppers, beef, and guacamole also make good toppings.

Totopos

Totopos literally means "toppers." It's also the word used for the condiments served with tacos or when serving "make your own" tostadas.

1. Peel the onion and chop finely. Peel and pit the avocados and slice into crescents ¼" thick. Shred the lettuce. Slice the pickles into ¼" rounds. Remove the stem from the tomato and cut into ¼" slices. Warm the chicken in a small pan on low heat.

2. Melt the butter in a medium-sized frying pan on medium heat. Add the onion and sauté until limp but not brown. Add the kidney beans with their liquid and the salt and pepper. Cook until the liquid is reduced by half.

3. Heat 1 cup of the vegetable oil in a large skillet to medium-high. Fry tortillas one at a time. Drain and cool.

4. Mix together the vinegar, sugar, garlic salt, and the ⅓ cup remaining vegetable oil in a small container with a cover. Cover and shake until well mixed.

5. Combine the lettuce, avocados, pickles, and chicken in a medium-sized bowl. Mix with the vinegar and oil dressing.

6. Spread the beans about ½" thick on the tortillas. Pile the salad mixture on top. Add the tomato slices and sprinkle with cheese.

CHAPTER 5

Soups

Jalapeño and Potato Soup

Add a dollop of sour cream and sprigs of fresh cilantro before serving.

INGREDIENTS | SERVES 8

5 pounds red potatoes

¼ cup fresh or ⅛ cup canned jalapeño peppers

1 medium yellow onion

¼ cup butter

8 cups chicken broth

1 teaspoon ground cumin

¼ teaspoon baking soda

4 cups evaporated milk

Jalapeño Chili Peppers

Jalapeños are perhaps the most common hot pepper sold in the United States. They come in both green and red colors that taste only slightly different. When in doubt, use jalapeños, because they definitely add heat and spice but they are mild enough that most people can tolerate them.

1. Clean the potatoes and cut into quarters (do not peel). Remove the stem and seeds from the jalapeños and cut into ⅛" pieces. Remove the skin from the onion and cut into ¼" pieces.

2. In a medium sauté pan over medium heat, sauté the onions in butter until the onions are clear but not brown, 5–8 minutes.

3. Combine the potatoes, onions, broth, and cumin in a large stockpot. Cook uncovered for about 30 minutes, until the potatoes are tender.

4. Coarsely mash the potatoes with a potato masher. Stir in the jalapeños, baking soda, and evaporated milk; stir well.

5. Simmer on low heat for 15 minutes, stirring constantly.

Mexican Onion Soup

Serve with Brie and Papaya Quesadillas (see recipe in Chapter 4) for a light yet filling lunch.

INGREDIENTS | SERVES 6

3 large yellow onions

2 cloves garlic

¼ cup butter

2 cups tomato juice

2 cups beef broth (canned or homemade)

1 cup water

½ cup salsa

1 cup grated Monterey jack cheese

Use Fresh Garlic

Beware of prepared garlic. While preminced garlic looks like a good buy and certainly sounds easier, it releases an oil while stored after chopping. This affects both the taste and consistency in your recipes. Fresh garlic is always best.

1. Remove the skins from the onions and slice into thin rings. Remove the skin from the garlic cloves and mince.

2. Melt the butter over medium-low heat in a large frying pan. Add the onions and cook for about 20 minutes, stirring frequently. Onions should be tender and light brown.

3. Stir in the tomato juice, broth, water, and salsa. Bring to a boil. Reduce heat to low.

4. Simmer uncovered for 20 minutes. Top with grated cheese before serving.

Asparagus and Pistachio Soup

When reheating this soup, make sure it never comes to a boil, because the cream will turn brown. Serve with warm flour tortillas.

INGREDIENTS | SERVES 8

1 medium onion

2 cups fresh asparagus tips (about 1" long)

½ cup natural pistachio meats

1 tablespoon butter

6 cups chicken broth

½ teaspoon salt

1 teaspoon ground black pepper

¼ cup cooking sherry

½ cup heavy cream

The Green Nut

Pistachios are a very common treat in Mexico. When walking the streets of virtually any town, you're likely to have a young child come up to you offering fresh roasted pistachios. Be sure to avoid the red and white dyed pistachios sold in the United States, as the dye will discolor your food.

1. Remove the skin from the onion and chop into ¼" pieces.

2. Cook the asparagus tips in water on medium heat until slightly tender, about 5–8 minutes.

3. Cover the pistachio meats with boiling water and let sit for 10 minutes. Remove the skins and let the meats dry.

4. Sauté the pistachio meats in the butter on medium heat until golden, 3–5 minutes. Set the pistachio meats aside and add the onion to the butter; sauté until limp, about 5 minutes.

5. Combine 1 cup of the broth, the pistachio meats, onion, salt, black pepper, and cooking sherry in a blender and mix until it's a smooth paste.

6. Place the mixture in a medium-sized pot over medium heat. Add the remaining broth and stir until well mixed. Add the asparagus tips and cook for 20 minutes on low heat.

7. Stir in the cream right before serving.

Chicken Tortilla Soup

An alternative for cooking this soup is to put all the ingredients except the lime juice, tostada, and cilantro in a slow cooker, cover, and cook on low setting for 8–10 hours.

INGREDIENTS | SERVES 8

1 whole chicken (precooked)

1 medium white onion

4 garlic cloves

1 red bell pepper

3 medium red tomatoes

2 (15-ounce) cans black beans, drained

2 tablespoons chili powder

2 teaspoons salt

1 tablespoon ground cumin

½ teaspoon ground red pepper

1 teaspoon granulated sugar

2 cups canned (and drained) or frozen corn

6 cups chicken broth

¼ cup lime juice

4 Tostadas (see recipe in Chapter 2)

1 bunch fresh cilantro

1. Remove the skin from the chicken and cut into 1" cubes, discarding the bones.

2. Remove the skin from the onion and garlic. Chop the onion into ¼" pieces. Mince the garlic. Remove the stem and core from the red bell pepper and chop into ¼" pieces. Chop the tomatoes into 1" pieces.

3. Combine all the ingredients except the lime juice, tostadas, and cilantro in a large stockpot. Bring to a boil and cook for 20 minutes. Reduce heat to low, cover, and simmer for 2 hours. Stir in the lime juice right before serving.

4. Break the tostadas into small pieces. Cut the stems from the cilantro. Sprinkle the tostada pieces and cilantro leaves on the soup before serving.

Roasted Red Pepper and Cabbage Soup

Make this a heartier meal by adding 2 cups of dry white rice to the soup before simmering.

INGREDIENTS | SERVES 8

2 red bell peppers

1 tablespoon olive oil

1 large white onion

2 large carrots

4 garlic cloves

1 medium cabbage

2 medium zucchini (8"–12" long)

2 cups canned (and drained) or frozen corn

2 teaspoons salt

1 teaspoon ground black pepper

6 cups chicken broth

1. Preheat oven to 350°F.

2. Remove the stems and seeds from the red bell peppers. Cut the peppers into 2"-wide strips. Place skin-side down on a baking sheet. Spread the olive oil over the pepper strips. Place in oven and bake for 30 minutes or until the peppers are lightly blackened on the edges.

3. Remove the skin from the onion and chop into ¼" pieces. Clean the carrots and chop into ¼" rounds. Remove the skin from the garlic and mince. Tear the cabbage leaves into pieces about 3" square. Clean the zucchini and cut into ½" pieces. Cut the roasted red pepper strips into 1" squares.

4. Add all the ingredients to a large stockpot. Bring to a boil, cover, and cook for 20 minutes. Reduce heat to medium-low and simmer for 2 hours.

Cold Avocado Soup

This makes a wonderful summer lunch served with a fresh fruit salad.

INGREDIENTS | SERVES 8

1 medium yellow onion

3 garlic cloves

1 medium green tomato

2 ripe avocados

2 fresh habanero chilies (¼ cup canned jalapeños can be substituted)

½ cup fresh cilantro leaves

4 cups chicken broth

1 teaspoon salt

½ teaspoon ground red pepper

¼ cup chopped cilantro

¼ cup lime juice

What's an Avocado?

An avocado actually is a fruit that comes in several different varieties. It is fairly high in calories (about 300 for an average avocado). Although many people think otherwise, avocados contain only monounsaturated fat, which may help reduce bad cholesterol. When choosing a ripe avocado, the flesh should give slightly to your touch.

1. Remove the skin from the onion and chop into ¼" pieces. Remove the skin from the garlic and mince. Remove the skin from the tomato and mash with a potato masher. Peel and pit the avocados, then cut into 2" pieces. Remove the stems and seeds from the chilies and chop into ¼" pieces.

2. Combine all the ingredients except the sour cream and lime juice in a food processor or blender. You may need to do it in 2 or 3 batches. Blend on medium setting for 3 minutes or until the ingredients are well combined. Strain and discard any chunks.

3. Refrigerate for 3 hours. Remove any fat that has congealed on the top of the soup. Stir and refrigerate for an additional hour.

4. Top with cilantro and lime juice before serving.

Creamy Corn Soup

Garnish with strips of roasted red peppers to create a festive look and a unique combination of flavors.

INGREDIENTS | SERVES 8

1 large white onion

3 medium red tomatoes

3 cups canned (and drained) or frozen whole-kernel corn

4 cups chicken broth

1 teaspoon salt

½ teaspoon ground black pepper

1 cup heavy whipping cream

Peeling Tomatoes

Although a tomato can be peeled cold, the easiest way to peel it is to drop it in boiling water for 20 seconds. Then cool it by running it under cold water. The peel will easily strip off with a paring knife.

1. Remove the skin from the onion and cut into quarters. Remove the skin from the tomatoes and cut into quarters.

2. Put the corn, onion, tomatoes, and 1 cup of the broth in a food processor or blender. Blend on medium setting for 3 minutes or until all the ingredients are melded. They do not have to be liquefied—small pieces of corn, onion, and tomato are fine.

3. Place the remaining broth in a large saucepan on medium-low heat. Stir in the blended mixture. Add the salt and pepper. Heat thoroughly, but do not allow to boil.

4. Stir in the whipping cream and turn the heat to low, stirring constantly, for 5 minutes.

Cornball Soup

This can also be made using a beef stock with beef and vegetable chunks.

INGREDIENTS | SERVES 8

1 small yellow onion

1 garlic clove

2 cups masa harina or cornmeal

1 cup milk

2 large eggs

¼ cup freshly grated Parmesan cheese

1 teaspoon dried cilantro

2 large red tomatoes

¼ cup vegetable oil

8 cups chicken broth

2 teaspoons salt

1 teaspoon ground black pepper

Cross-Cultural Soups

It's interesting how soups travel through different cultures, changing to fit the available ingredients and tastes of different peoples. This soup seems awfully similar to matzo ball soup, yet it has a distinctly Mexican touch with the tomatoes, cilantro, and garlic.

1. Peel and mince the onion and garlic.

2. Combine the onion, garlic, cornmeal, milk, eggs, Parmesan cheese, and cilantro. Roll into balls about the size of golf balls.

3. Remove the skin from the tomatoes and cut into quarters. Put in blender or food processor and blend on medium setting until thick and creamy.

4. Heat the vegetable oil on medium-high in a medium-sized frying pan. Add the cornmeal balls and fry until lightly brown. (Cut one open to make sure they are cooked into the center.) Keep them warm by putting them in a warm oven.

5. Heat the broth. Stir in the tomato purée, salt, and black pepper. Add the cornmeal balls. Serve immediately.

Cowboy Soup

This thick soup, more like a stew, is an excellent choice for lunch on a cold winter day. Serve with warmed flour tortillas, sour cream, and guacamole.

INGREDIENTS | SERVES 4–6

1 pound lean ground beef

1 onion, chopped

2 jalapeño chilies, minced

4 cloves garlic, minced

2 tablespoons flour

1 (10-ounce) can condensed tomato soup

1 tablespoon chili powder

1 teaspoon cumin

5 cups beef stock

2 cups frozen corn

½ cup Texmati rice

1 cup cubed processed American cheese

1. In a heavy stockpot, cook beef, onion, chilies, and garlic over medium heat, stirring to break up beef, until browned, about 7–8 minutes. Add flour; cook and stir for 3–4 minutes until bubbly. Add soup, chili powder, cumin, and beef stock; bring to a boil, then cover and simmer for 5 minutes.

2. Stir in frozen corn and bring back to a simmer. Stir in the rice, cover, and simmer for 15–20 minutes until rice is tender. Stir in cheese until melted, and serve.

Turkey and Filbert Soup

This is a great way to use leftover turkey. It also works well with chicken.

INGREDIENTS | SERVES 8

1 medium white onion
2 cups cubed skinless turkey meat
¼ cup butter
½ cup filberts
8 cups chicken broth
¼ cup dry red wine
½ teaspoon ground nutmeg
1 tablespoon dried parsley
1 teaspoon salt
1 teaspoon ground black pepper

Edible Soup Bowls

Use squash as a soup bowl. Many small squashes make excellent complements to soups and stews. Cut them in half, remove the seeds, and prebake in the microwave or oven. Ladle your soup or stew into the squash for a festive look.

1. Remove the skin from the onion and chop into ¼" pieces.

2. Melt the butter in a small frying pan at medium heat and sauté the filberts for 5 minutes. Drain off the butter and discard.

3. Place the filberts, ½ cup of the turkey meat, the onions, and 1 cup of the stock in a blender or food processor. Blend at medium speed until you have a purée—a thick substance with all the ingredients melded.

4. Combine the mixture with the remaining chicken stock in a large stockpot. Add the remaining ingredients. Heat on medium temperature for 30 minutes, stirring frequently.

Mexican Chicken Chowder

Serve with Jalapeño Corn Bread (see recipe in Chapter 6).

INGREDIENTS | SERVES 4

1½ pounds boneless, skinless chicken breasts

2 medium white onions

2 garlic cloves

2 celery ribs

½ cup canned, chopped jalapeño peppers, or 3 fresh jalapeños

½ pound Monterey jack cheese

1 tablespoon olive oil

4 cups chicken broth

1 package dry chicken gravy mix

2 cups whole milk

2 cups salsa

1 (32-ounce) bag frozen hash brown potatoes

1. Preheat oven to 300°F.

2. Cut the chicken into ½" cubes. Peel the onion and cut into ¼" pieces. Peel and mince the garlic. Cut the celery into ¼" pieces. Drain the chilies and cut into ⅛" pieces. Cut the cheese into ½" cubes.

3. Combine the chicken, onions, garlic, celery, oil, and broth in a large mixing bowl; stir until well blended. Pour into a casserole dish, cover, and bake in oven for 1 hour.

4. Dissolve the gravy mix in the milk in a medium-sized mixing bowl. Stir into the cooked chicken mixture. Add the salsa, potatoes, chilies, and cheese; mix well. Cover and cook for an additional hour.

Hold the Salt

Resist the urge to salt. Salt draws flavors and juices out of meat and vegetables. Let the flavors release on their own time for the best results. Guests can salt their own dishes if they prefer. They'll also use less than if you add it while cooking.

Market Basket Soup

This soup is also called wastebasket soup, probably because it is often made at the end of the week when the refrigerator and cupboards are being cleaned out.

INGREDIENTS | SERVES 8

2 pounds smoked link sausages

1 small white onion

¼ cup canned jalapeño chili peppers

2 celery ribs

4 medium red tomatoes

1 green bell pepper

1 medium zucchini (8"–12" long)

1 cup black olives

1 cup canned or frozen whole-kernel corn

1 cup canned green lima beans

2 cups canned pinto beans

4 ounces Bloody Mary mix

2 cups water

1 package dry onion soup mix

2 teaspoons salt

2 teaspoons ground white pepper

1 teaspoon dried oregano

1. Cook the sausages in a medium-sized frying pan on medium-low heat until lightly browned. Cut into 1" pieces.

2. Peel the onion and chop into ¼" pieces. Drain the jalapeños and cut into ¼" pieces. Cut the celery into ¼" pieces. Cut the tomatoes into 1" pieces. Remove the stem and seeds from the bell pepper and cut into ¼" pieces. Cut the zucchini into 1" pieces. Cut the black olives into ¼" pieces.

3. Add all the ingredients to a large stockpot and stir well. Bring to a boil, then lower the temperature to medium-low and simmer uncovered for 1 hour.

Lower the Cholesterol

When sautéing or browning foods, you don't have to use oil. Many chefs simply use a little bit of water to cook these items. When browning a fatty meat, such as sausages, start cooking them at a low temperature to cook some of the fat out before you turn up the temperature for browning.

Creamy Gazpacho with Avocado

Use as an appetizer for a heavier meal or as the main course for a summer luncheon.

INGREDIENTS | SERVES 6

4 large eggs
5 medium fresh red tomatoes
1 large cucumber
1 medium white onion
1 ripe avocado
¼ cup vegetable oil
1 tablespoon prepared yellow mustard
1 tablespoon Worcestershire sauce
¼ cup lime juice
1 teaspoon garlic salt
½ teaspoon ground black pepper
1 cup sour cream

1. Boil the eggs in water for about 10 minutes. Cool and peel. Slice the eggs in half and remove the yolks. Set the whites aside. Peel the tomatoes. Set 1 tomato aside and chop the other 4 into quarters. Peel and seed the cucumber. Chop ¾ of the cucumber into 1" pieces and set aside the rest. Peel the onion and cut into quarters. Peel the avocado and remove the pit; set aside half.

2. Put the chopped tomatoes, cucumber, onion, and half of the avocado in a blender or food processor; blend until smooth.

3. Put the egg yolks in a small bowl and mash with a fork. Blend in the oil, mustard, Worcestershire sauce, lime juice, garlic salt, and pepper. Add the mixture to the blender and blend until thoroughly mixed. Add the sour cream gradually, blending well.

4. Pour the mixture into a medium-sized container with a cover. Chop the remaining tomato, cucumber, and hard-cooked egg whites and add to soup. Slice the remaining avocado half thinly and add to the soup. Stir in lightly.

5. Cover and refrigerate for at least 8 hours before serving.

CHAPTER 6

Breads

Jalapeño Corn Bread

This is a great side to serve with a bunch of different recipes. For example, try serving this with Mexican Pot Roast (see recipe in Chapter 12).

INGREDIENTS | SERVES 4

1 small yellow onion
2 garlic cloves
2 tablespoons canned chopped jalapeños
1½ cups bread flour
¾ cup masa harina or cornmeal
¼ cup granulated sugar
4½ teaspoons baking powder
1 teaspoon salt
1 large egg
1 cup whole milk
½ teaspoon vegetable oil
½ cup canned cream-style corn
½ cup grated Cheddar cheese

1. Preheat oven to 350°F.

2. Remove the skin from the onion and chop into ¼" pieces. Remove the skin from the garlic and mince. Drain off the water from the jalapeños.

3. Mix all the ingredients together in a medium-sized mixing bowl.

4. Pour the mixture into a greased bread pan.

5. Bake for 30–45 minutes or until lightly brown on top.

Know When Bread Is Done

Bread that is fully cooked will spring back when you lightly touch the top with your finger. In addition, a toothpick inserted into the center of the bread should come out clean. Most breads will also be lightly browned on top when they are done.

Pineapple Sopapillas

These can be made using any jam or heated fruits.

INGREDIENTS | MAKES 20

2 cups flour
1 tablespoon baking powder
1 teaspoon salt
4 cups peanut oil
¾ cup water
3 cups canned pineapple, drained
2 tablespoons ground cinnamon
1 cup white granulated sugar

1. Mix together the flour, baking powder, and salt in a medium-sized mixing bowl.

2. Blend 1 cup of the oil into the dry ingredients. Stir in just enough water to make a soft dough.

3. Divide the dough into 4 parts. Roll out 1 part at a time to about ¼" thick. Cut into triangles about 4" long and 2" at their widest.

4. In a large skillet, heat the remaining peanut oil to about 385°F. Add 3 to 4 pieces of dough at a time. Stir the oil until the sopapillas puff up like pillows. Fry until light brown. Lay on paper towels to drain off excess grease.

5. Chop the pineapple into ½" pieces. Drain off juice. Heat the pineapple to lukewarm in a small saucepan over medium-low heat, about 2–4 minutes.

6. Open a small hole in the side of each sopapilla and spoon about 2 tablespoons of pineapple inside it.

7. Mix together the cinnamon and sugar in a bowl. Sprinkle on the top of each sopapilla.

Easy Mexican Sweet Rolls

If you would rather use fresh-made dough for the sweet rolls, look at the dough recipe for Pineapple Sopapillas (see recipe in this chapter).

INGREDIENTS | SERVES 10

2 large eggs
⅔ cup flour
½ cup white granulated sugar
¼ cup softened butter
1 (10-ounce) can refrigerator flaky biscuits
½ teaspoon shortening
1 tablespoon whole milk

Separating Eggs

If you don't have an egg separator in your kitchen, break the egg neatly in half and transfer the yolk back and forth, catching the egg white in a small bowl underneath. In some recipes even the smallest amount of yolk in an egg white can cause the recipe to fail, so don't break that yolk!

1. Preheat oven to 375°F.

2. Separate the egg yolks from the egg whites.

3. Combine the flour and sugar in a bowl. Cut in the butter until the mixture resembles coarse crumbs. Add the egg yolks and mix until well blended. Set aside ¼ cup of this mixture.

4. Separate the canned biscuits into 10 pieces. Press or roll each to a ⅗" oval. Crumble 1–2 tablespoons of the sugar and flour mixture over each oval to ¼" from the edge.

5. Roll each biscuit, starting at the shorter side, wrapping the dough around the filling and rolling to the opposite side. Place the seam side down on a baking sheet lightly greased with shortening.

6. Beat the egg whites with the milk. Brush over the rolls with a pastry brush. Sprinkle evenly with the reserved ¼ cup of sugar and flour mixture. Press lightly into the rolls.

7. Bake for 13–17 minutes or until medium brown.

Mango Corn Bread

Serve this as part of a big breakfast for friends or during a family brunch.

INGREDIENTS | SERVES 6

1 tablespoon active dry yeast

¼ cup warm water

1 medium white onion

1 mango

1 fresh jalapeño chili pepper

3 cups masa harina or cornmeal

1½ cups grated Cheddar cheese

½ cup vegetable oil

1 cup canned cream-style corn

3 tablespoons granulated sugar

⅓ cup whole milk

⅓ cup buttermilk

1. Preheat oven to 425°F.

2. Dissolve the yeast in the warm water. Peel the onion and chop into ¼" pieces. Remove the skin and seed from the mango; cut into ¼" pieces. Remove the stem and seeds from the jalapeño and cut into ¼" pieces.

3. Combine all the ingredients in a large mixing bowl. Mix until well blended.

4. Pour into a greased bread pan and bake for 35 minutes.

About Yeast

Yeast is a live entity that grows when it gets warm. However, if it's added to boiling water, you can kill it. You can make a heavy, dense bread by leaving out the yeast and substituting baking soda.

Rosquillas Fritas

These treats, similar to doughnuts, are frequently served at holiday celebrations.

INGREDIENTS | MAKES 24

4 cups vegetable oil

2 teaspoons active dry yeast

¼ cup warm water

½ cup roasted almonds

2 large eggs

3 cups flour

1¼ cups white granulated sugar

1 teaspoon baking soda

½ teaspoon salt

½ teaspoon cinnamon

½ teaspoon almond extract or flavoring

2 tablespoons butter

¼ cup whole milk

½ cup white sugar, confectioners' sugar, or sugar and cinnamon mixed, to taste

Extracts and Flavorings

Extracts are flavorings that have actually been extracted from the fruit or seed by squashing it and removing the oil. Flavorings are usually artificially produced and added to a water base.

1. Pour the vegetable oil into a medium-sized skillet. The oil should be about 2" deep. Heat to about 370°F.

2. Dissolve the yeast in the warm water. Chop the almonds into small pieces.

3. In a medium bowl, mix the eggs with half of the flour, the sugar, dissolved yeast, almonds, baking soda, salt, cinnamon, almond extract, butter, and milk. Beat until the dough begins to thicken. Add the remaining flour and mix well. If the dough is not stiff enough to knead, add more flour, ¼ cup at a time.

4. Flour a flat surface and remove the dough from the bowl. Knead the dough until it is pliable and smooth. Roll out the dough about ½" thick and cut into doughnut shapes.

5. Put 2 to 3 fritas in the hot oil at a time. Fry for 2–3 minutes or until golden brown. Flip and fry for 2–3 minutes on the other side. Place on paper towels to absorb the excess oil.

6. Sprinkle with white sugar, confectioners' sugar, or a mixture of sugar and cinnamon.

Kings' Bread Ring

This bread is usually served on January 6, Three Kings' Day. The person who gets the small china doll is expected to host a Candlemas Day party on February 2.

INGREDIENTS | SERVES 8

2 cups candied fruits (citron, cherries, orange peel)

3 large eggs

2 teaspoons (or 1 package) active dry yeast

½ cup warm water

½ cup milk

⅓ cup white granulated sugar

⅓ cup shortening

2 teaspoons salt

4 cups all-purpose flour

Tiny china doll (approximately 1" high)

½ cup melted butter

1⅓ cups confectioners' sugar

4 teaspoons water

½ teaspoon vanilla extract

1. Chop candied fruits into ¼" pieces. In a bowl, beat the eggs until the yolks and whites are blended. In a separate bowl, dissolve the yeast in the warm water.

2. Heat the milk in a small saucepan at medium-high temperature until scalded.

3. Combine the granulated sugar, shortening, and salt in a large bowl. Pour in the scalded milk and mix until sugar is dissolved and the shortening is melted. Let cool to lukewarm.

4. Beat in 1 cup of the flour, the eggs, and yeast. Add more flour until a stiff dough is formed. Stir in 1½ cups of the candied fruits.

5. Turn the dough onto a floured surface and knead until smooth and satiny. Roll the dough to form a long rope; shape into a ring, sealing the ends together. Transfer to a greased baking sheet. Push the tiny china doll into the dough so that it is completely covered. Brush the ring with melted butter.

6. Cover with a towel and let rise in a warm place until it doubles in size, about 1½ hours.

7. Preheat oven to 375°F.

8. Bake for 25–30 minutes or until golden brown. Cool on a wire rack.

9. Blend together the confectioners' sugar, 4 teaspoons water, and vanilla extract to make an icing. When the bread is cool, spread the icing over the top.

Molletes

Serve as a breakfast treat with Easy Huevos Rancheros (see recipe in Chapter 8).

INGREDIENTS | MAKES 16 LARGE ROLLS

4 large eggs, divided

½ cup warm water

2 teaspoons (or 1 package) active dry yeast

½ cup butter

½ cup granulated sugar

½ teaspoon salt

1 tablespoon anise seeds

4½ cups (approximately) all-purpose flour

2 tablespoons light corn syrup

1. Leave the eggs out until they reach room temperature. Add the warm water to a large bowl and sprinkle the yeast on top. Stir until it dissolves. Melt the butter in a small pan on low heat.

2. Add 3 of the eggs, melted butter, sugar, salt, anise seeds, and 2 cups of the flour to the bowl with the yeast; beat until smooth. Stir in enough additional flour to make a soft dough.

3. Turn the dough onto a lightly floured surface; knead until smooth and elastic, about 10 minutes.

4. Put the dough into a greased bowl and turn the dough over to grease the top. Cover and let rise in a warm place until the dough doubles in size, about 1 hour.

5. Punch the dough down and turn onto a lightly floured surface. Roll into a 12" square. Cut into fourths and cut each square into 4 triangles. Place the triangles on a greased baking sheet, allowing space for rising. Cover and let rise in a warm place until they double in size, about 1 hour.

6. Preheat oven to 350°F.

7. Separate the yolk and white of the remaining egg. Discard the white. Beat the egg yolk and corn syrup together until well blended. Generously brush over the triangles.

8. Bake for 10–15 minutes or until lightly browned. Serve warm.

Pastelitos

For variety, use any dried fruit in this recipe. Peaches and pears make an especially tasty pastry.

INGREDIENTS | MAKES ABOUT 24 PASTRIES

1 cup dried apricots
1 cup water
½ cup granulated sugar
1 teaspoon vanilla extract, divided
2 cups all-purpose flour
¾ teaspoon salt
½ teaspoon baking powder
⅔ cup shortening
5 tablespoons ice water
1 cup confectioners' sugar
3 tablespoons cream

1. Put the apricots and 1 cup of water into a medium-sized saucepan. Cover and bring to a boil. Reduce to a simmer and cook for 20 minutes. Pour the mixture into a blender or food processor and blend until smooth.

2. Combine the blended apricots and the granulated sugar in a saucepan. Cook on medium heat until thick, about 5 minutes. Let cool slightly. Stir in ½ teaspoon of the vanilla extract.

3. Preheat oven to 400°F.

4. Mix together the flour, salt, and baking powder in a bowl. Cut in the shortening until crumbly. Add the ice water, 1 tablespoon at a time. Toss with a fork until the dough holds together. Divide the dough in half.

5. Roll out each half of dough into a 14" × 10" rectangle on a lightly floured surface.

6. Line a 13" × 9" × 2" baking pan with 1 rectangle of dough. Spread the apricot mixture evenly over the dough. Place the remaining dough on top. Seal the edges. Prick the top crust with a fork.

7. Bake for 25 minutes or until lightly browned. Let cool slightly.

8. Combine the confectioners' sugar and the remaining vanilla extract. Blend in the cream. Use as a frosting for the baked pastry. When cool, cut the pastry into squares.

Torrejas de Coco

While many people call this Mexican-style French toast, it is actually used as a dessert in Mexico.

INGREDIENTS | SERVES 12

1½-pound loaf egg bread
¼ cup blanched almonds
4 cups granulated sugar, divided
1½ cups water, divided
2 cups shredded coconut
3 large eggs
1 tablespoon flour
1 cup shortening
1 cinnamon stick
3 tablespoons raisins

1. Slice the egg bread into 24 slices. Chop the almonds into small pieces.

2. Dissolve 1 cup of the sugar in ½ cup of the water in a saucepan over medium heat. Bring to a boil and boil for 3 minutes. Add the shredded coconut. Cook for about 15 minutes. Remove from heat and let cool slightly.

3. Spread the coconut paste on 12 slices of egg bread. Cover each with another slice of egg bread.

4. Beat the eggs with the flour. Dip both sides of the sandwiches in the egg.

5. Heat the shortening in a large frying pan to medium-high heat. Fry the sandwiches on each side for about 1 minute. Set on paper towels to cool.

6. Make a syrup by heating the remaining sugar and water with the cinnamon stick in a large frying pan; boil for 5 minutes. Add the browned sandwiches, reduce heat, and simmer for 5 minutes. Turn the sandwiches over and simmer for an additional 5 minutes.

7. Arrange the sandwiches on a serving dish. Garnish with raisins and almonds. Top with strained syrup.

Pan de Muerto

This bread is traditionally served on the Day of the Dead, November 1, although you can exclude the gruesome decoration and make it any time of the year.

INGREDIENTS | MAKES 1 LOAF

1 tablespoon (or 1 package) active dry yeast

½ cup warm water

5 large eggs

1 tablespoon anise seeds

¼ cup butter

½ cup granulated sugar

½ teaspoon salt

½ teaspoon ground nutmeg

2½ cups flour

1. Dissolve the yeast in ¼ cup of the warm water. Separate 2 of the eggs' yolks from their whites. Beat together 2 eggs plus the 2 egg yolks. Steep the anise seeds in the remaining ¼ cup warm water for 10–15 minutes. Melt the butter in a small saucepan on low heat.

2. Combine the dissolved yeast and 1 tablespoon of the sugar in a large mixing bowl; stir gently. Let sit for about 10 minutes or until it appears foamy.

3. Stir in the salt, ⅓ cup of the sugar, the nutmeg, the melted butter, the anise seeds and water mixture, and the beaten eggs and yolks. Mix well while slowly adding the flour. The dough should be slightly sticky. Knead for 10–15 minutes.

4. Lightly coat a large mixing bowl with oil or shortening. Place the dough inside and cover with a towel. Place in a warm place and let rise until it has doubled in size, usually 1–2 hours.

5. Punch the dough down and place it on a floured surface. Remove a handful of dough and set aside. Shape the remaining dough into a round loaf about 1" thick and place it on a greased baking sheet.

6. Make a deep indentation in the center of the loaf with your fist. Form the small piece of dough set aside into 2 "bone" shapes about 4" long and 1 "skull" shape. Place these in the center indentation.

7. Cover the dough with a towel and place in a warm place to rise for 45 minutes to 1 hour. The dough should hold a fingerprint when pressed.

continued on following page

Pan de Muerto—*continued*

8. Preheat oven to 375°F.

9. Bake for 30 minutes or until golden brown.

10. Beat the remaining egg and use it as a wash on the bread while the bread is still warm. Sprinkle with the remaining sugar.

Mexican Spoon Bread

This is used as a side dish to meals that don't have tortillas. Spoon it out as you would mashed potatoes.

INGREDIENTS | SERVES 6

½ cup shortening
1 pound Cheddar cheese
¼ cup canned jalapeño chili peppers
1 cup cornmeal or masa harina
2 large eggs
1 (15-ounce) can cream-style corn
1 teaspoon salt
½ cup milk
½ teaspoon baking soda

Low-Fat Milk Products

Low-fat cheese and sour cream can be substituted in most recipes. However, they do not melt as well and do not hold up over a long time of heating, so they do not work well in dips and baked dishes.

1. Preheat oven to 350°F.

2. Melt the shortening in a small saucepan on medium heat. Grate the Cheddar cheese. Cut the chili peppers into ¼" pieces.

3. Mix together the cornmeal and eggs until well blended. Add the melted shortening, corn, salt, milk, and baking soda; mix well.

4. Pour half of the mixture into a greased 9" × 9" casserole dish. Add a layer of jalapeños and half of the cheese. Add the remaining mixture and top with the rest of the cheese.

5. Place in the oven and bake for 45–50 minutes or until lightly browned.

CHAPTER 7

Salads

Fresh Cauliflower Salad

Try making this with any fresh vegetables, such as green beans, broccoli, or even carrots.

INGREDIENTS | SERVES 8

1 head cauliflower
2 celery ribs
1 large red onion
1 garlic clove
6 slices bacon
1 teaspoon salt
1 teaspoon ground cumin
½ cup sour cream
1 cup salsa

1. Break the cauliflower florets into bite-sized pieces. Slice the celery into ⅛"-thick slices. Peel the onion and chop into ¼" pieces. Peel and mince the garlic. Cook the bacon until crisp; drain off the bacon grease and discard. Crumble the bacon.

2. In a medium bowl, combine the salt and cumin. Add the cauliflower florets, celery, onion, garlic, and bacon; mix well. Chill covered for 2 hours.

3. Right before serving, combine the sour cream and salsa. Pour over vegetable mixture and toss lightly.

Black Bean and Corn Salad

You can add more peppers to this to give it more spiciness. Also try adding fresh green beans and carrots when they're in season.

INGREDIENTS | SERVES 6

1 red bell pepper
1 fresh habanero pepper
1 medium red onion
1 celery rib
¼ cup olive oil
3 tablespoons lime juice
2 (15-ounce) cans black beans, drained
2 (15-ounce) cans kernel corn, drained
¼ cup chopped cilantro

1. Remove the stem and seeds from the bell pepper and cut into ½" pieces. Remove the stem and seeds from the pepper and cut into ¼" pieces. Remove the skin from the onion and cut into ½" pieces. Cut the celery into ¼" pieces.

2. Combine the olive oil and lime juice until well blended.

3. Combine the beans, corn, red pepper, habanero, onion, and celery in a large mixing bowl. Stir in the dressing until well coated.

4. Cover and refrigerate overnight. Garnish with cilantro and serve chilled.

Mexican Potato Salad

Use this as a side dish to complement a spicy fish or poultry meal.

INGREDIENTS | SERVES 8

1 pound small red potatoes

1 quart water

1 large tomato

½ cup ripe olives

6 green onions

1 tablespoon fresh cilantro

¼ cup salsa

1 tablespoon olive oil

2 tablespoons lime juice

½ teaspoon salt

½ teaspoon ground black pepper

Different Types of Potatoes

Most of us eat a great deal of potatoes, but are we aware of how many different types there are? New potatoes are usually very small, brown potatoes that have a sweet flavor. Red potatoes can be either new or larger and have a mild flavor. Bakers are large, tough potatoes. New varieties such as golden-fleshed and purple-fleshed potatoes offer other tastes.

1. Clean and quarter the potatoes. Boil in 1 quart of water until tender but not mushy. (They may also be cooked in the microwave.) Drain and set aside.

2. Cut the tomato into ½" cubes. Remove the pits from the olives and slice into ¼" pieces. Remove the skins from the onions and slice into ¼" pieces. Remove the stems from the cilantro.

3. Combine all the ingredients except the tomatoes and cook uncovered on low heat for 5 minutes.

4. Pour the sauce over the potatoes and store in a covered bowl in the refrigerator for 8–12 hours before serving.

Shrimp Salad

This works well as a main course, especially for lunch. Serve with Jalapeño Corn Bread (see recipe in Chapter 6).

INGREDIENTS | SERVES 6

3 cups baby shrimp

3 large eggs

1 small white onion

2 large red tomatoes

1 avocado

½ cup pimiento-stuffed green olives

1 bunch fresh cilantro

½ cup olive oil

¼ cup lime juice

1 teaspoon salt

1 teaspoon ground black pepper

1. In a large saucepan, boil the shrimp for 5 minutes in 6 cups water. Drain and rinse with cold water. Remove shells if necessary.

2. In a medium saucepan, boil the eggs in 4 cups of water for 10 minutes. Rinse with cold water. Peel and chop into small pieces.

3. Remove the skin from the onion and chop into ¼" pieces. Chop the tomatoes into ½" pieces. Peel and pit the avocado and chop into ½" pieces. Chop the olives into quarters. Remove the stems from the cilantro and chop the leaves roughly.

4. Combine the olive oil, lime juice, salt, and pepper; mix well.

5. Combine the shrimp, eggs, onion, tomatoes, avocado, olives, and cilantro in a large mixing bowl. Pour the lime juice and olive oil dressing over the top. Stir gently until the ingredients are well blended.

6. Chill before serving.

Crab Salad

You can easily turn this into a mixed seafood salad by adding cooked shrimp, lobster meat, and scallops.

INGREDIENTS | SERVES 4

2 cups precooked crabmeat
1 medium jicama
1 celery rib
½ cup pitted black olives
1 small white onion
1 fresh jalapeño pepper
⅓ cup mayonnaise
⅓ cup sour cream
1 cup diced, peeled cucumber
1 teaspoon salt
1 teaspoon cayenne pepper

Jicama

Jicama is a root vegetable with a crisp, white flesh. It has a very mild flavor that will pick up the flavor of dressings or spices. It's an excellent addition to salads because it looks so beautiful nestled among all the other colorful foods!

1. Shred the crabmeat. Peel the jicama and cut into ½" pieces. Cut the celery into ¼" pieces. Cut the black olives in half. Remove the skin from the onion and cut into ¼" pieces. Remove the stem and seeds from the jalapeño and cut into ¼" pieces.

2. Mix together the mayonnaise and sour cream.

3. Combine the crabmeat, jicama, celery, cucumber, black olives, onion, jalapeño, salt, and cayenne pepper in a large mixing bowl. Add the mayonnaise and sour cream mixture. Mix until well blended.

4. Serve chilled.

Cucumber Mousse

This is a great, light salad course to pair with a heavier main dish.

INGREDIENTS | SERVES 4

1 small white onion

1 medium cucumber

1 (3-ounce) package lime-flavored gelatin

¾ cup boiling water

1 cup cottage cheese

1 cup mayonnaise

1 cup slivered almonds

1. Peel the onion and grate until you have 2 tablespoons. Grate the cucumber until you have ¾ cup.

2. Dissolve the gelatin in the boiling water. Stir in the onion, cottage cheese, and mayonnaise until well blended.

3. Fold in the cucumber and almonds.

4. Pour the mixture into a 1-quart mold. Refrigerate until set.

Broccoli Salad

Serve on a bed of lettuce with a cold meat and cheese tray for a complete, summertime meal.

INGREDIENTS | SERVES 6

4 cups broccoli florets
1 medium yellow onion
1 cup yellow raisins
1 cup dry cooking sherry
1 cup canned mandarin oranges, undrained
½ cup lime juice
1 tablespoon dried cilantro
½ cup olive oil
1 teaspoon salt
1 teaspoon ground white pepper
½ cup blanched almond slivers

1. Cut the broccoli florets into bite-sized pieces. Remove the skin from the onion and cut into ¼" pieces. Place the raisins in the sherry and let soak for 15 minutes.

2. Combine the juice from the mandarin oranges, the lime juice, cilantro, olive oil, salt, and white pepper; mix well.

3. Combine the broccoli, onion, raisins, mandarin oranges, and blanched almond slivers; mix until well blended.

4. Pour dressing on top of the broccoli mixture and stir until well blended.

5. Refrigerate for at least 1 hour before serving.

Cactus Salad

Canned cactus strips are available at most large grocery stores today, although you can substitute any vegetable such as broccoli or cauliflower.

INGREDIENTS | SERVES 6

2 cups canned cactus strips

2 large red tomatoes

½ cup pitted black olives

2 tablespoons fresh cilantro leaves

4 medium red radishes

¼ cup olive oil

¼ cup red wine vinegar

1 teaspoon garlic salt

1 teaspoon ground white pepper

½ teaspoon cayenne pepper

1. Drain off the water from the cactus strips. Cut the tomatoes into 1" pieces. Cut the black olives in half. Chop the cilantro leaves. Remove the stems and roots from the radishes and cut into ½" pieces. Combine these ingredients in a large mixing bowl.

2. In a small container with a cover, mix the olive oil, vinegar, garlic salt, white pepper, and cayenne pepper; shake well to mix.

3. Pour the dressing over the vegetables and toss until well mixed.

4. Chill before serving.

What about the Stickers?

For those of us in northern climates, the idea of eating cactus is, well, terrifying. However, it really is quite juicy and flavorful. Many people in the southwestern United States will simply pick their own backyard cactus. The canned variety is much mushier and loses some of its flavor but is a good place to start for those new to this delicacy.

Mixed Vegetables with Hot Pepper Dressing

Experiment by adding smoked or pickled peppers to the dressing instead of fresh peppers.

INGREDIENTS | SERVES 6

1 cup broccoli florets

1 cup cauliflower florets

1 cup fresh green beans

1 carrot

4 radishes

½ cup pimiento-stuffed green olives

1 cup canned or frozen corn kernels

2 large red tomatoes

2 fresh or canned serrano chili peppers

2 garlic cloves

1 cup dry red wine

1 cup olive oil

½ teaspoon dried oregano

½ teaspoon salt

½ teaspoon cayenne pepper

What Happened to the Salad?

Mexicans typically don't serve a salad course with their meals. If a green salad is served, it typically takes the place of the vegetable. As a result, many of their salads feature a wide variety of vegetables.

1. Cut the broccoli and cauliflower florets into bite-sized pieces. Cut the ends off the green beans and cut the beans in half. Peel the carrot and cut into ¼" rounds. Cut the roots and stems from the radishes and cut the radishes into ¼" rounds. Cut the green olives into quarters. Drain off the water from the corn. (Thaw if using frozen corn.) Cut the tomatoes into 16 wedges each.

2. Mix these ingredients in a large mixing bowl.

3. Remove the stems (but not seeds) from the chili peppers and mince. Remove the skin from the garlic cloves and mince. Mix together the chilies, garlic, red wine, and olive oil. Add the oregano, salt, and cayenne pepper. Place in a small container with a cover. Cover and shake until well mixed.

4. Pour the dressing over the other ingredients; toss gently until well mixed.

5. Best if chilled before serving.

Carrot and Chili Pepper Salad

Serve with Empanaditas de Carne (see recipe in Chapter 17).

INGREDIENTS | SERVES 4

1 large carrot
2 celery ribs
3 green onions or scallions
1 fresh jalapeño pepper
1 cup canned pineapple chunks, drained
1 cup light mayonnaise

1. Grate the carrot. Cut the celery into ¼" pieces. Remove the roots from the green onions and chop into ¼" pieces, including the green tops. Remove the stem and seeds from the jalapeño and cut into ¼" pieces.

2. Combine the carrot, celery, green onions, jalapeño, and pineapple in a medium-sized mixing bowl; stir until well mixed.

3. Add the mayonnaise and stir until all the ingredients are covered.

Carrot Salad

This makes an excellent side dish to accompany fried chicken.

INGREDIENTS | SERVES 4

6 large, fresh carrots
½ cup golden raisins
¾ cup orange juice
1 teaspoon granulated sugar
⅛ teaspoon salt
¼ cup pistachio meats

1. Peel and grate the carrots.

2. Combine the carrots, raisins, orange juice, sugar, and salt in a medium-sized bowl. Cover and refrigerate for 3–4 hours before serving.

3. Right before serving, mix in the pistachio meats.

Zesty Cheese Salad

Serve this refreshing salad alongside grilled steak or swordfish.

INGREDIENTS | SERVES 12

1 medium red onion

4 garlic cloves

2 small poblano chilies

1 large avocado

1 medium jicama

⅔ cup fresh cilantro leaves

1 pound mozzarella cheese

1 teaspoon ground cumin

½ teaspoon fresh oregano (or ¼ teaspoon dried)

⅔ cup olive oil

½ teaspoon salt

½ teaspoon ground black pepper

½ cup lime juice

How to Substitute Dry Spices

Because dried spices have the water taken out of them, you usually substitute half the amount of dried for the fresh variety. However, many spices lose their flavor when dried, so it's best to use what the recipe calls for if at all possible.

1. Peel the onion and cut into ¼" pieces. Peel and mince the garlic. Remove the stem and seeds from the chilies and cut into ¼" pieces. Peel and pit the avocado and slice into 2" lengths about ¼" thick. Peel the jicama and cut into pieces about the size of matchsticks. Remove the stems from the cilantro and chop the leaves into ¼" pieces. Cut the mozzarella into ½" cubes.

2. In a large mixing bowl, combine the onion, chilies, avocado, jicama, and cheese; toss until well mixed.

3. In a medium-sized container with a lid, combine the garlic, cumin, oregano, olive oil, salt, black pepper, and lime juice. Cover and shake until well mixed.

4. Pour the dressing over the vegetables and cheese; toss lightly.

Mexican Coleslaw

Serve as a salad with Barbecued Pork Ribs (see recipe in Chapter 12).

INGREDIENTS | SERVES 6

3 tablespoons salad oil

½ cup cider vinegar

2 tablespoons white granulated sugar

1½ teaspoons salt

1 teaspoon paprika

½ teaspoon dry mustard

1 teaspoon celery seeds

1 large cabbage

1 green bell pepper

1 small yellow onion

¼ cup canned pimientos

½ cup pitted black olives

Paprika

Paprika is made from red peppers, which are dried and powdered into a coarse-grained spice. It is used in many Spanish recipes and a handful of Mexican recipes. Interestingly, paprika comes in many different strengths. What's typically sold in the United States is the most mild.

1. In a small container with a cover, combine the salad oil, cider vinegar, white sugar, salt, paprika, dry mustard, and celery seeds. Cover and shake until well mixed.

2. Remove the outer leaves of the cabbage and discard. Shred the remaining cabbage into pieces about the size of wooden matchsticks.

3. Remove the seeds and stem from the bell pepper and cut into ¼" pieces. Peel the onion and cut into ¼" pieces. Dice the pimientos. Cut the black olives into ¼" rounds.

4. In a large serving bowl, combine the cabbage, bell pepper, onion, pimientos, and black olives; toss gently until well mixed.

5. Pour the dressing on top and toss gently until well covered.

6. Cover and refrigerate for at least 1 hour before serving.

Vegetable-Stuffed Avocados

Use this dish as the main course for a summer luncheon or serve as the salad course for a large dinner.

INGREDIENTS | SERVES 6

1 head cauliflower
½ cup black olives
¼ cup canned pimientos
2 tablespoons red wine vinegar
1½ teaspoons granulated sugar
¼ teaspoon salt
⅓ cup vegetable oil
1 cup canned green peas
3 large ripe avocados

Appetizer Advice

Appetizers should complement the meal to come, not overpower it. Serve items that have milder but similar flavors to the main dish. Remember not to have so many appetizers that the guests aren't hungry for the main meal.

1. Cut the cauliflower florets into pieces about the size of a dime until you have about 2 full cups. Chop black olives into ¼" pieces. Chop pimientos into ¼" pieces.

2. Combine the red wine vinegar, sugar, salt, and vegetable oil in a small container with a cover. Cover and shake until well mixed.

3. Combine the cauliflower, peas, olives, and pimientos in a medium-sized bowl. Cover with vinegar and oil dressing; mix well. Cover and refrigerate for 4–6 hours.

4. Peel, halve, and remove the pits from the avocados. Fill with cauliflower salad.

CHAPTER 8

Eggs

Chile Relleno Soufflé

This is a perfect meal for Sunday brunch, or it can be served as the main course in a vegetarian meal.

INGREDIENTS | SERVES 4

1 pound mild Cheddar cheese
1 pound Monterey jack cheese
½ cup canned green chili peppers
4 large eggs
1 cup evaporated milk
⅔ cup flour
1 (8-ounce) can tomato sauce

1. Preheat oven to 350°F.

2. Grate the cheese. Cut the chili peppers into ¼" strips.

3. Mix together the eggs, milk, and flour.

4. Layer ⅓ of the cheese, then ½ of the egg mixture, then ½ of the chilies in a rectangular baking pan. Repeat layers. Top soufflé with the tomato sauce.

5. Bake uncovered for 30–45 minutes. Cover with the remaining cheese and bake for 15 minutes.

Spinach Egg Bake

Substitute fresh smoked peppers such as chipotle chilies to give this dish a distinctive flavor.

INGREDIENTS | SERVES 6

1 (10-ounce) package frozen chopped spinach
8 ounces fresh mushrooms
1 small white onion
¼ cup canned jalapeño peppers
¾ pound Cheddar cheese
6 large eggs
2 cups chopped cooked ham
2 cups small-curd cottage cheese
½ cup butter
6 tablespoons flour

1. Preheat oven to 350°F.

2. Thaw the spinach and squeeze out the water. Cut the mushrooms into thin slices. Remove the skin from onion and chop into ¼" pieces. Drain off the water from the jalapeños. Grate the cheese. Beat the eggs until the whites and yolks are well blended.

3. Mix together all the ingredients in a large mixing bowl. Stir well until all ingredients are blended. Pour into a 9" × 13" baking dish. Bake for 1 hour. Let stand for 10 minutes before cutting.

Mexican Frittata

This is a perfect breakfast meal served with Mexican Coffee (see recipe in Chapter 21).

INGREDIENTS | SERVES 4

3 cups whole milk

1½ cups flour

½ teaspoon salt

6 large eggs

1 tablespoon vegetable oil

1½ pounds fresh chili peppers (type of your choosing)

1½ pounds medium Cheddar cheese

1½ pounds Monterey jack cheese

1 avocado

1 red bell pepper

All about Eggs

Egg yolks contain all of the fat and cholesterol in an egg. Use egg whites instead of whole eggs when making pasta, cakes, and other dishes. Usually 2 egg whites can be substituted for 1 whole egg.

1. Preheat oven to 375°F.

2. Blend the milk, flour, salt, and eggs.

3. Spread the oil over the bottom and sides of a 9" × 13" baking pan.

4. Remove the stems and seeds from the chili peppers and cut into 1" pieces.

5. Shred the cheeses and mix.

6. Place half of the chili peppers in a layer on the bottom of the pan. Top with half of the cheese. Add the rest of the chili peppers. Add the rest of the cheese. Pour the egg mixture over the top.

7. Bake for 40 minutes.

8. Remove the skin and pit from the avocado and cut into slices. Remove the seeds and stem from the red pepper and cut into 1" pieces. Use the avocado and red pepper as garnish.

Egg-Stuffed Rolls

When served with fresh fruit, this makes a perfect lunch for a large group.

INGREDIENTS | MAKES 36 ROLLS

2 quarts water

6 large eggs

2 pounds Velveeta cheese

1 (15-ounce) can pitted black olives

1 medium yellow onion

½ cup canned jalapeño peppers, or 4 fresh jalapeños

1 cup salsa

1 cup vegetable oil

¼ cup vinegar

1 tablespoon garlic salt

3 dozen small French rolls

Finding Fresh Eggs

Fresh eggs will be translucent when held up to the light. When you break the egg, the white should be clear and the yolk should be shiny. Yolks can vary in color, depending on the diet and breed of the chicken the egg came from.

1. Bring the water to a boil in a medium-sized pot. Add the eggs and cook at a boil for 6 minutes. Turn off the heat but keep the eggs in the water for 4 more minutes. Remove eggs from pot and run cold water over the eggs. When the eggs are cool enough to handle, remove the shells and chop the eggs into ¼" pieces.

2. Grate the cheese. Drain the black olives and cut them into ¼" pieces. Peel the onion and cut into ¼" pieces. Drain off the juice from the jalapeños and cut into ¼" pieces.

3. Combine the eggs, cheese, olive, onions, jalapeños, Tomato Salsa, vegetable oil, vinegar, and garlic salt in a medium-sized mixing bowl. Cover and refrigerate for 8–12 hours.

4. Preheat oven to 300°F.

5. Cut off the tops of the French rolls and dig out some of the bread. Fill with the egg mixture and wrap the stuffed rolls with parchment paper.

6. Place on a baking sheet and bake for 1 hour.

Easy Huevos Rancheros

Serve with a side of refried beans.

INGREDIENTS | SERVES 4

1 small red onion
1 tablespoon vegetable oil
4 large eggs
4 (6") corn tortillas
1 cup salsa
¼ cup shredded white Cheddar cheese
½ cup chopped cilantro

1. Peel and dice the onion.

2. Heat the oil to medium temperature in a medium-sized frying pan. Add the eggs. Fry to your liking.

3. Remove the eggs and put the tortillas in the frying pan. Fry for 30 seconds on each side. Cover the tortilla with salsa. Place 1 egg on top of each tortilla. Garnish with onions, cheese, and cilantro.

Huevos Bogotano

Spice up this dish any way you would like. Add hot peppers, oregano, or dill weed, for example.

INGREDIENTS | SERVES 6

½ pound ground sausage
½ pound fresh or frozen corn
12 large eggs
¼ teaspoon onion powder
½ teaspoon salt
½ teaspoon ground black pepper

1. Crumble the sausage and sauté over medium heat in a medium-sized frying pan until cooked but not browned, stirring frequently, about 6–8 minutes. Remove the sausage and spread on a paper towel to absorb excess fat. Wipe the grease from the frying pan with a paper towel.

2. In a small saucepan, heat the corn at medium temperature until thoroughly warmed.

3. Crack the eggs into a medium-sized mixing bowl. Add the onion powder, salt, and pepper. Beat until light and fluffy.

4. Pour the eggs into the frying pan and stir in the sausage and corn. Cook over low heat, stirring frequently, until the eggs are done.

Royal Eggs

Serve this as a dessert at your next traditional Mexican meal.

INGREDIENTS | SERVES 6

¼ cup raisins
½ cup dry sherry
12 large eggs
2 cups granulated sugar
1 cup water
1 cinnamon stick
¼ cup slivered almonds

Nuns As Cooks

Many of the Mexican recipes that combine European ingredients such as sherry with traditional Mexican ingredients such as eggs were actually invented by Spanish nuns who first came to Mexico as missionaries.

1. Preheat oven to 325°F.

2. Soak the raisins in ¼ cup of the sherry. Separate the eggs and discard the whites.

3. Beat the egg yolks until they form a ribbon when poured from the bowl. Pour into a buttered, shallow pan. Set this pan in another larger pan with about 1" of water in it.

4. Bake for 20–25 minutes, or until set. Remove from oven and cool on a wire rack. When cool, cut into 1" cubes.

5. While the eggs are cooling, combine the sugar, water, and cinnamon stick in a saucepan and bring to a boil. Reduce heat to medium-low and simmer for about 5 minutes, stirring until all the sugar is dissolved. Remove the cinnamon stick.

6. Carefully place the egg cubes in the sauce. Continue simmering over very low heat until the cubes are well-saturated with the syrup. Add the soaked raisins and remaining sherry. Sprinkle with slivered almonds.

Egg Chilaquiles

Serve with fresh cantaloupe and honeydew melon slices.

INGREDIENTS | SERVES 4

4 (6") corn tortillas
2 medium red tomatoes
1 small white onion
4 large eggs
2 tablespoons butter or margarine
½ teaspoon salt
¼ teaspoon ground black pepper
½ teaspoon Tabasco or other hot sauce
½ cup grated Parmesan cheese

1. Cut the tortillas into ½" strips. Destem the tomatoes and chop into ¼" pieces. Peel the onion and chop into ¼" pieces. Beat the eggs.

2. Melt the butter in a skillet. Fry the tortilla strips until golden brown.

3. Stir in the tomatoes and onion and heat to boiling.

4. Stir in the eggs, salt, pepper, and Tabasco sauce; cook until the eggs are set, stirring frequently.

5. Top with Parmesan cheese. Serve immediately.

Scrambled Egg Tacos

Use a hot salsa or mix some diced jalapeños into the eggs if you like things spicy.

INGREDIENTS | SERVES 4

1 teaspoon butter
½ cup salsa
8 large eggs
⅓ cup cream
½ teaspoon salt
4 (6") corn tortillas
½ cup shredded Monterey jack cheese

1. Melt the butter in a large frying pan over medium heat. Add the salsa and heat until the onion is soft, about 5 minutes.

2. Beat the eggs with the cream and salt. Pour the egg mixture into the salsa and cook, stirring constantly, until the eggs are set.

3. While the eggs are cooking, heat the tortillas in an ungreased, medium-hot skillet or griddle, turning frequently.

4. Place a hot, soft tortilla on a plate and spoon eggs on top. Sprinkle with cheese. Serve immediately.

Chili Egg Noodles

Serve as a side dish for Mexican Meat Loaf (see recipe in Chapter 12).

INGREDIENTS | SERVES 6

6 large eggs
½ teaspoon chili powder
½ teaspoon salt
1 cup flour
2 dried ancho chilies
1 cup whipping cream
1 cup grated Cheddar cheese
½ teaspoon paprika

Different Eggs

While Americans typically only eat chicken eggs, other birds' eggs can provide some interesting taste sensations. Try duck or goose eggs when baking to give more fluffiness to your cakes and dessert bars. They also have a sweeter taste in casseroles and even as scrambled eggs.

1. Separate the eggs and discard the whites. Combine the egg yolks, chili powder, and salt in a small bowl. Mix, adding the flour until you have a workable dough.

2. Roll out the dough on a flat, floured surface. Let air-dry about 1 hour. Cut into noodles by drawing a knife through the dough.

3. Bring 2 quarts of water to a boil in a large saucepan. Add the noodles; boil for 10 minutes. Drain and rinse in cold water.

4. Preheat oven to 350°F.

5. Wash, peel, and seed the chilies. Cut into quarters and put in a blender or food processor. Add the whipping cream and blend until the chilies are finely chopped.

6. In a greased, 2-quart casserole dish, layer the noodles, cheese, then cream-chili sauce. Sprinkle the top with paprika.

7. Bake for 30 minutes or until bubbling hot.

CHAPTER 9

Stews and Moles

Beef Mole

When fresh vegetables are in season, don't hesitate to add carrots, corn, or any of your favorite vegetables to this dish.

INGREDIENTS | SERVES 6

3 pounds stewing beef

3 fresh jalapeño peppers

2 medium white onions

2 garlic cloves

3 medium red tomatoes

3 tablespoons vegetable oil

4 medium potatoes

1 medium zucchini (about 10" long)

2 teaspoons salt

1 teaspoon ground black pepper

Mole

Moles are stews made with thick, intensely flavorful sauces, usually featuring different chili peppers and nuts. Sometimes the mole is poured over uncut pieces of meat, such as chicken, so the meat can stew that way. Most often, however, the meat is cut up and made part of the sauce.

1. Place the beef in a large saucepan and fill with water to about 2" from the top of the pan. Bring to a boil, cover, and reduce heat to medium. Cook for 2 hours. Drain and set aside.

2. Remove the stems and seeds from the jalapeños and cut into quarters. Remove the skin from the onions and cut into quarters. Remove the skin from the garlic cloves. Remove the skin from the tomatoes and cut into quarters. Place these ingredients in blender or food processor and blend on medium until all the ingredients are puréed. They should look as though they are chopped into very small pieces, but not blended into a paste.

3. Heat the oil on medium-high setting in a large frying pan. Add the purée and cook, stirring constantly, for 5 minutes.

4. Peel the potatoes and cut into 1" cubes. Place in a medium-sized saucepan, cover with water, and boil until tender. Drain and set aside.

5. Cut the zucchini into 1" cubes.

6. Combine all the ingredients in a frying pan; stir gently. Heat on medium setting for 10 minutes.

Beef and Cactus Stew

This is excellent served with Red Rice (see recipe in Chapter 2).

INGREDIENTS | SERVES 4

2 pounds beef steak

2 tablespoons olive oil

1 medium yellow onion

4 garlic cloves

1 cup canned cactus pieces

4 fresh jalapeño chilies

2 chipotle chilies

4 green tomatoes

2 medium red tomatoes

1 teaspoon dried oregano

1 teaspoon salt

1 teaspoon ground black pepper

1. Cut the beef into 1" pieces. Place in a large frying pan with the olive oil. Heat to medium temperature. Cook beef until brown on all sides.

2. Remove the skin from the onion and cut into 1" pieces. Remove the skin from the garlic and mince. Drain off the water from the cactus and cut into 1" pieces. Remove the stems and seeds from the chilies and cut into ¼" pieces. Cut the green and red tomatoes into 1" pieces.

3. Add all the ingredients to the beef and reduce the heat to low. Cover and cook for 1 hour, stirring periodically.

What Oil to Use?

In most recipes you can substitute virgin olive oil for the vegetable oil. It gives a slightly more tangy taste. Sunflower and soy oil have the lightest flavors and are the healthiest. Corn oil is slightly heavy and gives a heartier feel to a dish. Traditionally, Mexican cooking uses lard.

Chicken Dry Soup

Mexican dry soups are more like casseroles than typical soups.

INGREDIENTS | SERVES 4

4 boneless, skinless chicken breasts
1 medium yellow onion
2 garlic cloves
1 tablespoon olive oil
1 cup salsa
4 cups chicken broth
5 (6") corn tortillas

Onion Varieties

Onions vary in sweetness. Vidalia tend to be the sweetest, followed by red, then yellow. White onions are the least sweet and are better in meat dishes than in soups.

1. Cut the chicken breasts into 1" cubes. Remove the skin from the onion and cut into ¼" pieces. Remove the skin from the garlic and cut into thin slices.

2. Heat the olive oil in a large frying pan on medium. Add the chicken, onion, and garlic to the frying pan and cook until the chicken is brown on all sides.

3. Reduce the heat to low and add the salsa and broth; mix well. Cook for 30 minutes, uncovered, stirring periodically.

4. Tear the tortillas into 1" pieces. Add to the frying pan and stir well. Cover and simmer for 1 hour.

5. Remove cover and simmer until the dish is moist, but not runny.

Mexican Chicken Casserole

Serve over a bed of lettuce with fresh Tostadas (see recipe in Chapter 2).

INGREDIENTS | SERVES 4

4 boneless, skinless chicken breasts

1 small onion

12 (8") flour tortillas

1½ cups grated Cheddar cheese

1 (10.75-ounce) can cream of mushroom condensed soup

1 (10.75-ounce) can cream of chicken condensed soup

1 cup sour cream

½ cup canned chopped jalapeño peppers, drained (or 4 fresh jalapeños, chopped)

1 cup salsa

1. Preheat oven to 300°F.

2. Cut the chicken into 1" cubes. Peel the onion and grate using the fine side of a vegetable grater. Tear the tortillas into eighths.

3. Combine the onion, cheese, soups, sour cream, and jalapeños in a medium-sized bowl. Make layers in a casserole dish using ⅓ of the torn tortillas, soup mixture, chicken, then salsa. Repeat twice, in that order.

4. Cover and bake for 2 hours.

Beef and Bean Stew

Serve with white rice and a fresh fruit salad.

INGREDIENTS | SERVES 6

2 pounds round steak

1 yellow onion

4 red tomatoes

1 beef bouillon cube

2 cups canned kidney beans

½ cup canned chopped jalapeño peppers

¼ teaspoon ground black pepper

½ teaspoon garlic salt

1 tablespoon chili powder

1 tablespoon prepared yellow mustard

Tomato Types

All tomatoes are not alike. Substitute plum tomatoes for a more robust flavor. Choose golden tomatoes for a mellower taste. Reserve pricier hot-house tomatoes for recipes in which tomatoes are the main ingredient.

1. Cut the beef into 1" cubes. Peel and chop the onion into ¼" pieces. Cut the tomatoes into quarters. Crush the bouillon cube. Drain the kidney beans and jalapeños.

2. Mix together the meat, black pepper, garlic salt, chili powder, and mustard in a large pot. Cover with the onion, tomatoes, crushed bouillon cube, beans, and jalapeños; mix well.

3. Cover the pot, and cook on medium-low heat for 2 hours. Stir periodically.

Caldo de Rez

Serve with Pineapple and Coconut Salad (see recipe in Chapter 15).

INGREDIENTS | SERVES 6

1½ pounds beef stew meat

1 medium cabbage

1 small white onion

1 celery rib

4 medium red tomatoes

½ green bell pepper

4 medium baking potatoes

1 teaspoon dried cilantro

1 teaspoon salt

½ teaspoon ground black pepper

1 teaspoon Tabasco or other hot sauce

1. Remove any fat from the stew meat. Cut the cabbage into wedges. Peel the onion and chop into ¼" pieces. Chop the celery into ¼" pieces. Remove the stem and seeds from the bell pepper, then chop into ¼" pieces. Peel the potatoes and cut into 1" cubes.

2. Place all the ingredients in a large pot and stir until well mixed. Cover and bring to a boil; reduce temperature to medium-low and simmer for 30 minutes.

Too Salty?

If the dish tastes too salty, add a teaspoon each of cider vinegar and sugar to the recipe. They will neutralize the salt without adding additional flavor.

Pork Posole

Serve with fruit salad for a complete meal.

INGREDIENTS | SERVES 8

4 medium yellow onions
6 medium red tomatoes
12 fresh serrano chilies
5 garlic cloves
4 pounds lean pork roast
2 pounds fresh or frozen hominy
¼ cup granulated sugar
3 tablespoons salt
1 teaspoon ground black pepper
2 cups fresh or canned tomato sauce
2 tablespoons lemon juice

What Is Posole?

Mexican cooking has many dishes with no European equivalents. Although this is a stew because many ingredients are mixed with liquids, posole tends to be heavier and thicker than a traditional stew. If the hominy is not overcooked, it will be a bit crunchy, adding a unique texture to what most North Americans think of as a stew.

1. Peel the onions and chop into ¼" pieces. Cut the tomatoes into ¼" pieces. Remove the stems and seeds from the chili peppers. Peel the garlic and chop into ¼" pieces.

2. In a large stew pot, combine the roast, onions, chili peppers, garlic, hominy, sugar, salt, and pepper. Cover with water and bring to a boil. Turn heat to medium-low and cook until the meat is done and the hominy is tender but not mushy, about 3 hours. Stir occasionally and add more water if necessary.

3. Remove the meat and shred. Return the meat to the pot.

4. Add the tomatoes and tomato sauce. Cook uncovered over medium heat for 30 minutes.

5. Stir in the lemon juice right before serving.

Beef Picadillo

This is excellent served with Broccoli Salad (see recipe in Chapter 7).

INGREDIENTS | SERVES 6

1 small white onion
2 garlic cloves
1 medium Granny Smith apple
1 pound ground beef
1 cup canned or fresh tomato sauce
½ cup raisins
¼ cup toasted almond slivers
1 tablespoon vinegar
1 teaspoon granulated sugar
1 teaspoon salt
¼ teaspoon ground cinnamon
¼ teaspoon ground cumin
⅛ teaspoon ground black pepper

1. Peel the onion and cut into ¼" pieces. Peel and mince the garlic. Peel and remove the core and stem from the apple; cut into ¼" pieces.

2. Place the ground beef, onion, and garlic in a medium-sized frying pan. Cook on medium heat until the ground beef is browned.

3. Stir in the remaining ingredients.

4. Continue cooking on medium heat, stirring periodically, until all the ingredients are well blended.

Substitute Mushrooms

To turn any meat dish into an instant vegetarian entrée, substitute morel mushrooms for the meat. Be sure to substitute by volume, not weight, because even these heavier mushrooms weigh less than meat.

Mexican Meatball Stew

This is a great cold-weather dinner. Serve it with bread or tortillas to mop up the savory sauce.

INGREDIENTS | SERVES 6

1 large white onion

6 carrots

6 new potatoes (small)

1 (15-ounce) can plum tomatoes or 4 fresh plum tomatoes

2 large fresh jalapeño peppers

3 garlic cloves

1½ pounds lean ground beef

½ pound ground sausage

1 teaspoon dried cilantro

1 teaspoon salt

1 teaspoon ground black pepper

1 teaspoon ground cumin

1 teaspoon celery salt

1 teaspoon garlic powder

2 tablespoons vegetable oil

1 cup canned hominy

1 (15-ounce) can red kidney beans

6 cups water

3 beef bouillon cubes, crushed

Potatoes au Naturel

Potato skins contain many vitamins not found in the "meat" of the potato. Unless your recipe calls for a clean, "white" look, leave the skins on and savor the extra nutrition.

1. Peel the onion and cut into ¼" pieces. Peel the carrots and cut into quarters. Wash the potatoes and quarter. If using fresh tomatoes, cut into quarters. Remove the stems and seeds from the jalapeño peppers and cut into ¼" rounds. Peel and mince the garlic.

2. Combine the ground beef and ground sausage. Add the cilantro, salt, black pepper, cumin, celery salt, and garlic powder. Mix well with your hands. Form meatballs slightly smaller than golf balls.

3. Heat the oil in a large skillet at medium-high. Add the meatballs and garlic. Cook until browned, flipping meatballs so all sides are browned. Drain off the grease. Set the meatballs on paper towels to soak up excess grease.

4. Transfer to a large stew pot. Add the onion, carrots, potatoes, jalapeños, hominy, kidney beans, and water. Cook for 1 hour on medium-low heat or until the potatoes and carrots are tender.

5. Add the bouillon and tomatoes.

Tomato Dry Soup

Use flour tortillas in this dish for a slightly different taste.

INGREDIENTS | SERVES 6

1 large white onion
2 garlic cloves
2 cups canned tomatoes, with juice
10 (6") corn tortillas
½ cup vegetable oil, divided
1 teaspoon salt
½ teaspoon ground black pepper
½ teaspoon dried oregano
1 cup whipping cream
1 cup grated Parmesan cheese
1 teaspoon paprika

Dry Soup?

Many Mexican dishes feature bread or tortillas that are soaked in a sauce until the dish resembles more of a casserole or heavy stew than a soup. In Mexico, they refer to these dishes as dry soups. It's not certain where this name came from, but it's an apt description.

1. Preheat oven to 350°F.

2. Peel the onion and chop into ¼" pieces. Peel and mince the garlic. Roughly chop the tomatoes, reserving the juice. Cut the tortillas into ½"-wide strips.

3. In a large saucepan, heat 2 tablespoons of the oil to medium temperature. Add the onion and garlic. Cook until the onion is soft but not brown. Add the tomatoes, salt, pepper, and oregano, and stir until blended. Heat to simmering and cook for about 10 minutes.

4. Heat the remaining oil in a large frying pan. Fry the tortilla strips until limp, not crisp. Set on paper towels to absorb excess grease.

5. In an ovenproof casserole dish, arrange layers as follows: a little tomato juice, a handful of tortilla strips, some cream, then cheese. Repeat until all the ingredients are used, ending with cheese. Sprinkle the paprika on top.

6. Bake for 20 minutes, uncovered, or until the dish is bubbling.

Pig Feet Stew

Serve with fresh chilies, limes, lettuce, onion, and radishes to add to the soup as garnishes.

INGREDIENTS | SERVES 6

1 pound pork roast

3 medium potatoes

1 large white onion

3 medium carrots

8 garlic cloves

6 pigs' feet

2 quarts water

1 teaspoon salt

1 teaspoon dried oregano

1 cup fresh or frozen peas

1. Cut the pork roast into 1" cubes. Peel the potatoes and cut into 1" cubes. Peel the onion and chop into ¼" pieces. Peel the carrots and cut into ¼" rounds. Peel the garlic and slice thinly.

2. Put the pigs' feet and onion into a large stockpot with the water. Add the salt and oregano; stir well. Bring to a boil. Boil uncovered for 30 minutes.

3. Add the remaining ingredients. Reduce heat to medium and simmer uncovered for 3–4 hours or until the carrots are soft and the meat is tender.

Cashew Chili

Because the nuts provide all the protein, you don't need meat to have a complete meal. Serve with a side of fresh fruit.

INGREDIENTS | SERVES 8

1 medium white onion

1 small green bell pepper

2 celery ribs

6 large tomatoes

1 tablespoon vegetable oil

1 teaspoon dried oregano

1 teaspoon ground cumin

1 teaspoon garlic powder

1 tablespoon chili powder

4 cups canned (or precooked) kidney beans

2 cups cashews

1. Peel the onion and cut into ¼" pieces. Remove the seeds and stem from the green pepper and cut into ¼" pieces. Cut the celery into ¼" pieces. Dice tomatoes, reserving the juice.

2. Heat the oil to medium heat. Add the onion, green pepper, and celery. Cook until the onion is browned, about 10–12 minutes. Add the spices; stir well.

3. Transfer the mixture to a soup pot. Add the tomatoes, reserved juice, and beans. Simmer on low for 3 hours, stirring periodically. Add the cashews and heat through just before serving.

CHAPTER 10

Fish and Seafood

Sea Bass with Filberts

This is excellent served with Zucchini with Jalapeños (see recipe in Chapter 13).

INGREDIENTS | SERVES 6

1 (5–6-pound) whole sea bass
1 tablespoon lemon juice
1 medium white onion
12 pitted green olives
¼ cup olive oil
¼ cup canned, chopped pimientos
½ teaspoon salt
1 teaspoon ground black pepper
½ teaspoon crushed coriander seeds
2 tablespoons orange juice
½ cup crushed filberts
¼ cup chopped fresh parsley

Coriander

Coriander is an herb of the parsley family. The fresh leaves of the plant, called "cilantro" or "Chinese parsley," are commonly used in Mexican cooking. The seeds are the dried ripe fruits of the herb, and they come either whole or ground. It is especially good when the whole seeds are slightly roasted in a small frying pan before being ground and added to a dish.

1. Preheat oven to 375°F.

2. Remove the head and guts from the fish and slice in half. (You might ask the fish department manager to do this for you!) Lay the fish in an ovenproof baking pan, skin-side down. Sprinkle with lemon juice.

3. Remove the skin from the onion and chop into ¼" pieces. Chop the olives into ¼" pieces.

4. Sauté the onions in olive oil over medium heat in a small skillet for 3 minutes. Add the olives, pimientos, salt, black pepper, and coriander seeds, and sauté for an additional 3 minutes.

5. Remove from heat and add the orange juice and filberts; stir well.

6. Pour the mixture over the fish and place in the oven for 30 minutes or until the fish flakes easily. Sprinkle with parsley before serving.

Shrimp Tamales

It's best to keep the filling for tamales simple yet very flavorful, since you don't use a lot of it.

INGREDIENTS | YIELDS 16 TAMALES

16 corn husks

1 batch dough from Plain Tamales (see recipe in Chapter 2)

⅔ cup chopped cooked shrimp

3 tablespoons sour cream

2 tablespoons adobo sauce

2 green onions, chopped

1 tablespoon chili powder

1. Soak corn husks in hot water for 1 hour. Prepare Plain Tamale dough. In small bowl, combine remaining ingredients and mix well.

2. Drain husks and spread tamale dough on husks to within 1" of edges. Place 1 tablespoon shrimp filling in center of dough. Fold sides of husks to the middle so edges meet, then fold up bottom and fold down top to enclose filling; tie with kitchen string. Place in colander and steam for about 1 hour or until corn husks peel away from tamales.

Grilled Swordfish

Serve with a fresh fruit salad for a light summer meal.

INGREDIENTS | SERVES 4

1 teaspoon chili powder

2 tablespoons lime juice

1 teaspoon dried oregano

1 teaspoon dried cilantro

¼ cup canned anchovies

½ teaspoon ground cayenne pepper

1 teaspoon salt

1 cup picante sauce

4 large swordfish fillets (about 6 ounces each)

1. Preheat grill to medium-high heat.

2. Add the chili powder, lime juice, oregano, cilantro, anchovies, cayenne pepper, and salt to the picante sauce.

3. Place the fillets on the grill and baste liberally with the sauce, reserving about ¼ cup for serving. Turn once and baste again.

4. When the fillets are done, drizzle the remaining sauce over the top.

Shark Steak with Green Tomato Sauce

Serve with Red Rice (see recipe in Chapter 2) and fresh fruit.

INGREDIENTS | SERVES 4

4 medium shark steaks (about 6 ounces each)

½ teaspoon salt

½ teaspoon ground black pepper

1 teaspoon olive oil

4 garlic cloves

4 scallions

2 habanero chilies

2 teaspoons dried cilantro

1 cup Green Tomato Salsa (see recipe in Chapter 2)

1. Preheat oven to 350°F.

2. Sprinkle both sides of the shark steaks with the salt and pepper. Grease the bottom of a 9" × 13" baking pan with the olive oil. Place the steaks in the pan.

3. Remove the skin from the garlic cloves and scallions; slice thinly. Remove the stems and seeds from the chilies and slice thinly. Top the steaks with the garlic, scallion, and chili peppers. Sprinkle cilantro on top.

4. Pour the Green Tomato Salsa over the steaks evenly. Bake for 20 minutes.

Let's Hear It for Green Tomatoes

Although we tend to think of green tomatoes as unripe and therefore not fit to eat, the opposite is true. Because they have a firmer flesh and more tart taste, they add a distinctly different flavor from their ripe counterparts. Eating green tomatoes also means we get to enjoy the fresh garden tomatoes for a longer season.

Soused Langoustines

While this is excellent served with white rice for a light dinner, it is good served cold atop a bed of mixed greens, too.

INGREDIENTS | SERVES 4

6 garlic cloves

6 capers

½ cup fresh lime juice

½ cup dry white wine

½ teaspoon cayenne pepper

½ teaspon salt

2 pounds langoustines

(If you must substitute lobster tails, cut them into 1" slices.)

What Are Langoustines?

Langoustines are small lobsters commonly found in tropical climates. They are excellent for cooking in stews and soups because the pieces of flesh are so small that they easily take up the spices. You likely won't find langoustines in the shell anywhere except the southern coastal states, but fresh or freshly frozen usually work just fine in a recipe.

1. Peel and mince the garlic. Mince the capers.

2. In a bowl, combine the lime juice, white wine, capers, garlic, cayenne pepper, and salt.

3. Put the langoustines in a medium-sized frying pan and pour the liquid mixture over the top. Slowly bring the mixture to a simmer over medium heat. Simmer for 5 minutes or until the langoustines are opaque.

4. Remove from heat and pour the entire mixture into a bowl; refrigerate for 24 hours.

5. Drain off the liquid and reheat the langoustines by placing in a medium-sized, covered pot on medium-low heat for 5 minutes. Stir and test by eating a small piece. If not hot enough, add ¼ cup water, cover and raise heat to medium for 2 more minutes.

Smothered Shrimp

This is excellent served with a variety of cheeses and wine.

INGREDIENTS | SERVES 4

2 pounds medium fresh shrimp
1 small white onion
4 garlic cloves
3 medium red tomatoes
1 cup canned, stewed green tomatoes, with juice
½ cup canned or fresh jalapeño peppers
½ cup olive oil
¼ cup dry cooking sherry

1. Boil the shrimp for 10 minutes in 1 gallon of water. Rinse with cold water. Remove the shell and use a fork tine to remove the back vein.

2. Peel and mince the onion and garlic. Chop the tomatoes into ¼" pieces, reserving the juice from the green tomatoes. Remove the stems and seeds from the jalapeños and mince.

3. Heat the olive oil in a medium-sized frying pan. Add the onion, garlic, and jalapeños; sauté on medium heat until the onions are limp but not brown. Add the red and green tomatoes, including the juice from the green tomatoes. Continue cooking at medium heat, stirring constantly, for 15 minutes. Stir in the cooking sherry.

4. Preheat oven to 300°F.

5. Arrange the shrimp in a large baking pan. Pour the sauce over the shrimp. Place the pan in the oven for 15 minutes.

Red Snapper with Pecan Sauce

This unique blend of flavors is suitable for almost any white fish. It also works for seafood such as shrimp and scallops.

INGREDIENTS | SERVES 4

1 cup chicken broth

1 cup water

4 (6- to 10-ounce) red snapper fillets

1 small yellow onion

2 garlic cloves

1 cup pecans, divided

1 teaspoon salt

1 teaspoon saffron powder

2 key limes

Use Saffron Sparingly

Pure saffron is one of the rarest spices in the world. It has a very subtle yet distinctive flavor that is brought out in fish dishes. Saffron powder is usually diluted with other ingredients that help carry the flavor of the saffron throughout the food.

1. Combine the broth and water in a large frying pan and bring to a boil. Add the fish fillets. Reduce heat to medium-low and cook until the fish flakes easily with a fork. Lift the fish out and place on a serving platter. Reserve ½ cup of the cooking liquid.

2. Remove the skin from the onion and garlic cloves. Cut the onion into quarters.

3. Put the onion, garlic cloves, ½ cup of reserved cooking liquid, ¾ cup of the pecans, salt, and saffron powder into a blender or food processor; blend at medium speed for about 2 minutes or until you have a smooth purée.

4. Heat the sauce in a medium-sized saucepan at medium heat. Do not let it boil. Pour the sauce over the fish fillets.

5. Top with the remaining whole pecans. Squeeze the juice from the limes on the top right before serving.

Tuna Steaks with Chili Sauce

To add some color to this dish, garnish the fish with fresh sprigs of parsley or cilantro.

INGREDIENTS | SERVES 4

1 cup chicken broth
1 cup water
4 (6- to 10-ounce) tuna steaks
1 medium yellow onion
2 garlic cloves
8 chili peppers (type of your choosing)
1 teaspoon salt
½ teaspoon cayenne pepper
1 teaspoon ground white pepper

Choosing Chili Peppers

Chili peppers can be fun to experiment with, as there are so many varieties available today. Don't hesitate to try something new. You will soon get beyond the heat of the first bite and discover a wide range of flavors to match the many shapes, colors, and sizes available.

1. Combine the broth and water in a large frying pan and bring to a boil. Add the tuna steaks. Reduce heat to medium-low and cook until the fish flakes easily with a fork. Lift the fish out and place on a serving platter. Reserve ½ cup of the cooking liquid.

2. Remove the skin from the onion and garlic cloves. Cut the onion into quarters. Remove the seeds and stems from the chilies. Cut into quarters.

3. Put the onion, garlic, chilies, ½ cup reserved cooking liquid, salt, cayenne pepper, and white pepper into a blender or food processor and blend at medium speed for about 2 minutes or until you have a smooth purée.

4. Heat the sauce in a medium-sized saucepan at medium heat. Do not let it boil. Pour the sauce over the fish.

Fried Flounder with Spicy Green Sauce

Try adding some freshly grated Parmesan cheese on top of the fish fillets during the last 10 minutes of baking for an additional flavor treat.

INGREDIENTS | SERVES 4

4 (6- to 10-ounce) flounder fillets

1 cup flour

3 tablespoons vegetable oil

½ small white onion

2 garlic cloves

8 fresh chili peppers (type of your choosing)

6 green tomatoes

¼ teaspoon ground cloves

½ teaspoon ground cinnamon

½ teaspoon ground nutmeg

½ teaspoon dried oregano

½ teaspoon ground cumin

½ teaspoon dried thyme

½ teaspoon dried rosemary

1 teaspoon dried parsley

¼ cup lime juice

Which Fish Tastes Best?

Because most Mexican fish recipes call for adding sauces and spices to the fish, look for a firm, mild-flavored, white-fleshed fish that holds up well to cooking. Bass, flounder, shark, swordfish, and red snapper all work well. Some fish can have surprisingly strong flavors so if you want to try a new fish, take a small piece home and steam it to see if you like the flavor before putting it in your recipe.

1. Wash the fillets with warm water and cover with the flour.

2. Heat the oil to medium-high heat in a large frying pan. Add the fillets and fry on both sides until golden brown. Drain off the oil and place the fillets in a baking dish.

3. Remove the skin from the onion and garlic. Remove the stems and seeds from the chili peppers. Cut the green tomatoes into quarters.

4. Preheat oven to 350°F.

5. Place the onion, garlic, cloves, cinnamon, nutmeg, oregano, cumin, thyme, rosemary, parsley, tomatoes, and lime juice in a food processor or blender. Blend at medium speed until you have a smooth purée.

6. Pour the sauce over the fish. Place the fish in the oven and bake for 1 hour or until the fish flakes easily with a fork.

Crab with Spinach and Rice

Serve with flour tortillas and assorted fresh fruits.

INGREDIENTS | SERVES 4

4 cups chicken broth
2 cups dry white rice
1 small yellow onion
2 garlic cloves
1 fresh jalapeño pepper
2 cups frozen or canned spinach
2 pounds crabmeat
1 teaspoon salt
1 teaspoon ground black pepper
1 cup grated mozzarella cheese

Crabby or Not?

Many people try to substitute "imitation crab" for the real thing. These inexpensive "sea legs" are actually a fine substitute if you are eating the meat right away. However, they quickly lose their flavor and soon taste like gummy noodles. You're better off paying for the real thing.

1. Bring the broth to a boil in a medium-sized saucepan. Add the rice. Cover and boil for 5 minutes. Reduce heat to medium-low and cook for 20 minutes or until the rice is tender.

2. Remove the skin from the onion and garlic. Cut the onion into ¼" pieces. Mince the garlic. Remove the stem and seeds from jalapeño pepper and mince.

3. Preheat oven to 350°F.

4. In a large mixing bowl, combine the rice, onion, garlic, jalapeños, spinach, crabmeat, salt, and black pepper until well mixed.

5. Spread the mixture evenly in a large baking dish. Top with cheese. Bake for 1 hour.

Mussel Ceviche

Serve atop a bed of lettuce with fresh Tostadas (see recipe in Chapter 2).

INGREDIENTS | SERVES 4

1 pound fresh shelled mussels
½ cup lime juice
1 small Vidalia onion
2 habanero chilies
3 green tomatoes
½ cup red tomato juice
½ cup clam juice
1 teaspoon salt
3 key limes

Mussels with Muscle

Fresh mussels will not smell fishy. The water they sit in will be clear and the shells will be bright, not filmy. Frozen and canned mussels simply don't have the same flavor as the fresh ones. However, some people substitute canned oysters for fresh mussels and consider it a good tradeoff.

1. Combine the mussels and lime juice in a small glass or ceramic container. Cover and refrigerate for 1 hour.

2. Remove the skin from the onion and cut into ¼" pieces. Remove the stems and seeds from the chilies and cut into ¼" pieces. Chop the tomatoes into ¼" pieces; reserve the juice.

3. Drain off and discard the lime juice and put the mussels in a medium-sized mixing bowl. Add the onions, chilies, green tomatoes with their juice, red tomato juice, clam juice, salt, and freshly squeezed juice from the key limes; stir well.

4. Refrigerate in a glass or ceramic container for 4–12 hours.

Halibut Ceviche

Serve with Black Bean and Corn Salad (see recipe in Chapter 7) for a wonderful mix of flavors.

INGREDIENTS | SERVES 4

1½–2 pounds fresh halibut
½ cup lime juice
1 small red onion
2 serrano chilies
1 large red tomato
½ cup fresh cilantro leaves
½ cup orange juice
1 teaspoon salt

Do I Have to Eat It Raw?

Ceviche is always served with raw fish because the lime juice effectively cooks the outside layer of flesh. However, if you're squeamish about eating raw fish, steam the fish chunks for 5 minutes to make sure they are fully cooked. You will lose some of the authentic flavor of a true ceviche, but it will still taste marvelous.

1. Cut the halibut into ½" cubes. Combine the fish and lime juice in a small glass or ceramic container. Cover and refrigerate for 1 hour.

2. Remove the skin from the onion and cut into ¼" pieces. Remove the stems and seeds from the chilies and cut into ¼" pieces. Chop the tomato into ¼" pieces; reserve the juice. Chop the cilantro into ¼" pieces.

3. Drain off and discard the lime juice and put the fish in a medium-sized mixing bowl. Add the onion, chilies, tomatoes with their juice, cilantro, orange juice, and salt; stir well. Refrigerate in a glass or ceramic container for 4–12 hours.

Shrimp in Vinaigrette

This makes an excellent substitute for a salad course for a formal meal. It is also a good lunch on a hot summer day when served with a green lettuce salad.

INGREDIENTS | SERVES 4

2 small red onions
½ teaspoon cayenne pepper
2 pounds fresh medium-sized shrimp
1 jalapeño chili pepper
1–2 cups red wine vinegar
1 teaspoon granulated sugar
½ teaspoon salt
½ teaspoon ground white pepper

Canned or Fresh?

Canned jalapeños are mushy, so they blend better with the other ingredients. If you prefer to use fresh jalapeños, you could substitute 1 small pepper, removing the seeds and stem.

1. Remove the skin from the onions. Cut 1 onion into ½" rings and add it to 2 gallons of water in a large stockpot. Add the cayenne pepper. Bring to a boil and add the shrimp. Cook for 10 minutes. Drain and discard the onions. Run the shrimp under cold water. Remove the shells and back veins.

2. Chop the other onion into ¼" pieces. Remove the stem and seeds from the jalapeño and chop into ¼" pieces.

3. Mix together 1 cup of the red wine vinegar, the chopped onions and chili, sugar, salt, and ground white pepper.

4. Put the shrimp in a large glass or ceramic dish. Pour the sauce over the top, making sure all the shrimp are covered. If you need more sauce, add the remaining cup of red wine vinegar.

5. Chill in the refrigerator for 4–12 hours before serving.

Rosquillas Fritas (Chapter 6)

Tomato Salsa (Chapter 2)

Cold Avocado Soup (Chapter 5)

Churros (Chapter 17)

Gazpacho (Chapter 17)

Easy Huevos Rancheros (Chapter 8)

Fried Plantains (Chapter 4)

Tequila Sunrise (Chapter 21)

Black Bean and Corn Salad (Chapter 7)

Mexican Tea Cakes (Chapter 16)

Natilla (Chapter 16)

Halibut Ceviche (Chapter 10)

Guacamole (Chapter 2)

Arroz con Pollo (Chapter 14)

Grilled Corn on the Cob (Chapter 13)

Chiles Rellenos (Chapter 17)

Red Sangria (Chapter 21)

Sherried Raisin and Rice Pudding (Chapter 14)

Chicken Tortilla Soup (Chapter 5)

Seafood Paella (Chapter 10)

Biscochitos (Chapter 16)

Enchiladas (Chapter 17)

Plain Tamales (Chapter 2)

Lime Margaritas (Chapter 21)

Scallops with Sesame Seed Sauce

Serve with Eggplant Casserole (see recipe in Chapter 13).

INGREDIENTS | SERVES 4

1½ pounds fresh scallops
1 garlic clove
½ cup plain hulled pepitas (pumpkin seeds)
3 tablespoons sesame seeds
2 tablespoons vegetable oil
¾ teaspoon chili powder
¼ teaspoon ground cinnamon
⅛ teaspoon ground cloves
¾ cup chicken broth
½ teaspoon salt
1½ tablespoons lime juice

Pepitas

Pepitas are simply pumpkin seeds. They are a favorite snack food in Mexico but also a popular cooking ingredient. In many non-Mexican U.S. markets, when the green interior of the seed is sold separately, it is labeled as pepitas while the whole seed is labeled as pumpkin seeds. However, in a Mexican market, you will need to specify whether you want hulled or nonhulled. Note that pumpkin seeds can be eaten with the shell on for a less oily, fruity flavor.

1. Put the scallops in a medium-sized saucepan. Add ½" water. Cover and heat on low until the scallops are opaque and firm.

2. Peel the garlic. Combine the pepitas, sesame seeds, garlic, and oil in a saucepan. Stir and cook over medium heat until the sesame seeds are light golden brown.

3. Remove from heat and stir in the chili powder, cinnamon, and cloves. Put the sauce in an electric blender or food processor and grind. Add the broth and salt. Grind again.

4. Transfer the mixture to a saucepan. Mix in the lime juice and heat over low heat, stirring until thickened.

5. Arrange the scallops on a platter and spoon the sauce over them.

Seafood Paella

Enjoy this with fresh fruit and a spinach salad.

INGREDIENTS | SERVES 8

1 small rock lobster tail
24 fresh mussels in shells
1½ pounds medium-sized shrimp
1 pound scallops
1 pound fresh crabmeat
1 small yellow onion
2 garlic cloves
2 medium ripe tomatoes
1 cup fresh or frozen green peas
1 cup whole pimientos
1 cup olive oil
1½ teaspoons salt
1 quart hot water
2 cups uncooked rice
¼ cup chopped, fresh parsley

1. Boil the lobster, mussels, shrimp, scallops, and crab for about 10 minutes. Remove the shells and devein the shrimp. Cut the lobster into 1" cubes. Cut the crabmeat into 1" pieces.

2. Peel and mince the onion and garlic. Remove the stems from the tomatoes and chop into ¼" pieces. Thaw the peas if using frozen. Cut the pimientos into ¼"-wide strips.

3. Heat the oil in a large frying pan. Add the onion and garlic. Cook until the onion is limp, about 2 minutes. Add the tomatoes and salt.

4. Add the hot water, rice, peas, and parsley; mix well. Cover and cook, stirring occasionally, for about 20 minutes or until the rice is tender.

5. Mix in the lobster, shrimp, scallops, half of the pimientos, and the mussels. Heat until very hot. Serve garnished with remaining pimientos.

CHAPTER 11

Poultry

Chicken-Stuffed Avocados

Serve as a summer lunch or as the salad before a heartier Mexican meal.

INGREDIENTS | SERVES 4

2 medium avocados
¼ cup fresh lime juice
2 cooked boneless chicken breasts
2 medium tomatoes
4 scallions or green onions
12 pimiento-stuffed green olives
1 cup finely chopped lettuce
½ teaspoon salt
1 teaspoon black pepper
2 tablespoons red wine vinegar
½ cup shredded Cheddar cheese

1. Peel the avocados. Slice in half and remove the pits. Sprinkle with lime juice.

2. Remove the skin from the chicken and chop into ½" pieces to yield about 1 cup of meat.

3. Chop the tomatoes into ¼" pieces. Remove the skin from the scallions and chop into ¼" pieces. Cut the olives into quarters.

4. Combine all the ingredients except the avocados and cheese in a medium-sized bowl.

5. Place ¼ of the mixture into each avocado half. Sprinkle the cheese on top.

Tequila Lime Chicken

Chicken should marinate for only a few hours in the refrigerator; any longer and the flesh will become too soft. This simple marinade can be used with turkey or pork, too.

INGREDIENTS | SERVES 4

¼ cup tequila
¼ cup lime juice
2 tablespoons adobo sauce
1 teaspoon sugar
1 teaspoon salt
⅛ teaspoon cayenne pepper
4 cloves garlic, minced
4 chicken breasts

1. In large bowl, combine all ingredients except chicken breasts and mix well. Add chicken and turn to coat. Cover and refrigerate for 2–4 hours.

2. Prepare and heat grill. Remove chicken from marinade and place, skin-side down, on grill. Cover and cook for 10 minutes. Turn chicken, cover again, and cook for 10–20 minutes or until chicken is thoroughly cooked. Discard remaining marinade.

Cinnamon Chicken

If there is extra room in the roasting pan, wash potatoes, leaving the skin on, and quarter them. Place them in with the chicken to bake.

INGREDIENTS | SERVES 4

4 skin-on chicken breasts
1 cup milk
1 cup flour
2 tablespoons ground cinnamon
1 teaspoon cayenne pepper
1 tablespoon salt
1 teaspoon ground nutmeg
1 teaspoon ground cloves
4 tablespoons vegetable oil

1. Preheat oven to 300°F.

2. Wash the chicken thoroughly. Pour the milk into a soup bowl and dunk the chicken breasts in milk until completely coated. Discard the remaining milk.

3. In another soup bowl, mix together the flour, cinnamon, cayenne pepper, salt, nutmeg, and cloves. Roll each breast in the flour mixture until well coated.

4. Put the vegetable oil in a roasting pan. Place the chicken breasts skin-side down in the roasting pan and bake for 30 minutes.

5. Flip the chicken so that the skin side is up and put back in the oven for 1 hour.

The Subtler Spices

Subtle spices abound in Mexican cooking. Cinnamon, nutmeg, and cloves, for example, are common ingredients in many recipes that don't contain an abundance of hot chili peppers.

Fruit-Stewed Turkey

*This simple dish is wonderful served over white rice with a side of
Zucchini with Jalapeños (see recipe in Chapter 13).*

INGREDIENTS | SERVES 4

4 cups precooked turkey meat (leftovers are great)

1 small yellow onion

6 pitted prunes

¼ cup dried apricots

1 tablespoon olive oil

1 cup canned pineapple chunks, drained

½ cup fresh raspberries

1 teaspoon salt

1 teaspoon ground white pepper

1. Cut the turkey into 1" chunks. Remove skin from onion and cut into quarters. Cut the prunes and apricots in half.

2. In a large frying pan preheat the olive oil to medium temperature. Add the turkey chunks and fry until lightly browned on all sides.

3. Drain off the oil and add the onion, pineapple, apricots, prunes, raspberries, salt, and pepper to the pan. Turn heat to low and cook for 1 hour, stirring periodically.

Nutty Chicken

Because this is a mild entrée, it goes well with a spicy vegetable or rice dish.

INGREDIENTS | SERVES 4

1 (2½- to 3½-pound) whole chicken
½ cup olive oil
¼ cup hulled pepitas (pumpkin seeds)
¼ cup sesame seeds
¼ cup pecans
¼ cup slivered almonds
¼ cup pistachio meats
¼ cup filberts

Nuts Galore

Mexico's subtropical climate means a large variety of nuts grow easily there, making nuts very easy to buy and cook with. As a result, Mexicans often use them as the equivalent of flour, as a thickening agent for sauces or batters.

1. Preheat oven to 350°F. Wash the chicken and cut it into 8 serving pieces. Brush each piece with some of the olive oil.

2. Combine all the nuts. In a food processor or nut grinder, grind the nuts into small pieces. Place the nut mixture in a soup bowl and roll each piece of chicken in the nuts. Reserve the remaining nuts.

3. Put the remaining olive oil in a baking pan. Place the chicken, skin-side down, in the pan. Bake for 30 minutes. Flip the chicken and sprinkle with the remaining nuts. Bake for an additional hour.

Chicken Tacos

Authentic Mexican tacos are usually served with just meat and salsa. However, you can add the American fixings such as cheese and lettuce if you'd like.

INGREDIENTS | SERVES 6

6 cups water
1 medium yellow onion
4 garlic cloves
1 carrot
1 green bell pepper
1 celery rib
4 chicken breasts (with skin and bones)
1 teaspoon salt
1 teaspoon black pepper
12 (6") corn tortillas

Tortilla or Tostada

Although many North Americans associate crispy corn tortillas with tacos, the tostada is the only item that calls for frying the tortilla until it is crisp and hard. Mexicans rarely use the formed, fried tortillas we see at Mexican restaurants. Instead, they heat the soft corn tortilla, place the meat in the middle, and fold it over.

1. Place the water in a large stockpot and bring to a boil.

2. Remove the skin from the onion and cut into 1" pieces. Remove the skin from the garlic cloves and cut into thin slices. Peel the carrot and cut into ½" rounds. Remove the core and seeds from the green pepper and cut into 1" pieces. Cut the celery into 1" pieces.

3. Place the chicken breasts, onion, garlic, carrot, green pepper, salt, black pepper, and celery in the boiling water; boil for 20 minutes. Skim the foam from the top, reduce heat to medium, and continue cooking until the meat falls off the bones when picked up with a fork.

4. Pour the contents of the stockpot into a strainer. Pull out the chicken breasts. Remove the bones and skin. Discard all the vegetables, chicken bones, and skin.

5. Shred the meat. Use as a filling for the tacos.

Soused Chicken

Serve with white rice. Ladle the fruit onto the top of the chicken and the rice before serving.

INGREDIENTS | SERVES 4

1 (2½- to 3½-pound) whole chicken
½ cup prunes
½ cup dried pears
1 large green apple
1 medium red onion
4 garlic cloves
½ cup black olives
3 cups dry white wine
½ cup raisins
1 teaspoon salt
1 teaspoon ground black pepper
1 tablespoon dried cilantro
1 cup whole roasted almonds

Is It Soused or Potted?

Mexican dishes that have meat soaking in a sauce, especially an alcohol-based sauce, are often called soused or potted dishes. Funny that those two words are used to describe someone who is drunk, too!

1. Preheat oven to 300°F.

2. Wash the chicken and cut into 8 serving pieces. Remove the skin.

3. Remove the pits from the prunes and cut in quarters. Cut the pears into quarters. Remove the stem and core from the apple; cut into 1" pieces. Remove the skin from the onion and cut into ¼" rounds. Remove the skin from the garlic cloves and cut into quarters. Cut the black olives into quarters.

4. Put the chicken in an oven-safe pot. Pour the wine over the top. Add the raisins, prunes, pears, apple, onion, garlic, olives, salt, pepper, and cilantro to the pot.

5. Cover and bake for 2 hours. Remove the cover, add the almonds, and bake for 30 minutes.

Chicken in Nutty Green Sauce

Have fun with this dish by experimenting with different types and amounts of chili peppers.

INGREDIENTS | SERVES 4

1 (2½- to 3½-pound) chicken
2 cups chicken broth
6 habanero chilies
1 medium yellow onion
4 garlic cloves
6 green tomatoes
1 green bell pepper
1 bunch fresh cilantro
½ cup blanched almond slivers
½ cup chopped walnuts
1 teaspoon salt
1 teaspoon ground black pepper
1 tablespoon olive oil
½ cup cooking sherry

1. Preheat oven to 300°F.

2. Wash the chicken and cut into 8 serving pieces.

3. Place the chicken and broth in an ovenproof casserole dish with a lid. Cover and cook for 30 minutes.

4. Remove the stems and seeds from the chilies. Peel the onion and garlic, and cut into quarters. Remove the stems from the tomatoes and cut into quarters. Remove the stems and seeds from the green bell pepper and cut into quarters. Remove and discard the stems from the cilantro.

5. Combine the chilies, onion, garlic, tomatoes, bell pepper, cilantro, almonds, walnuts, salt, black pepper, olive oil, and cooking sherry in a mixing bowl. Scoop out about 1 cup at a time and place in a blender or food processor. Blend until all the ingredients are melded but not puréed. Repeat until all the ingredients are blended.

6. Drain off and discard the chicken stock from the chicken. Pour the sauce over the chicken, cover, and return to the oven. Cook for 1½ hours.

Cocoa Turkey

*Try this for a unique Thanksgiving treat. You'll be surprised how
well chocolate and turkey meat go together!*

INGREDIENTS | SERVES 8

1 (8- to 10-pound) turkey
1 medium red onion
4 garlic cloves
¾ cup vegetable oil
2 cups powdered cocoa
1 teaspoon ground cinnamon
¼ teaspoon anise seeds

Cocoa as a Spice

While Americans think of cocoa only in
terms of chocolate, many Mexican dishes
use it as a main spice. They will mix it with
cheeses, meats, and even vegetables.
Although it can take some getting used to,
it's definitely worth trying.

1. Preheat oven to 350°F.

2. Thaw the turkey, remove the neck and giblets from the cavities, and wash the cavities thoroughly. Place turkey in a roasting pan.

3. Remove the skin from the onion and chop into ¼" pieces. Peel and mince the garlic. Stir the onion and garlic into ¼ cup vegetable oil and, using a paper towel, rub the inside of the turkey cavity with the garlic and onion mixture. Leave all the garlic and onion pieces inside the cavity.

4. Mix the cocoa, cinnamon, and anise into the remaining ½ cup vegetable oil. Use this to baste the turkey. Place the turkey in the oven and baste every 15 minutes for 3 hours.

5. Remove the turkey and let it rest for 30 minutes before serving.

Five-Pepper Chicken Stew

*If your local market doesn't have the varieties of chilies mentioned
here, experiment with your own variations.*

INGREDIENTS | SERVES 6

4 boneless, skinless chicken breasts
4 fresh jalapeño chilies
4 fresh mulato chilies
4 fresh ancho chilies
1 fresh poblano chili
4 fresh habanero chilies
4 medium tomatoes
1 large yellow onion
4 garlic cloves
4 medium baking potatoes
2 large carrots
½ cup hulled pepitas (pumpkin seeds)

1. Cut the chicken into 1" pieces.

2. Remove the stems and seeds from the chilies and chop
   chilies into ¼" pieces. Cut the tomatoes into quarters.
   Remove the skin from the onion and chop into ¼"
   pieces. Remove the skin from the garlic cloves and cut
   into thin slices. Peel the potatoes and carrots, and cut
   into 1" pieces.

3. Combine all the ingredients in a large pot, cover, and
   cook on medium-low heat for 3 hours. Stir
   occasionally.

The Poblano Chili

Poblano chilies are one of the largest and
mildest-tasting green peppers in the chili
category. They are meaty and relatively
juicy, which makes them excellent for roasting and baking. Because they are fairly
large, they also work well for stuffing.

Chicken Achiote

Serve with Pineapple and Coconut Salad (see recipe in Chapter 15).

INGREDIENTS | SERVES 4

1 (2½- to 3½-pound) whole chicken
4 garlic cloves
1 medium red onion
4 jalapeño chili peppers
½ cup white grapefruit juice
½ cup red cooking sherry
2 tablespoons achiote paste
1 cup green seedless grapes

Achiote

Achiote is a blend of ground annatto seeds, garlic, black pepper, other spices, and vinegar. It is most common in Yucatán cooking but has migrated into middle Mexican cooking as well. It leaves food (as well as clothing, plastic cookware, and anything else it touches) a bright orange color.

1. Cut the chicken into 8 serving pieces. Remove the skin, but not the bones.

2. Remove the skin from the garlic and onion. Cut the onion into quarters. Remove the stems (but not the seeds) from the jalapeños. Combine the garlic, onion, jalapeños, grapefruit juice, sherry, and achiote paste in a blender or food processor. Blend on medium setting until all the ingredients are melded.

3. Place the chicken in a large mixing bowl. Cover with sauce. Cover the bowl and place in the refrigerator for 6–12 hours.

4. Preheat oven to 350°F.

5. Cut the grapes in half.

6. Remove the chicken from the bowl and place in a baking dish; discard the sauce. Cover with grapes.

7. Cook, uncovered, for 1 hour.

Marinated Chicken

Serve this dish cold, garnished with pickled vegetables.

INGREDIENTS | SERVES 8

2 fryer chickens (about 2½ pounds each)

1 cup canned or frozen sliced carrots

2 celery ribs

1 large white onion

1 garlic clove

1½ cups vegetable oil

⅛ teaspoon thyme

⅛ teaspoon marjoram

1 bay leaf

12 peppercorns

1 teaspoon salt

3 cups vinegar

1. Cut each chicken into 8 serving pieces. Thaw the frozen carrots or drain canned carrots. Chop the celery into 1" pieces. Peel the onion and cut into 1" pieces. Peel and mince the garlic.

2. Heat the oil to medium temperature in a large skillet. Brown the chicken pieces, then place them in a large pot. Top with the carrots, onions, celery, garlic, thyme, marjoram, bay leaf, peppercorns, and salt. Pour the vinegar over the top.

3. Remove from heat and let cool to room temperature. Cover and refrigerate for 3–4 hours.

Duck in Prune Sauce

Serve with Green Beans with Pine Nuts and Feta Cheese (see recipe in Chapter 13).

INGREDIENTS | SERVES 6

2 cups pitted prunes

¼ cup raisins

1 cup dry sherry

1 (4- to 5-pound) duckling

1 cup flour

1 large white onion

2 garlic cloves

4 tomatillos

½ cup butter

1 teaspoon salt

½ teaspoon ground black pepper

½ teaspoon ground nutmeg

1. Cut the prunes into ¼" pieces. Combine the prunes and raisins in a small bowl and add the sherry; let soak for at least 2 hours.

2. Preheat oven to 325°F.

3. Cut the duck into serving pieces and roll in flour. Peel the onion and chop into ¼" pieces. Peel and mince the garlic cloves. Peel the tomatillos and chop into ¼" pieces.

4. Melt the butter in a large frying pan over medium heat. Add the duck pieces and cook until browned on both sides. Sprinkle with salt and pepper during the last couple minutes of browning. Place the duck pieces in a large, ovenproof casserole dish. Do not drain the grease from the frying pan.

5. Put the onion in the frying pan and cook on medium heat until limp but not brown. Stir in the garlic, tomatillos, and nutmeg; pour over the duck. Cover the casserole dish and cook for 1½ hours. Pour the prune and raisin mixture over the duck, cover, and cook for an additional 15 minutes.

Squabs in Orange Sauce

Use the juice in the bottom of the pan as a dipping sauce for the meat.

INGREDIENTS | SERVES 4

1 medium white onion
1 garlic clove
2 medium red tomatoes
2 tablespoons pecans
4 squabs
½ cup butter
1 cup freshly squeezed orange juice
½ cup dry white wine
½ teaspoon thyme
1 tablespoon grated orange rind

1. Preheat oven to 325°F. Peel the onion and cut into ¼" rounds. Peel and mince the garlic. Remove the stems from the tomatoes and chop into ¼" pieces. Chop the pecans finely.

2. Split each squab in half lengthwise, leaving it in 1 piece. Melt the butter in a large frying pan on medium heat. Sauté each squab until golden brown on all sides. Do not drain grease. Place the squabs in an ovenproof casserole dish. (It's fine if they overlap.)

3. Put the onion and garlic in the frying pan and sauté until the onion is limp but not brown. Reduce heat to low. Add the tomatoes, pecans, orange juice, wine, and thyme; cook for 5 minutes, stirring occasionally. Pour over the squabs.

4. Cover the casserole dish and bake for 1½ hours.

5. Arrange the squabs on a serving platter. Sprinkle with orange rind.

Green Chicken with Almond Sauce

Serve with white rice and Carrot and Chili Pepper Salad (see recipe in Chapter 7).

INGREDIENTS | SERVES 4

1 fryer chicken
4 fresh tomatillos
4 fresh serrano chilies
1 large white onion
1 cup blanched almonds
1 cup flour
1 teaspoon garlic salt
1 teaspoon ground white pepper
2 tablespoons olive oil
1 handful fresh cilantro leaves
1 handful fresh parsley leaves
1 cup white cooking sherry
1 cup chicken broth

Remove the Alcohol

If you don't want alcohol in your non-cooked recipe, take slightly more than you need for the recipe and sauté it over medium heat for a few minutes. The alcohol will evaporate but you will be left with all the flavor.

1. Preheat oven to 350°F.

2. Cut the chicken into 8 serving pieces. Peel and quarter the tomatillos. Remove and discard the stems from the chilies and quarter. Peel and quarter the onion. Chop the almonds into small pieces.

3. Combine the flour, garlic salt, and white pepper. Moisten the chicken with water and roll in the flour.

4. Heat the olive oil to medium temperature in a large frying pan. Add the chicken. Fry until the chicken is golden brown on all sides. Place chicken in an ovenproof casserole dish.

5. Put the tomatillos, chilies, onion, cilantro, parsley, sherry, and broth in a blender. Blend on medium speed until puréed. Stir in the almonds. Pour the mixture over the chicken. Bake for 1 hour.

Creamy Red Chicken with Mushrooms

Serve with Cucumber Mousse (see recipe in Chapter 7) for an interesting blend of flavors.

INGREDIENTS | SERVES 4

1 pound fresh white button mushrooms
1 large red onion
1 garlic clove
2 medium red tomatoes
1 red bell pepper
2 fresh jalapeño chilies
4 boneless, skinless chicken breasts
2 cups chicken broth
1 sprig epazote
½ cup heavy cream

1. Preheat oven to 350°F.

2. Clean the mushrooms and slice thinly. Peel the onion and slice into ¼" rounds. Peel and quarter the garlic. Peel the tomatoes and remove the stems; cut into quarters. Remove the stem and seeds from the red pepper; cut the pepper into quarters. Remove the stems and seeds from the jalapeños and cut into ¼" rounds.

3. Place the chicken breasts in an ovenproof casserole. Add the mushrooms and onion slices on top. Pour 1 cup of the chicken broth over the top. Cover and bake for 1 hour.

4. In the meantime, combine the remaining 1 cup chicken broth, garlic, tomatoes, red pepper, jalapeño peppers, and epazote in a blender; blend on medium speed until puréed.

5. Pour the mixture into a medium-sized skillet over medium heat. Gently stir in the heavy cream until it is well mixed, making sure the mixture does not boil.

6. Pour the creamy mixture over the chicken. Replace the cover and bake for an additional 15 minutes.

CHAPTER 12

Beef and Pork

Mexican Pot Roast

Thicken the sauce by adding ¼ cup flour and cooking it on the stove until it becomes a gravy. Serve drizzled over the meat or over mashed potatoes.

INGREDIENTS | SERVES 6

3 tablespoons olive oil
1 (3-pound) pot roast
½ cup flour
1 large yellow onion
1 garlic clove
6 medium red tomatoes
4 fresh morita chilies
¼ teaspoon dried oregano
1 teaspoon salt

The Morita Chili Pepper

Morita chilies are a type of jalapeño that has been dried and smoked. They tend to be a bit hotter than regular jalapeños and less smoky than chipotles.

1. Preheat oven to 350°F.

2. Heat the olive oil in a large skillet over medium heat. Dredge the beef in the flour by pounding the flour into the meat until no more flour will stick. Place the beef in the skillet. Cook, turning until the meat is brown on all sides.

3. Peel the onion and garlic clove. Cut the onion into ¼"-thick rings and mince the garlic. Cut the tomatoes into 1" pieces. Stem and seed the chilies and cut into ¼" pieces.

4. Place the pot roast in a roasting pan. Sprinkle with oregano and salt, and cover with the remaining ingredients.

5. Cook in the oven, covered, for 2 hours.

Citrus Veal

Serve this with a fresh fruit salad to bring out the fruity flavor of the dish.

INGREDIENTS | SERVES 4

4 veal cutlets
¼ teaspoon ground cinnamon
¼ teaspoon ground cloves
1 teaspoon salt
1 large white onion
2 garlic cloves
2 oranges
1 tablespoon vegetable oil
1 cup orange juice
¼ cup lime juice

Choosing Good Veal

A good veal steak will be nearly as white and textureless as chicken breasts. It should have less than ½" of fat around the edges.

1. Preheat oven to 350°F.

2. Season both sides of the veal cutlets with cinnamon, cloves, and salt.

3. Remove the skin from the onion and cut into 1" pieces. Remove the skin from the garlic and cut thinly. Cut the oranges into ¼" rounds with the rind remaining on the oranges.

4. Pour the oil into the bottom of a medium-sized baking dish. Place the veal cutlets in the dish so that they don't overlap. Pour the orange juice and lime juice over the veal. Place the onion, oranges, and garlic on top.

5. Cover, and cook for 1 hour.

Mexicali Rice and Beef

This hearty and rich casserole is perfect for a cold winter night. Serve it with some warmed flour tortillas or a green salad with a mild ranch salad dressing.

INGREDIENTS | SERVES 6

1 cup long-grain rice
3 cups beef broth, divided
1 tablespoon chili powder
½ teaspoon cumin
1 pound ground beef
1 onion, chopped
3 cloves garlic, minced
2 green bell peppers, chopped
2 chipotle peppers in adobo sauce, minced
1 (8-ounce) can tomato sauce
1 (6-ounce) can tomato paste
2 tablespoons adobo sauce
¼ teaspoon pepper
1½ cups shredded Colby cheese

1. In heavy saucepan, combine rice with 2 cups beef broth, chili powder, and cumin, and bring to a boil. Cover, reduce heat, and simmer for 15–20 minutes until rice is tender and liquid is absorbed. Meanwhile, in heavy saucepan cook ground beef with onion and garlic until beef is browned. Add bell peppers and chipotle peppers; cook and stir for 2 minutes longer. Drain well.

2. Preheat oven to 375°F. Add tomato sauce, paste, adobo sauce, 1 cup beef broth, and pepper to ground beef mixture. Cook over medium heat, stirring frequently, for 15 minutes. Combine cooked rice and beef mixture in a 2-quart casserole dish and mix thoroughly. Top with cheese and bake at 375°F for 20–25 minutes until cheese melts.

How to Cook Rice

To cook fluffy rice, use double the amount of liquid as rice, do not uncover while rice is cooking, and let rice stand off the heat for 5 minutes before using, then fluff and serve. Use a fork to fluff rice; a spoon will crush the grains.

Hot and Spicy Tripe

*Serve with broken Tostadas (see recipe in Chapter 2) in bowls,
much as you would serve Chinese soft noodles.*

INGREDIENTS | SERVES 4

1 medium yellow onion
4 garlic cloves
6 fresh habanero peppers
½ cup filberts
2 pounds fresh beef tripe
1 quart water
1 tablespoon salt
1 tablespoon olive oil
1 teaspoon dried oregano
1 teaspoon ground black pepper
1 cup canned pinto beans

Trying Tripe

Although many people find the idea of eating tripe a bit scary, it really can be an excellent meal because it picks up the flavor of the ingredients it is cooked with. Expect the tripe itself to be fairly tasteless and rubbery, but enjoy the mingling of flavors that are carried with the tripe.

1. Remove the skin from the onion and chop into ¼" pieces. Remove the skin from the garlic and cut into thin slices. Remove the stems and seeds from the peppers and cut into ¼" pieces. Chop the filberts into small pieces.

2. Place the tripe and the water in a pot. Add the salt and stir until well mixed. Let stand for 2–3 hours.

3. Place the onion, garlic, and habanero peppers in a large frying pan. Add the olive oil. Cook on medium heat until the onion and garlic are browned. Reduce heat to low, and add the tripe, oregano, and black pepper. Cover and simmer for 1 hour.

4. Add the beans. Cover and simmer for 15 minutes.

5. Add the filberts right before serving.

Barbecued Pork Ribs

*Serve with Jalapeño Corn Bread (see recipe in Chapter 6) and
Grilled Corn on the Cob (see recipe in Chapter 13).*

INGREDIENTS | SERVES 4

1 small red onion

12 garlic cloves

8 fresh chipotle chilies

½ cup water

¼ cup red wine vinegar

1 cup honey

½ cup Dijon mustard

1 tablespoon dried oregano

1 teaspoon salt

1 teaspoon ground black pepper

4 pounds pork ribs

Cooking Ribs

Ribs must be cooked very slowly. If the cooking temperature is too hot, the meat will burn off. Some people boil the ribs in beer or water for 10 minutes before grilling to ensure that the meat doesn't dry out.

1. Preheat grill to medium setting.

2. Peel the onion and cut into ¼" pieces. Peel and mince the garlic. Remove the stems from the chilies.

3. Place the chilies in a small saucepan with the water; cover and simmer on low setting for 10 minutes or until the chilies are plump. Drain off the water. Cut the chilies into ¼" pieces.

4. Combine all the ingredients except the ribs in a medium-sized saucepan; stir well. Bring the mixture to a boil. Cover and simmer for 10 minutes.

5. Use as a basting sauce while grilling the ribs. Reserve ½ cup to be served as a dipping sauce with the meal.

Salpicon

This can be used as a dip, as a filling for tacos, or as a side dish.

INGREDIENTS | SERVES 6

3 cups Shredded Beef (see recipe in Chapter 2)
1 bottle Italian salad dressing
1 cup canned garbanzo beans
½ pound Monterey jack cheese
1 cup canned jalapeños
2 avocados
1 bunch parsley

1. Arrange the beef in a 9" × 11" casserole dish. Pour salad dressing over beef, cover, and refrigerate overnight.

2. Preheat oven to 300°F.

3. Drain the garbanzo beans. Shred the cheese. Drain the chili peppers and cut into ¼" pieces. Remove the skin and pit from the avocados and cut the avocados into ½" slices. Remove the stems from the parsley and roughly chop the leaves.

4. Spread layers over the beef in this order: garbanzo beans, cheese, jalapeños, avocados, parsley. Place in the oven for 20 minutes.

Chorizo (Mexican Sausage)

This goes very well with huevos rancheros or any other egg dish.

INGREDIENTS | MAKES 2 POUNDS

2 pounds ground pork
2 tablespoons paprika
1 teaspoon ground black pepper
1 teaspoon dried oregano
1 teaspoon ground cumin
¼ teaspoon ground coriander seeds
⅔ cup vinegar
1 teaspoon garlic powder
2 tablespoons salt
2 tablespoons cayenne pepper

1. Place all the ingredients in a large mixing bowl. Mix with your hands until all the ingredients are well blended.

2. Place in an airtight container. Refrigerate for at least 2 days.

3. Form into patties for frying.

Fideo con Carne

Serve with Pineapple and Coconut Salad (see recipe in Chapter 15).

INGREDIENTS | SERVES 6

2 medium red tomatoes

¼ head cabbage

3 garlic cloves

¼ cup vegetable oil

8 ounces vermicelli noodles

1 pound lean ground beef

¼ teaspoon ground cumin

¼ teaspoon salt

¼ teaspoon ground black pepper

2 quarts water

1. Chop the tomatoes into ¼" pieces. Chop the cabbage into 1" pieces. Peel and mince the garlic.

2. Heat the oil to medium temperature in a large frying pan. Add the vermicelli noodles; sauté until the noodles are lightly browned. Remove the noodles and set aside.

3. In the same pan, sauté the garlic and beef until the beef is browned. Drain off the oil.

4. Add the tomatoes, vermicelli, cumin, salt, and ground pepper; stir until all the ingredients are mixed. Add the water. Bring to a simmer, cover, and cook for 10 minutes.

5. Add the cabbage and stir to combine. Simmer, uncovered, for 15 minutes.

Mexican Meat Loaf

This meat loaf packs a ton of flavor and is easy to prepare.

INGREDIENTS | SERVES 4

1 large white onion
¼ cup pimiento-stuffed green olives
3 large eggs
1 pound ground beef
½ pound ground pork
⅔ cup uncooked oats
1 teaspoon salt
¼ teaspoon ground black pepper
1 cup Red Chili Sauce (see recipe in Chapter 2)

1. Preheat oven to 350°F.

2. Peel the onion and chop into ¼" pieces. Slice the olives into ¼" rounds. Boil 2 of the eggs for 10 minutes. When cool, slice into ¼" rounds. Beat the remaining egg until the white and yolk are well mixed.

3. Combine the ground beef, ground pork, onion, oats, salt, pepper, ½ cup of the chili sauce, and the beaten egg. Mix with your hands until well blended.

4. Pack half of the meat mixture into an 8" × 4" × 2" loaf pan. Arrange the hard-cooked eggs in a row down the center of the loaf. Arrange the olive slices on either side of the eggs. Press the eggs and olives slightly into the meat mixture. Cover with the remaining half of the meat mixture. Pour the remaining ½ cup chili sauce on top.

5. Bake for 1 hour.

Beef Taco Salad

*Processed cheese food, a classic Tex-Mex ingredient, is made with emulsifiers
so it melts perfectly, every time. There's really no substitute.*

INGREDIENTS | SERVES 6–8

1 pound ground beef

1 onion, chopped

3 cloves garlic, minced

1 serrano chili, minced

2 tablespoons chili powder

½ teaspoon cumin

1 tablespoon Worcestershire sauce

1 (14-ounce) can tomatoes with green chilies, undrained

1 (16-ounce) package processed cheese food

1 (10-ounce) bag chopped romaine lettuce

1 green bell pepper, chopped

1 red bell pepper, chopped

3 cups corn chips

2 cups shredded Cheddar cheese

1. In a heavy skillet, cook ground beef, onion, garlic, and serrano chili until beef is browned, stirring to break up meat. Drain if necessary, then add chili powder, cumin, Worcestershire sauce, and tomatoes with green chilies. Bring to a boil, then reduce heat and simmer for 20 minutes.

2. Cut processed cheese food into ½" pieces and stir into beef mixture; cover and let stand off the heat for 5 minutes.

3. In a serving bowl, combine lettuce with bell peppers and corn chips. Top with beef mixture and sprinkle with Cheddar cheese; serve immediately.

Make-Ahead Tips

Ground beef, processed cheese food, tomatoes with green chilies, and corn chips are the "authentic" Tex-Mex ingredients in this yummy salad. You can make the beef mixture ahead of time, but don't add the cheese. Refrigerate until you're ready to eat, then reheat beef mixture, add cheese, and proceed with the recipe.

Pork Picadillo

Serve as a stew over white rice or use as a filling for enchiladas.

INGREDIENTS | SERVES 6

1 (1½-pound) pork roast

1 large white onion

2 garlic cloves

¼ cup canned jalapeño chilies, or 2 fresh jalapeños

1 cup frozen or canned peas

1 cup frozen or canned carrots

1 bay leaf

¼ cup vegetable oil

1 cup Green Chili Sauce (see recipe in Chapter 2)

½ cup chicken broth

¼ teaspoon dried ginger

1 teaspoon salt

¼ teaspoon ground black pepper

Picadillo

Picadillo is meat and vegetable hash. As a result, the variations are endless. Some versions call for vegetables, while others call for fruits and nuts. Get creative and see if you can discover your own unique variation.

1. Place the pork roast in a large stew pot and add just enough water to cover. Cook the meat on medium temperature for 1–3 hours or until tender. Shred the meat by pulling it apart into strips.

2. Peel the onion and chop into ¼" pieces. Peel the garlic and chop into ¼" pieces. Stem, seed, and chop the jalapeños. If using frozen vegetables, thaw and warm to room temperature. If using canned vegetables, drain off the water. Crumble the bay leaf and discard stem.

3. Heat the vegetable oil to medium-high temperature in a large frying pan. Add the onion and garlic. Sauté until the onion is limp but not brown.

4. Add all the ingredients to the frying pan; stir well. Reduce heat to low, cover, and cook for 30 minutes.

Tongue in Almond Sauce

If you are a little too squeamish to try tongue, try the sauce with any lean red meat.

INGREDIENTS | SERVES 4

1 medium yellow onion
2 whole cloves
1 veal tongue (about 2½ pounds)
1 celery rib, with leaves
1 bay leaf
6 black peppercorns
2 teaspoons salt
2 dried ancho chilies
½ cup canned tomatoes, with juice
½ cup blanched whole almonds
½ cup raisins, divided
2 tablespoons vegetable oil
¼ cup blanched slivered almonds

1. Peel the onion and stick the cloves in it. Put the tongue, onion, whole celery rib, bay leaf, peppercorns, and salt into a pot. Cover with water. Bring to a boil. Reduce heat to medium and cook for about 2 hours or until the meat is tender. Allow the meat to cool in the liquid.

2. Remove the skin from the cooled tongue, trim off the roots, and cut the meat into ½" slices. Strain the stock and save 1 cup of the liquid. Return the meat to the pot.

3. Remove the skin, seeds, and stems from the dried chilies. Put the chilies, tomatoes with juice, whole almonds, and ¼ cup of the raisins in a food processor or blender; blend to a thick purée.

4. Heat the vegetable oil to medium temperature in a medium-sized frying pan. Add the puréed mixture and cook for about 5 minutes. Stir in the reserved tongue stock and the remaining ¼ cup of raisins. Cook for 5 more minutes.

5. Pour the sauce over the meat in the pot. Heat to medium and simmer until the meat is heated through.

6. Garnish with slivered almonds.

Pork with Pineapple

Serve with Red Rice (see recipe in Chapter 2).

INGREDIENTS | SERVES 8

1 (3-pound) pork loin
1 large white onion
1 large red tomato
⅓ cup sliced pimientos
1 tablespoon vegetable oil
2 cups canned pineapple chunks, with juice
1 cup canned beef stock (or 1 beef bouillon cube dissolved in 1 cup water)
¼ cup dry sherry
½ teaspoon chili powder
1 teaspoon salt
½ teaspoon black pepper
2 tablespoons flour

1. Cut the meat into 2" chunks. Peel the onion and chop into ¼" pieces. Remove the stem from the tomato and chop into ¼" pieces.

2. Heat the vegetable oil in a large frying pan. Add the meat and brown well on all sides. Add the onion and cook for about 5 minutes or until soft.

3. Add the tomato, pimientos, pineapple with juice, beef stock, sherry, and chili powder to the skillet; stir until well mixed. Bring to a boil, reduce heat to a simmer, and add the salt and pepper.

4. Cover and simmer until the meat is tender, about 1½ hours. Stir occasionally.

5. Just before serving, sprinkle the flour over the simmering sauce and stir in. Cook and stir until the sauce is thickened.

Baked Noodles with Chorizo

This makes an easy, unique breakfast dish when served with fresh fruit.

INGREDIENTS | SERVES 6

¼ pound chorizo sausage or any hot, spicy sausage

1 small yellow onion

4 tablespoons vegetable oil

7 ounces small egg noodles

2 cups chicken broth

1 cup cottage cheese

1 cup sour cream

1 teaspoon Tabasco or other hot sauce

1 teaspoon salt

½ teaspoon ground black pepper

½ cup grated Parmesan cheese

Sausage

Virtually every culture that slaughters animals has invented some type of sausage. Traditionally it is made with the little pieces of meat that are leftover from the slaughter—ears, nose, and so on. Spices are added for both flavor and preservation. Many cultures, including the Mexicans, force the meat mixture into cleaned-out intestines to make links.

1. Preheat oven to 350°F.

2. Fry the sausage in a large frying pan until cooked through. Crumble the sausage as it fries. Remove meat from frying pan and set aside. Peel the onion and chop into ¼" pieces.

3. Add the oil to the frying pan. Stir in the onion and uncooked noodles; fry until the noodles are lightly browned and the onion is soft. Stir often to prevent burning.

4. Return the chorizo to the frying pan and stir in the broth.

5. Transfer the mixture to an ovenproof casserole dish. Bake uncovered for about 15 minutes or until all the liquid is absorbed by the noodles.

6. Remove from the oven. Stir in the cottage cheese and sour cream. Add the hot sauce, salt, and pepper. Sprinkle the Parmesan cheese on top. Return to the oven and bake uncovered for about 10 minutes or until bubbling hot.

CHAPTER 13

Vegetables

Home-Canned Spicy Tomatillos

Serve as an appetizer or put them on top of any vegetable salad.

INGREDIENTS | SERVES 16

30–40 small tomatillos
8 jalapeño peppers
4 celery ribs
4 teaspoons dill weed
2 teaspoons dried oregano
1 quart cider vinegar
½ cup granulated pickling salt

Tomatillos

Tomatillos are an essential ingredient in many Mexican dishes. They are pale green or yellow and encased in a papery husk, which is removed before cooking. Avoid any with shriveled husks. Don't hesitate to substitute these for green tomatoes in any recipe, although they are slightly more tart than tomatoes.

1. Wash the tomatillos, jalapeño peppers, and celery. Remove the stems from the tomatillos and jalapeño peppers.

2. Place 2 of the jalapeño peppers, 1 celery rib, 1 teaspoon of dill weed, and ½ teaspoon of oregano into each of 4 hot canning jars.

3. Finish packing the jars with the tomatillos.

4. Combine the cider vinegar and pickling salt in a saucepan. Bring to a boil and stir until the salt dissolves. Pour the mixture into the jars to ½" from the top.

5. Place the lids tightly on the jars and put the jars into a boiling water bath for 5 minutes. Let sit at least 1 month before using.

Zucchini with Jalapeños

This is excellent served with a mild meat or fish dish.

INGREDIENTS | SERVES 8

4 medium zucchini (8"–10" long)
2 medium tomatoes
1 medium yellow onion
2 garlic cloves
1 small green bell pepper
4 canned or fresh jalapeño peppers
½ teaspoon salt
½ teaspoon ground black pepper
1 tablespoon butter

1. Chop the zucchini and tomatoes into 1" pieces.

2. Remove the skins from the onion and garlic and chop into ¼" pieces.

3. Remove the stems and seeds from the bell pepper and jalapeños and chop into ¼" pieces.

4. Add all the ingredients to a medium-sized frying pan and sauté on medium heat until the zucchini is tender but not limp, about 5–8 minutes.

Jalapeño Mashed Potatoes

You can try almost any peppers in this recipe to complement the main dish being served.

INGREDIENTS | SERVES 4

1 quart water
4 medium potatoes
2 fresh jalapeño peppers
1 teaspoon salt
1 tablespoon butter
½ cup plain yogurt
1 teaspoon ground white pepper
1 teaspoon fresh epazote

1. Place the water in a large pot and bring to a boil on medium-high heat.

2. Peel the potatoes and cut into 1" cubes. Remove the stems and seeds from the jalapeño peppers and cut into ¼" pieces.

3. Place the potatoes, peppers, and salt in water and boil for about 15 minutes or until potatoes are easily pierced with a fork. Drain the potatoes and peppers.

4. Combine the butter, yogurt, white pepper, and epazote in a small mixing bowl. Add to the potatoes and jalapeño peppers. Mash with a potato masher or hand mixer on low speed.

Green Beans with Pine Nuts and Feta Cheese

This makes a wonderful potluck dish or a tame counterpart to a spicy beef dish.

INGREDIENTS | SERVES 6

1½ pounds fresh green beans

4 quarts water

1 large red onion

1 garlic clove

½ cup packed fresh spearmint leaves
or ¼ cup dried spearmint

1 cup pine nuts

¾ cup olive oil

¼ cup white vinegar

¾ teaspoon salt

½ teaspoon ground black pepper

1 cup crumbled feta cheese

1. Wash the green beans in cold water. Remove the stems and cut the beans in half. Bring the water to a boil in a large saucepan on medium-high heat. Add the green beans and cook for about 4 minutes or until tender but still crisp. Drain and immerse in ice-cold water for 2 minutes. Remove and spread on paper towels to dry.

2. Remove the peel from the onion and finely chop. Remove the peel from the garlic and mince. Finely chop the leaves. Finely chop the pine nuts.

3. Combine the garlic, spearmint leaves, oil, vinegar, salt, and pepper in a food processor or blender; blend until the ingredients are melded together. Cover and refrigerate for at least 2 hours.

4. Pat the beans to remove any remaining water. Place the beans in a serving bowl. Sprinkle the pine nuts and onion on top. Pour the dressing over the top and toss gently.

Yams with Mango

If you prefer mashed yams, don't bother layering the ingredients; instead, combine everything and then mash the yams and mango right before serving.

INGREDIENTS | SERVES 4

4 medium fresh yams
1 fresh ripe mango
½ cup honey
½ cup unflavored yogurt
1 tablespoon cinnamon
1 tablespoon butter

Yams or Sweet Potatoes?

Many people think yams and sweet potatoes are the same thing, but they are definitely different. Sweet potatoes are shaped more like a potato and have a brighter, orange flesh. Yams are more elongated and have stringy hairs on their skin. Their flesh is paler and less sweet.

1. Preheat oven to 350°F.

2. Peel the yams and cut into ¼"-thick rounds. Peel and seed the mango; cut the mango into ¼" slices.

3. Mix together the honey, yogurt, and cinnamon.

4. Grease a medium-sized baking dish (that has a lid) with the butter. Layer half the yams, then the mango, then the remaining half of the yams in the dish. Cover with the sauce.

5. Cover and place in the oven for 1 hour. Remove cover and place back in the oven for 30 minutes.

6. Drain the remaining liquid from the pan before moving the yams and mango to a serving dish. Lightly toss before serving.

Peppered Corn

This is a fun dish to serve with a milder seafood dish. The flavors complement each other very well.

INGREDIENTS | SERVES 6

2 (10-ounce) cans whole-kernel sweet corn
2 poblano chilies
1 ancho chili
2 serrano chilies
1 small white onion
2 tablespoons butter
1 tablespoon dried cilantro
1 teaspoon ground black pepper

1. Pour the corn into a medium-sized frying pan and place on medium-low heat.

2. Remove the stems and seeds from the chilies and cut into ¼" pieces. Remove the skin from the onion and cut into ¼" pieces.

3. Add the chilies and onion to the corn and cook until well-heated.

4. Remove from stove and drain off the liquid. Add the butter, cilantro, and black pepper; mix well, making sure the butter is melted.

Grilled Corn on the Cob

Try this as a surprising treat at your next outdoor barbecue.

INGREDIENTS | SERVES 8

8 ears fresh sweet corn
4 tablespoons butter
1 tablespoon cayenne pepper
1 teaspoon ground black pepper
1 teaspoon onion salt
1 teaspoon dried cilantro

1. Preheat the grill to medium temperature.

2. Peel back the corn husks and remove the hairs, leaving the husks attached.

3. Mix together the butter, cayenne pepper, black pepper, onion salt, and cilantro.

4. Use the mixture to coat the corn. Fold the husks back up over the corn cobs.

5. Place on the grill, turning frequently. Check every few minutes to make sure the corn is not burning. The corn is done when a few kernels on each cob begin to turn light brown.

Turnip and Mustard Leaf Rolls

Any combination of leaves works well. If your local store has a small supply of exotic leaves, try spinach and beet leaves.

INGREDIENTS | SERVES 6

1 bunch turnip leaves
1 bunch mustard leaves
¼ cup fresh epazote leaves
4 tablespoons butter
1 teaspoon salt
1 teaspoon ground black pepper

1. Remove the stems from the turnip and mustard leaves and wash the leaves thoroughly. Pat dry with a paper towel.

2. Remove the stems from the epazote leaves and mince the leaves.

3. Layer 1 turnip leaf, then 1 mustard leaf. Add ½ teaspoon of butter in the center of the mustard leaf. Sprinkle with epazote leaves, salt, and black pepper. Roll up the leaves. Repeat with remaining leaves.

4. Place the leaf rolls in a frying pan with a small amount of water. Cover and turn heat on low. Cook for 10 minutes on low heat.

Mashed Chard

Virtually any green works well in this recipe. If you live in a chemical-free area, try using dandelion leaves.

INGREDIENTS | SERVES 4

1 bunch chard leaves
1 small white onion
½ cup water
2 tablespoons butter
½ cup sour cream
1 tablespoon dried oregano
1 teaspoon salt
1 teaspoon ground black pepper

1. Remove the stems from the chard and wash the leaves thoroughly. Do not dry. Remove the skin from the onion and cut into ¼" pieces.

2. Put the chard and onion in a medium-sized pot on the stove on low heat. Add the water. Cook for about 15 minutes or until the chard is very limp.

3. Drain off the water. Add the butter, sour cream, oregano, salt, and black pepper to the pot. Mash with a potato masher.

Mushroom-and-Nut-Stuffed Chayote

Chayote can be hard to find in northern climates, but you can substitute acorn squash for an equally good treat.

INGREDIENTS | SERVES 4

2 chayote squash
1 cup button mushrooms
¼ cup pistachio meats
¼ cup pecans
¼ cup roasted almonds
½ cup honey

1. Preheat oven to 350°F.

2. Cut the squash in half and remove the seeds. Poke holes in the squash meat with a fork. Do not pierce the rind. Clean the mushrooms and cut into quarters.

3. Combine the pistachios, pecans, and almonds. Grind in a food processor or nut grinder until you have small pieces.

4. Combine the mushrooms, nuts, and honey; mix well. Add ¼ of the mixture to the cavity of each squash half.

5. Bake directly on the oven rack for 1–2 hours or until the squash is easily pierced with a fork.

Tomatoes with Guacamole

This cool and refreshing side is a perfect complement to a spicier main dish.

INGREDIENTS | SERVES 8

1 ripe avocado
1 small yellow onion
2 garlic cloves
4 large ripe tomatoes
2 tablespoons lime juice
1 teaspoon chili powder
4 tablespoons mayonnaise
1 cup whipping cream
½ teaspoon salt
½ teaspoon ground black pepper
Fresh cilantro sprigs

1. Peel the avocado and remove the pit. Peel the onion and garlic cloves. Cut into quarters. Slice the tomatoes ¼" thick.

2. Put the avocado, onion, garlic, lime juice, chili powder, mayonnaise, whipping cream, salt, and black pepper in a food processor or blender; blend on medium until smooth.

3. Pour the sauce over the tomatoes and garnish with cilantro sprigs.

Broccoli with Walnuts and Goat Cheese

Serve as a salad before a heavier dish such as Pork with Pineapple (see recipe in Chapter 12).

INGREDIENTS | MAKES 2 CUPS

1½ pounds fresh broccoli
4 quarts water
1 large red onion
1 garlic clove
½ cup packed fresh chives
¾ cup olive oil
¼ cup white vinegar
¾ teaspoon salt
¼ teaspoon ground black pepper
1 cup chopped walnuts
1 cup crumbled goat cheese

1. Cut off the broccoli florets and cut into bite-sized pieces. If desired, cut the stems into ¼" pieces. Bring the water to a boil in a large saucepan. Add the broccoli and cook for 4–5 minutes. Drain and immerse in cold water. Remove from cold water and pat dry.

2. Peel the onion and garlic. Cut the onion into ¼" pieces. Cut the chives into 2" lengths.

3. Combine the garlic, chives, oil, vinegar, salt, and pepper in a food processor and blend until smooth. Place in a bowl, cover, and refrigerate for at least 4 hours.

4. Place the broccoli in a serving bowl. Sprinkle with the onions, nuts, and cheese.

5. Just before serving, pour the dressing over the broccoli and toss.

Calabacitas (Zucchini with Cheese and Corn)

This is a great summer side dish. If fresh corn is available, replace the canned corn with kernels cut off the cob.

INGREDIENTS | SERVES 4

3 small zucchini
1 large red tomato
2 fresh jalapeño peppers
1 garlic clove
½ pound mild Cheddar cheese
2 cups canned whole-kernel corn

1. Cut the zucchini into 1" chunks. Chop the tomato into ¼" pieces. Remove the stems and seeds from the jalapeños and chop into ¼" pieces. Peel and mince the garlic. Cut the cheese into ½" chunks.

2. Combine the zucchini, tomatoes, peppers, and garlic in a large saucepan. Turn heat to medium-low. Heat slowly until the ingredients are hot, about 4–7 minutes.

3. Add the corn and cheese. Cover and continue to cook until the cheese is melted.

Eggplant Casserole

This goes very well as a side dish for Pork with Pineapple (see recipe in Chapter 12).

INGREDIENTS | SERVES 6

1 medium eggplant
½ teaspoon garlic salt
½ cup canned jalapeño peppers
2 cups canned tomato sauce
½ cup sour cream
½ teaspoon ground cumin
1½ cups grated Cheddar cheese

1. Preheat oven to 350°F.

2. Remove the stem from the eggplant. Wash the rind but do not peel. Slice into ½"-thick rounds. Arrange the rounds in a lightly greased 9" × 9" baking pan. Sprinkle with the garlic salt.

3. Combine the jalapeño peppers, tomato sauce, sour cream, and cumin; mix well. Pour over the eggplant rounds. Layer the cheese over the top.

4. Bake for 45–60 minutes or until the cheese is melted and the eggplant is soft.

Pastel de Elote (Corn Pie)

This dish often is served as a side dish for fried chicken.

INGREDIENTS | SERVES 6

Shortening
¼ pound Monterey jack cheese
¼ pound sharp Cheddar cheese
½ cup canned jalapeño chili peppers
1½ cups frozen corn
½ cup butter
3 large eggs
1 (15-ounce) can cream-style corn
½ cup masa harina or cornmeal
1 cup sour cream
½ teaspoon salt
¼ teaspoon Worcestershire sauce

1. Preheat oven to 350°F. Grease a pie plate with shortening.

2. Cut the cheeses into ½" cubes. Drain the jalapeños and cut into ¼" pieces. Thaw the frozen corn. Melt the butter in a saucepan over low heat or in the microwave.

3. In a large mixing bowl, beat the eggs until frothy.

4. Add all the remaining ingredients to the eggs; stir until thoroughly mixed. Pour into the prepared pie plate.

5. Bake for 20 minutes.

Mexican Stuffed Peppers

Serve as the vegetable course with a mild-flavored poultry dish.

INGREDIENTS | SERVES 4

8 large fresh jalapeño peppers
1 tablespoon olive oil
2–3 cups refried beans
¼ cup shredded mild Cheddar cheese

1. Preheat oven to 300°F.

2. Remove the stems from the peppers and cut in half lengthwise. Remove the seeds.

3. Brush the cavities of the peppers with olive oil.

4. Place enough refried beans in each cavity to fill just to the top. (Don't heap the beans over the top.)

5. Sprinkle a small amount of cheese on top of each stuffed pepper. Place on a baking sheet or in a baking pan. Bake for 30 minutes.

Tomatillos with Zucchini

This mild dish is the perfect accompaniment for a spicier main course.

INGREDIENTS | SERVES 6

3 medium zucchini
4 medium tomatillos
1 large yellow onion
2 tablespoons butter
½ teaspoon dried oregano
½ teaspoon salt
1 tablespoon water
¼ cup grated Parmesan cheese

1. Remove the stems from the zucchini (do not peel). Cut the zucchini into thin slices. Remove the skin from the tomatillos and chop into ¼" pieces. Peel the onion and chop into ¼" pieces.

2. Melt the butter in a large frying pan at medium heat. Add the onion and cook until limp but not brown.

3. Add the zucchini, tomatillos, oregano, salt, and water; stir well.

4. Cover, bring to a boil, then reduce heat. Cook until the zucchini is tender but still slightly crisp, about 6 minutes. Stir in the cheese before serving.

Pickled Chilies

*If you're planning to eat these within six months, you can simply
seal them and keep them in the refrigerator.*

INGREDIENTS | MAKES 8 PINTS

4 pounds mixed chili peppers

2 large red onions

20 garlic cloves

1 (2") piece fresh ginger

12 tablespoons olive oil

12 cloves

1 tablespoon freshly ground cinnamon

2 teaspoons dried thyme

2 teaspoons dried oregano

8 cups distilled white vinegar

2 tablespoons sea salt

Gingerroot

Ginger can come in many forms from jellied
and crystallized to ground and pickled.
Fresh gingerroot should have a silvery skin.
It will have a slightly spicy flavor. To prepare it, first remove the tough outer skin
with a heavy blade. It then can be chopped
or grated.

1. Rinse the chilies under cold running water to clean.
   Remove the stems. Prick each chili 3 or 4 times with a
   fork. Peel the onions and slice into ¼" rounds. Peel the
   garlic cloves. Peel the ginger and slice thinly.

2. Heat the olive oil to medium-high in a very large
   saucepan. Add the garlic. Sauté until golden, then
   smash the garlic into the oil with the back of a spoon
   or spatula. Add the onions, ginger, cloves, cinnamon,
   thyme, and oregano. Cook for 2–3 minutes or until the
   onion just turns clear. Add the chilies and cook for 5–6
   minutes, stirring constantly.

3. Heat the vinegar to boiling in a large saucepan. Add it
   to the chili mixture. Bring everything to a boil for
   about 5 minutes. Stir in the salt until dissolved.

4. Pour into sterilized jars and seal.

Cactus Paddles

Try topping this with a sprinkling of ground pistachio meats.

INGREDIENTS | SERVES 4

2 pounds fresh cactus paddles
1 small yellow onion
4 garlic cloves
2 tablespoons butter
1 teaspoon dried oregano
1 cup sour cream

1. Clean the cactus paddles and pat dry. Cut into 1" pieces. Remove the skin from the onion and cut into ¼" pieces. Remove the skin from the garlic and cut into thin slices.

2. Melt the butter in a skillet on low heat. Add the cactus pieces, onion, garlic, and oregano; cook, stirring periodically, until the onion is clear.

3. Drain off excess butter. Stir in the sour cream.

Grilled Zucchini

This is perfect served with barbecued pork ribs or any other grilled meat.

INGREDIENTS | SERVES 8

4 medium zucchini
2 garlic cloves
1 fresh habanero pepper
½ cup olive oil
1 teaspoon dried oregano
1 teaspoon chili powder
1 teaspoon salt
½ teaspoon ground black pepper

1. Preheat grill to medium heat.

2. Remove the stems from the zucchini (do not peel) and slice in half lengthwise. Peel and mince the garlic. Remove the stem and seeds from the habanero pepper and mince.

3. Combine the garlic, habanero, oil, oregano, chili powder, salt, and black pepper in a small, covered container; shake until well mixed.

4. Place the zucchini flesh-side down on the grill for 10 minutes. Then turn flesh-side up and grill until the zucchini is soft. Use the oil-and-spice sauce to baste the zucchini as it cooks.

CHAPTER 14

Rice and Bean Dishes

Red, White, and Green Rice Salad

This salad makes an excellent vegetable or starch substitute for any summer meal. It also is the perfect potluck pleaser.

INGREDIENTS | SERVES 6

2 cups uncooked brown rice

1 medium green bell pepper

2 small pimientos

2 medium tomatoes

3 green onions

2 large eggs

1 teaspoon chopped fresh marjoram

½ teaspoon chopped fresh basil

1 tablespoon chopped fresh parsley

¼ cup vegetable oil

¼ cup olive oil

¼ cup wine vinegar

1 teaspoon salt

1. Bring 4 cups of water to a boil. Add the rice; boil for 5 minutes. Reduce heat to medium-low and let cook for 20 minutes or until the rice is tender.

2. Remove the stems and seeds from the green pepper and pimientos. Slice into ¼" strips. Cut the tomatoes into ½" cubes. Remove the skin and roots from the green onions; slice into ¼" pieces. Hard-boil the eggs and chop into ¼" pieces.

3. Combine the rice, pepper, pimientos, tomatoes, green onions, and eggs in a medium-sized bowl; toss until well mixed.

4. Combine the marjoram, basil, and parsley in a small bowl. Add the vegetable oil, olive oil, vinegar, and salt; stir well.

5. Pour the dressing over the salad. Cover and chill for at least 1 hour before serving.

Gordo

This is an excellent complement to a poultry or red meat dish.

INGREDIENTS | SERVES 4

1 cup uncooked white rice
1 garlic clove
1 medium yellow onion
2 medium fresh jalapeños
1 cup sour cream
½ cup grated Parmesan cheese
1½ cups grated Cheddar cheese
1 teaspoon salt
¼ teaspoon ground black pepper

1. Add the rice to 2 cups of water in a medium-sized saucepan. Cover and bring to a boil. Boil for 5 minutes, then reduce heat to low and simmer for 20 minutes or until the rice is tender.

2. Preheat oven to 300°F. Lightly butter or grease a square baking dish.

3. Remove the skin from the garlic and onion and chop into ¼" pieces.

4. Mix together all the ingredients in a large mixing bowl. Spoon the mixture into the prepared baking dish and bake, covered, for 35 minutes. Remove cover and bake for an additional 5 minutes.

Jalapeño Rice

Serve as a side dish to any fish or chicken meal.

INGREDIENTS | SERVES 6

1½ cups uncooked white rice
½ teaspoon salt
½ pound Monterey jack cheese
¼ cup fresh green chilies, or ⅛ cup canned green chilies
2 cups sour cream
¼ cup butter

1. Preheat oven to 350°F. Grease a 9" square baking pan.

2. Bring 6 cups of water to a boil. Add the rice and salt. Cover and boil for 5 minutes. Reduce heat to medium-low and cook for 20 minutes or until the rice is tender.

3. Grate the cheese. If using fresh chilies, remove the stems and seeds. Chop the chilies into ¼" pieces.

4. Layer the rice, sour cream, cheese, and chilies in pan in that order. Dot with butter on top. Bake for about 30 minutes.

Casa Grande

Serve this dish with a crisp green salad and fresh fruit for a well-balanced meal.

INGREDIENTS | SERVES 6

1½ cups uncooked white rice
1 large bunch fresh spinach
1 large yellow onion
2 tablespoons butter
1½ cups shredded Colby cheese
¼ teaspoon garlic salt
4 large eggs
½ cup milk
2 teaspoons salt
½ teaspoon ground black pepper

Experimenting with Rice

There are many types of rice available in today's markets. Most are fairly easy to cook with, although you will need to experiment with the amount of water and cooking time each one needs. Generally, the less processed the rice, the more water it will take up and the more cooking time it will need.

1. Add the rice to 3 cups water in a medium-sized pot. Cover, bring to a boil, and cook for 5 minutes. Turn the heat to low and simmer for 20 minutes or until the rice is tender.

2. Remove the stems from the spinach and wash well. Pat dry. Place in a medium-sized pot with 1 cup water. Cover and cook on low heat until the spinach is limp and has diminished in size to about 1 cup. Drain off the water from spinach.

3. Preheat oven to 350°F.

4. Peel the onion and chop into ¼" pieces. In a large frying pan, melt the butter. Add the onion and cook until clear and tender but not brown. Add the rice, spinach, ½ cup of the cheese, and the garlic salt; mix well.

5. Combine the eggs, milk, salt, and pepper; mix well. Stir into the rice mixture.

6. Pour into a casserole dish, sprinkle on remaining cheese, and bake, uncovered, for 30 minutes.

Cold Rice and Beans

Serve as a summer luncheon with fresh flour tortillas.

INGREDIENTS | SERVES 6

1½ cups dry white rice

1 cup frozen peas

2 cups canned pinto beans

2 cups canned black beans

3 celery ribs

1 medium red onion

1 cup canned jalapeño chili peppers, or 8 fresh jalapeños

1 bunch fresh cilantro

⅓ cup white wine vinegar

¼ cup olive oil

1 teaspoon salt

½ teaspoon garlic powder

½ teaspoon ground black pepper

¼ teaspoon cayenne pepper

1. Bring 3 cups water to a boil in a medium-sized pot. Add the dry rice. Cover and boil for 5 minutes. Reduce heat to medium-low and simmer for 20 minutes. Drain off excess water.

2. Thaw the peas. Rinse and drain the beans. Cut the celery ribs into ¼" pieces. Peel the onion and cut into ¼" rounds. Drain the jalapeño peppers (if using canned) and cut into ¼" pieces. Remove the stems from the cilantro and roughly chop the leaves into ½" pieces.

3. Combine the rice, peas, pinto beans, black beans, celery, onion, jalapeño peppers, and cilantro in a large serving bowl; toss lightly to mix.

4. In a small glass jar, combine 2 tablespoons water, the white wine vinegar, olive oil, salt, garlic powder, black pepper, and cayenne pepper. Cover and shake until well mixed. Pour over the salad. Toss until all the ingredients are covered.

5. Cover and refrigerate for at least 24 hours before serving.

Rice with Sautéed Pork

This is a great dish to serve with flour tortillas.

Slicing Meat Thinly

To easily cut meat into small cubes or strips, thaw it only partially, then use a large kitchen knife and cut the meat as you would a brick of cheese. It should have about the same consistency.

1. Bring 3 cups of water to a boil in a medium-sized pot. Add the rice; boil for 5 minutes. Reduce temperature to medium-low and simmer for 20 minutes. Drain off excess water.

2. Cut the pork into thin slices. Peel the onion and cut into ¼" pieces. Rinse and drain the pinto beans.

3. Heat the oil to medium temperature in a large frying pan. Add the pork and cook until browned. Add the onion, garlic powder, salt, oregano, cumin, and chili powder; sauté lightly until the onion is soft and clear but not brown. Stir in the tomato paste and 1 cup of water.

4. Turn heat to low. Cover and simmer for 30 minutes.

5. Add the beans and stir lightly. Cover and simmer for 15 minutes longer.

6. Stir in the rice. Cook, uncovered, for 10 minutes.

Corn and Rice Salad

Tender roasted sweet corn along with fresh vegetables and fragrant rice is a great combination in this easy salad. Serve it with grilled steak and some warmed and buttered tortillas.

INGREDIENTS | SERVES 6

1½ cups Texmati or basmati rice

3 cups water

6 ears of corn

1 tablespoon olive oil

½ teaspoon salt

1 pint grape tomatoes

1 yellow squash, chopped

1 green bell pepper, chopped

1 cup ranch salad dressing

½ cup plain yogurt

½ cup green salsa

1 serrano chili, minced

1. Preheat oven to 400°F. In a heavy saucepan, combine rice and water. Cover and bring to a boil over medium-high heat. Reduce heat and simmer for 15–20 minutes until rice is tender and liquid is absorbed. Let stand for 5 minutes off the heat, then fluff with a fork.

2. Cut kernels off the corn cobs and spread on a baking pan. Drizzle with olive oil and sprinkle with salt; roast at 400°F for 12–15 minutes, stirring once during cooking time, until kernels are light golden brown around edges. Combine with rice, tomatoes, squash, and bell pepper in a serving bowl.

3. In a medium bowl, combine salad dressing, yogurt, green salsa, and minced chili and mix well. Pour over vegetables in serving bowl and toss gently. Serve immediately or cover and chill for 1–2 hours to blend flavors.

Arroz con Pollo

Add 1 chopped chili pepper of your choice to the recipe to make a spicier version of this meal.

INGREDIENTS | SERVES 4

1 large fryer chicken
2 teaspoons salt
1 medium onion
4 large tomatoes
1 garlic clove
4 tablespoons shortening
1½ cups uncooked brown rice
1 teaspoon black pepper
1 teaspoon cumin seeds
2–3 cups warm water

The Types of Arroz

Arroz is simply the Spanish word for "rice." As with most other warm-weather cultures around the world, the Mexicans have adopted rice as a staple of their diet. Although they usually use white rice in their cooking, brown rice is favored when seeking a more hearty dish.

1. Cut the chicken into 8 serving pieces. Sprinkle the salt over the chicken pieces. Remove the skin from the onion and dice into ¼" pieces. Dice the tomatoes into eighths. Remove the skin from the garlic and mince.

2. Melt the shortening in a large frying pan over medium heat. Add the rice and stir constantly until the rice is browned.

3. In a separate frying pan, brown the chicken over medium heat.

4. Place the chicken pieces on top of the rice. Add the tomatoes, onion, garlic, spices, and warm water.

5. Cover and simmer over low heat until the rice is tender and fluffy. If the mixture dries before the rice is cooked, add more warm water.

Baked Green Rice

Serve as a side dish for Cinnamon Chicken (see recipe in Chapter 11).

INGREDIENTS | SERVES 8

1½ cups dry white rice
2 fresh green chilies
4 tomatillos
1 bunch green onions
1 bunch parsley
½ pound mild Cheddar cheese
2 large eggs
⅓ cup butter
1 teaspoon salt
½ teaspoon ground black pepper
1 cup milk

1. Preheat oven to 350°F.

2. Put the rice in a medium-sized saucepan with 3 cups of water and bring to a boil. Reduce heat to low, cover, and simmer for 20 minutes or until the rice is tender.

3. Remove the stems, membranes, and seeds from the chilies. Remove the skins from the tomatillos and chop into ¼" pieces. Chop the green onions and their stems into ¼" pieces. Remove the stems from the parsley and chop the leaves into small pieces. Grate the cheese. Beat the eggs.

4. Combine the hot rice with the cheese and butter; toss until well mixed. Add the chilies, tomatillos, onions, parsley, salt, and pepper; mix well. Add the beaten eggs and milk; stir well.

5. Transfer the mixture to a greased 2-quart baking dish. Cover and bake for 30 minutes. Uncover and bake for an additional 10 minutes.

Arroz con Queso

Serve with Mexican Pot Roast (see recipe in Chapter 12).

INGREDIENTS | SERVES 8

2 cups dry white rice
¾ pound Monterey jack cheese
⅛ pound Cheddar cheese
¼ cup canned, diced green chilies
1 pint sour cream

1. Preheat oven to 350°F.

2. Bring 4 cups of water to a boil in a medium-sized saucepan. Add the rice; cover and boil for 5 minutes. Reduce heat to low and simmer for 20 minutes or until the rice is tender. Drain off any excess water.

3. Grate the cheeses. Drain the chilies and mix into the sour cream.

4. In a 1-quart casserole dish, layer the ingredients in the following order: ½ the rice, ½ the sour cream with jalapeños, ½ the Monterey jack cheese, the remaining rice, sour cream with jalapeños, and Monterey jack cheese.

5. Bake for 30 minutes. Top with Cheddar cheese and broil for 2–3 minutes before serving.

Cumin Rice

The cumin adds a nutty, peppery flavor to this delicious rice.

INGREDIENTS | SERVES 8

1 small onion
1 medium red bell pepper
1 medium green bell pepper
1 garlic clove
2 tablespoons butter
1 teaspoon ground cumin
1½ cups uncooked white rice
1½ cups hot chicken broth

1. Peel the onion and chop into ¼" pieces. Remove the stems, seeds, and membranes from the peppers and cut into ¼" pieces. Peel and mince the garlic.

2. Heat the butter to medium temperature in a saucepan. Add the peppers and onion; cook until the onion is limp but not brown. Add the garlic, cumin, rice, and hot broth. Mix well and cover the saucepan.

3. Bring to a boil, reduce heat, and cook for about 20 minutes or until the rice is tender and the liquid is absorbed.

Sherried Raisin and Rice Pudding

Add whipped cream and coconut to each dish right before serving for a festive touch.

INGREDIENTS | SERVES 6

⅔ cup raisins

¼ cup dry red sherry

1 large egg

1 cup uncooked white rice

1 teaspoon grated lemon peel

½ teaspoon salt

1½ cups water

3 cups whole milk

1 cup granulated sugar

½ teaspoon ground cinnamon

1. Soak the raisins in the sherry for 15 minutes. Beat the egg and set aside.

2. Put the rice, lemon peel, salt, and water in a saucepan; bring to a boil. Reduce heat to low, cover, and cook until all the water is absorbed, about 15 minutes.

3. Stir in the milk, sugar, and cinnamon; cook over very low heat, stirring frequently, until all the milk has been absorbed.

4. Stir in the soaked raisins, then the beaten egg. Continue to heat, stirring constantly, until the egg is cooked, about 1–2 minutes.

5. Transfer the pudding to a serving dish. Chill in the refrigerator for 2–3 hours before serving.

Creamed Rice with Chilies

Serve this dish with fried chorizo sausage.

INGREDIENTS | SERVES 4

4 cups water

2 cups dry white rice

4 habanero chilies

1 small yellow onion

2 garlic cloves

1 cup frozen or fresh peas

1 cup frozen or fresh corn kernels

½ pound Monterey jack cheese

2 tablespoons butter

2 cups sour cream

Canned or Fresh Peppers?

A local Wal-Mart in the northern United States had no fewer than seven varieties of fresh chili peppers in stock—showing that you will likely be able to find fresh chilies to meet your needs virtually anywhere. However, if you must use canned, plan to use about half as much as you would of fresh, because they become more packed during the canning process.

1. Bring the water to a boil in a medium-sized saucepan. Add the rice and bring back to a boil. Reduce heat to medium-low and simmer, covered, for 20 minutes or until the rice is tender. Drain off excess water and set the rice aside.

2. Preheat oven to 350°F.

3. Remove the stems and seeds from the chilies and cut into ¼" pieces. Peel the onion and cut into ¼" pieces. Peel and mince the garlic. Thaw the peas and corn if necessary. Grate the cheese.

4. Melt the butter in a medium-sized frying pan on medium heat. Add the onion and garlic; sauté until the onion is limp but not brown. Reduce heat to medium-low. Add the chilies, peas, and corn; cook until thoroughly heated. Stir in the sour cream and cheese. Cook, stirring often, until the cheese is melted.

5. Add the rice to the vegetable and cheese mixture; stir until well blended. Pour into an ovenproof casserole dish. Bake for 30 minutes or until it is slightly brown on top.

Extra-Special Frijoles Refritos

This is traditionally served with tortillas or dry toast triangles. However, it also makes an excellent meat substitute in tacos or enchiladas.

INGREDIENTS | SERVES 6

2½ cups uncooked pinto beans
5 slices bacon
1 large white onion
2 garlic cloves
4 large tomatoes
1 teaspoon salt
1 teaspoon ground black pepper
1 teaspoon dried oregano
1 teaspoon ground cumin
1 cup beef broth

1. Soak the beans overnight in 5 cups of water. Drain and place in a large saucepan on medium heat. Add 4 cups of water. Cover and cook until tender but not mushy (about 2 hours). Remove from heat and drain.

2. In a large frying pan, fry the bacon until crisp. Set the bacon on a paper towel to drain grease. Chop roughly.

3. Remove the skin from the onion and chop into ¼" pieces. Remove the skin from the garlic and mince. Add the onion and garlic to the bacon grease and sauté on medium heat until golden brown.

4. Cut the tomatoes into ½" pieces. Add the tomatoes and beans to the onions and garlic in the frying pan; stir together. Add the salt, pepper, oregano, and cumin; mix thoroughly. Stir in the chopped bacon. Stir in the beef broth. Cover and simmer on medium-low heat for 20 minutes.

Black Bean and Avocado Burritos

Add diced chicken or shredded beef to the filling for a heartier meal. Serve with tortilla chips and Chile con Queso (see recipe in Chapter 2).

INGREDIENTS | SERVES 4

4 flour tortillas

1 small onion

1 medium avocado

¼ cup canned or frozen whole-kernel corn

2 tablespoons fresh cilantro leaves

1 cup canned black beans, drained

1½ cups brown rice

½ cup shredded lettuce

¼ cup canned green chilies or 2 fresh green chilies

¼ teaspoon salt

½ teaspoon black pepper

½ cup shredded Monterey jack cheese

½ cup salsa

1. Preheat oven to 350°F. Place the tortillas in a covered container in the oven for 5–10 minutes.

2. Remove the skin and chop the onion into ¼" pieces. Remove the skin and pit from the avocado and chop into ½" pieces. Drain or thaw the corn. Roughly chop the cilantro leaves.

3. Combine the beans, rice, onion, corn, cilantro, lettuce, green chilies, salt, and pepper in a medium-sized bowl. Mix well.

4. Remove the tortillas from the oven and place ½ cup of the rice-bean mixture in the center of each tortilla. Top each with ¼ of the avocado, 2 tablespoons cheese, and 1 tablespoon salsa.

5. Roll up each tortilla. Fold over the ends before serving.

Mixed Bean Salad

For some extra zing, add a chopped hot pepper to the salad and some cayenne pepper to the dressing.

INGREDIENTS | SERVES 6

1 (15-ounce) can cooked garbanzo beans
1 (15-ounce) can cooked pinto beans
1 (15-ounce) can cooked black beans
1 (15-ounce) can cooked green beans
1 medium red onion
2 garlic cloves
1 medium carrot
1 medium cucumber
1 cup vegetable oil
½ cup white vinegar
¼ cup lemon juice
1 teaspoon salt
1 teaspoon ground black pepper
½ cup roasted pecans

1. Drain off the water from all the beans and rinse with cold water. Combine in a large mixing bowl.

2. Remove the skin from the onion and cut into ¼" rounds. Remove the skin from the garlic and cut into thin slices. Peel the carrot and cut into ¼" rounds. Peel the cucumber and cut into ¼" rounds. Mix these ingredients with the beans.

3. In a small container with a lid, mix together the vegetable oil, vinegar, lemon juice, salt, and ground black pepper. Cover and shake until well blended. Pour on the bean and vegetable mixture and toss gently until well mixed.

4. Chill overnight before serving. Right before serving, sprinkle pecans on top.

Mixed Bean Soup

Serve with fresh tortillas sprinkled with garlic salt.

INGREDIENTS | SERVES 8

1 cup each dried pinto, kidney, and black beans

1 large yellow onion

2 garlic cloves

2 medium red tomatoes

1 large carrot

1 fresh jalapeño or habanero pepper

1 teaspoon chili powder

½ teaspoon red chili pepper flakes

2 teaspoons salt

2 cups chicken broth

Blend at Will

Mexicans love to use their blenders and mashers. While similar dishes in other cultures leave the ingredients in chunky bites, the Mexican versions often have them blended together to create a unique meld of flavors.

1. Soak the beans overnight in 6 cups of water.

2. Remove the skin from the onion and chop into ¼" pieces. Remove the skin from the garlic and mince. Remove the stems from the tomatoes and chop into ½" pieces. Peel the carrot and chop into ¼" pieces. Remove the stem and seeds from the pepper.

3. Add all the ingredients except the chicken broth to a large stockpot. Bring to a boil for 5 minutes. Reduce heat to medium-low and simmer, uncovered, for 3 hours.

4. Drain off the water and transfer the mixture to a blender. (You may need to divide it into 2 or 3 groups.) Blend on medium setting for 2 minutes or until the mixture becomes a paste.

5. Stir in the chicken broth. Reheat to serving temperature.

Beer Beans

Serve as a side dish to barbecued pork ribs or another meat dish.

INGREDIENTS | SERVES 6

2 cups dry pinto beans

2 cups dark Mexican beer

2 pieces bacon

1 medium onion

3 garlic cloves

2 large red tomatoes

4 pickled jalapeño chilies

1 teaspoon salt

1 teaspoon ground black pepper

1. Soak the pinto beans in 6 cups of water overnight. Drain and rinse. Put the beans into a large pot and cover with water. Bring to a boil, then reduce heat. Simmer for 30 minutes or until the beans are cooked but still firm. Drain off water and add the beer. Stir and continue to cook on low heat.

2. Fry the bacon until very crisp. Reserve the grease in the frying pan. Transfer the bacon to a paper towel to cool. When cool, crumble into pieces about ¼" square.

3. Peel the onion and chop into ¼" pieces. Peel and mince the garlic. Remove the stems from the tomatoes and chop into ½" pieces. Remove the stems from the jalapeños and chop into ¼" pieces.

4. Add the onion and garlic to the bacon grease. Cook until the onion is clear and limp, about 5–7 minutes. Add the tomatoes and jalapeños; stir to blend. Cook for about 5 minutes.

5. Add the tomato mixture to the beans. Stir in the crumbled bacon, salt, and pepper. Bring to a boil, reduce heat to low, and simmer for about 15 minutes.

Bean Burritos

Serve with guacamole and extra salsa on the side.

INGREDIENTS | SERVES 6

2 teaspoons ground cumin

3 cups refried beans

¼ cup sour cream

1 cup salsa

6 (10") flour tortillas

½ cup grated Monterey jack cheese

1. Place the cumin in a small frying pan on low heat. Heat until toasted and fragrant, stirring constantly.

2. Place the beans in a blender or food processor and blend on medium speed until smooth. Add the cumin and sour cream; blend until well mixed. Remove from blender and stir in the tomato salsa.

3. Add about ⅔ cup of the mixture to the center of each tortilla. Sprinkle cheese on top. Fold over ends and roll up.

Bean-Stuffed Peppers

Serve as a side dish for Tequila Lime Chicken (see recipe in Chapter 11).

INGREDIENTS | SERVES 6

2 large eggs
6 red bell peppers
3 cups refried beans
¼ cup flour
1 cup shortening
½ cup cream
¼ pound Monterey jack cheese

1. Preheat oven to 350°F.

2. Separate the eggs. Beat the egg yolks until thick. Beat the whites until they are shiny and stiff. Fold the egg whites into the egg yolks. Remove the stems and seeds from the bell peppers. Stuff with refried beans. Dust the peppers with flour, then dip into the egg mixture.

3. Melt the shortening in a medium-sized frying pan. Put 2 or 3 peppers in the pan at a time and fry on all sides.

4. Arrange the peppers in an ovenproof casserole dish. Cover with the cream. Grate the cheese and sprinkle on top. Bake for about 20 minutes.

Bean-Stuffed Zucchini

Serve with Jalapeño Corn Bread (see recipe in Chapter 6).

INGREDIENTS | SERVES 4

2 medium zucchini (about 10" long)

2 medium onions

1 green bell pepper

½ pound Monterey jack cheese

3 tablespoons butter or margarine

2 teaspoons ground cumin

1 teaspoon dried basil

2 teaspoons red chili sauce

2 cups refried beans

¾ cup sour cream

1. Preheat oven to 350°F.

2. Wash the zucchini and slice off the ends. Slice each zucchini lengthwise and scoop out the centers. Place the zucchini in a 9" × 12" baking pan. Chop the zucchini centers and set aside.

3. Peel the onions and chop into ¼" pieces. Remove the stem and seeds from the green pepper and chop into ¼" pieces. Grate the cheese.

4. Melt the butter in a large frying pan at medium heat. Add the onions and green pepper; sauté until onions are clear and tender. Add the cumin, basil, chili sauce, and zucchini centers; sauté for an additional 5 minutes. Add the beans, stir well, and cook another 5 minutes. Add the cheese. Stir and cook until the cheese melts. Turn off the heat and stir in the sour cream.

5. Stuff the zucchini shells with the cooked mixture. Bake for 30 minutes or until the mixture is hot and bubbly.

Enrollados

You can also add beef, chicken, or pork to these fried tacos. They're wonderful served with guacamole and various salsas for dipping.

INGREDIENTS | SERVES 6

1 medium yellow onion
2 medium red tomatoes
3 cups refried beans)
1 cup Red Chili Sauce (see recipe in Chapter 2)
12 (8") flour tortillas
1½ cups shredded Monterey jack cheese
½ cup vegetable oil
2 large eggs
½ cup flour

1. Peel the onion and chop into ¼" pieces. Remove the stems from the tomatoes and chop into ¼" pieces.

2. Heat the beans on low in a medium-sized saucepan. Add the onion, tomatoes, and chili sauce; heat through.

3. Spoon about ⅓ cup of the mixture into the center of each tortilla. Add about 2 tablespoons of the cheese. Roll up the tortilla as you would an enchilada.

4. Heat the oil to medium-high in a large frying pan. Beat the eggs in a medium-sized bowl. Roll each tortilla in the flour and then in the beaten eggs. Place in the frying pan and fry until golden brown on all sides.

Mexican Pork and Beans

Serve this dish as a stew with fresh flour tortillas.

INGREDIENTS | SERVES 4

¼ pound boneless pork
tenderloin
¼ pound ham
1 large white onion
¼ pound sliced bacon
1½ cups canned diced tomatoes
1 teaspoon chili powder
½ teaspoon ground cumin
½ teaspoon dried oregano
2 cups canned pinto beans
1 cup tequila

1. Cut the pork and ham into 1" cubes. Peel the onion and slice into ¼" rounds.

2. Cook the bacon on medium heat in a frying pan until crisp. Reserve the grease in the pan and transfer the bacon to paper towels to drain. When cool, crumble.

3. Brown the pork and ham in the bacon fat over medium heat. Add the onion. Cover and cook until soft, about 5 minutes.

4. Add the tomatoes, chili powder, cumin, oregano, and the crumbled bacon; stir well. Add the beans. Bring to a boil. Gradually stir in the tequila.

5. Continue to cook, uncovered, for 1 hour or until the pork is well done and the mixture is the consistency of a rich stew. Stir occasionally.

Garbanzos with Sausage

This makes an excellent accompaniment to Citrus Veal (see recipe in Chapter 12).

INGREDIENTS | SERVES 4

1 medium white onion
1 garlic clove
2 cups canned garbanzo beans
½ cup canned pimientos
½ pound ground pork sausage
1 teaspoon chili powder
½ teaspoon salt
¼ teaspoon dried oregano
½ teaspoon ground black pepper

1. Peel the onion and chop into ¼" pieces. Peel and mince the garlic. Drain the garbanzo beans and rinse. Drain the pimientos and cut into ¼"-wide strips.

2. Brown the sausage in a frying pan on medium heat. Add the onion, garlic, and chili powder; cook until the onion is soft.

3. Add the garbanzos and pimientos; stir well. Bring to a simmer. Add the salt, oregano, and pepper.

Lima Bean Casserole

Serve with fresh fruit for a well-balanced meal.

INGREDIENTS | SERVES 6

1 pound dried lima beans
1 large white onion
¼ pound ham
¼ cup vegetable oil
¼ pound ground spicy sausage
1 cup Red Chili Sauce (see recipe in Chapter 2)
½ cup grated Monterey jack cheese

1. Put the lima beans in a large pot. Add water to cover them. Soak for 1 hour. Bring to a boil, reduce heat, and cook until tender, about 1 hour. If the beans seem dry after 30 minutes, stir in 1 cup more water.

2. Peel the onion and cut into ¼" rings. Cut the ham into ½" cubes.

3. Heat the oil to medium temperature in a medium-sized skillet. Add the onion and sausage; cook until the sausage is browned. Add the ham and chili sauce. Cover and cook for about 30 minutes.

4. Skim off excess fat. Add the cooked beans and cook another 15 minutes. Sprinkle with cheese before serving.

CHAPTER 15

Fruit

Pineapple and Coconut Salad

For a tropical change of pace, add 1 cup chopped fresh mango or papaya to the salad.

INGREDIENTS | SERVES 8

1 fresh pineapple

1 fresh coconut (substitute 2 cups preshredded if necessary)

1 medium fresh cabbage (or 2 cups preshredded)

1 cup mayonnaise

1 teaspoon lemon juice

6 large lettuce leaves

1. Remove the rind, core, and top from the pineapple. Cut into ½" cubes. Remove the shell from the coconut and shred until you have 2 cups. Shred the cabbage until you have 2 cups.

2. Combine the pineapple, coconut, cabbage, mayonnaise, and lemon juice in a large serving bowl; toss gently until well mixed.

3. Cover and chill for at least 1 hour before serving. Serve by scooping onto lettuce leaves.

Mango Paste

*Pastes can be made with any fruit and are often served with cream
cheese and crackers or used as an on-the-run treat.*

INGREDIENTS | SERVES 6–12

2 ripe mangoes
4 cups granulated sugar

1. Peel the mangoes and remove the seeds.

2. Place the fruit in a food processor or blender and
   blend on medium setting until you have a purée—the
   mixture should be free of large lumps.

3. Weigh the mango and measure out an equal weight
   of sugar.

4. Put the mango and sugar in a large pot on low heat;
   mix well. Cook, stirring often, until the mixture has the
   consistency of jelly. This usually takes 1–3 hours.

5. Remove from the heat and beat with a large spoon for
   about 10 minutes or until you have a heavy paste.

6. Pour the paste onto parchment paper and set in a
   sunny area for at least 24 hours.

Fruity Tamales

These are a favorite to take to the beach. Put the just-steamed tamales in a small cooler to keep them warm.

INGREDIENTS | SERVES 8

24 corn husks
2 cups masa harina or cornmeal
1 teaspoon salt
1 teaspoon baking powder
⅓ cup shortening
1 cup granulated sugar
1 cup water
1 teaspoon lime juice
½ cup dried peaches
½ cup dried apricots
½ cup raisins
½ cup slivered almonds

How to Steam with No Steamer

If you don't have a steamer, add 1" of water to a large pot and place a stainless steel mixing bowl in the pot. Put the tamales in the mixing bowl and turn the heat on medium-high. Cover and check every 5 minutes to make sure the water doesn't boil away.

1. Soak the corn husks in warm water for 1 hour. Drain off the water and pat the husks dry with a paper towel.

2. Mix together the cornmeal, salt, baking powder, shortening, sugar, water, and lime juice in a medium-sized mixing bowl to form a doughy texture. If the mixture seems too runny, add more cornmeal. If it seems too dry, add more water.

3. Place 1 heaping tablespoon of the cornmeal mixture in the center of each corn husk and pat down until it is about ¼" thick.

4. Cut the dried peaches and apricots into ¼" pieces. Mix together the peaches, apricots, raisins, and almonds.

5. Add 1 tablespoon of the fruit mixture to the center of the dough on each corn husk. Roll up the husks so the mixture is centered in the husk. Steam tamales for 30 minutes.

Peppery Mango Salad

This makes an excellent accompaniment to any beef dish.

INGREDIENTS | SERVES 12

10 ripe mangoes
2 large Vidalia onions
8 fresh jalapeño chili peppers
½ cup vegetable oil
1½ cups cider vinegar
½ teaspoon salt
½ teaspoon ground white pepper
½ teaspoon white granulated sugar

1. Peel the mangoes and slice the fruit into ½"-thick slices. Peel the onions and cut into ¼" rounds. Remove stems and seeds from jalapeño peppers and cut into ¼" rounds. Combine these ingredients in a large mixing bowl.

2. Stir together the oil, cider vinegar, salt, pepper, and sugar; pour over the fruit, onion, and pepper mixture. Toss gently until the mangoes, onions, and peppers are covered with the dressing.

3. Refrigerate at least 2 hours before serving.

Spicy Pineapple Salad

This makes an excellent counterpart to a heavy meat dish, such as Caldo de Rez (see recipe in Chapter 9).

INGREDIENTS | SERVES 6

1 pineapple
1 medium red onion
2 garlic cloves
1 bunch fresh cilantro
1 jalapeño pepper
½ teaspoon dried oregano
½ teaspoon cayenne pepper

1. Remove the stem, rind, and core from the pineapple. Cut into 1" cubes. Reserve the juice. Peel the onion and cut into ¼" rings. Peel the garlic and chop into ¼" pieces. Remove the stems from the cilantro and roughly chop the leaves into ½" pieces. Remove the stem and seeds from the jalapeño pepper and cut into ¼" rings.

2. Combine all the ingredients in a medium-sized serving bowl; mix well.

3. Cover and chill in the refrigerator for at least 4 hours before serving.

Fruit Tacos

Try any mix of fruits in this delightful treat. However, be sure to drain juicy fruits so they don't turn the tortillas into mush while baking.

INGREDIENTS | SERVES 4

2 ripe bananas
1 medium sweet apple
½ cup raisins
1 teaspoon ground cinnamon
1 teaspoon ground nutmeg
½ teaspoon lemon juice
4 (8") flour tortillas)

1. Preheat oven to 350°F.

2. Peel and mash the banana. Peel the apple and remove the core and stem. Dice the fruit into ¼" pieces.

3. Mix together the bananas, apple, raisins, cinnamon, nutmeg, and lemon juice.

4. Place ¼ of the mixture in the middle of each tortilla. Roll up and place on a baking sheet.

5. Bake for 5 minutes.

Banana Fritadas

Serve these as a dessert after any of your favorite meat dishes.

INGREDIENTS | SERVES 6

6 ripe bananas
3 cups flour
1 teaspoon baking powder
½ cup granulated sugar
2 teaspoons ground cinnamon
2 large eggs
2 teaspoons vanilla extract
2 tablespoons vegetable oil

1. Peel the bananas and mash well.

2. Combine the flour, baking powder, sugar, and cinnamon; mix well. Stir in the bananas.

3. Add the eggs and vanilla. Stir until all the ingredients are well blended.

4. In a medium-sized frying pan, heat the vegetable oil to medium-high heat. Make hand-sized patties about ½" thick out of the dough. Fry on both sides until light brown.

Fruit Compote

For a special treat, ladle over vanilla ice cream or raspberry sherbet.

INGREDIENTS | SERVES 8

1½ cups seedless green grapes
1½ cups fresh strawberries
2 medium oranges
4 medium kiwis
2 medium peaches
5 tablespoons confectioners' sugar
3 tablespoons triple sec
3 tablespoons tequila
1½ tablespoons lime juice

1. Cut the grapes in half. Remove the stems from the strawberries and cut the fruit in half. Peel the oranges and slice into ¼" rounds. Peel the kiwis and slice into ¼" rounds. Peel the peaches, remove the pits, and cut into ¼"-thick slices.

2. In a small jar, combine the sugar, triple sec, tequila, and lime juice. Cover and shake until well mixed. Combine all the fruit in a large serving bowl. Add the dressing and toss the fruit until well covered.

3. Cover and refrigerate for at least 4 hours before serving.

Mexican Fruitcake

An easy frosting for this cake is made with ¼ cup margarine, 8 ounces cream cheese, 2 cups confectioners' sugar, and 1 teaspoon vanilla. Mix well and spread on the cake while it's still warm.

INGREDIENTS | SERVES 8

2 large eggs
2 cups white granulated sugar
2 cups self-rising flour
2 teaspoons baking soda
1 (20-ounce) can crushed pineapple, with juice
1 cup chopped walnuts
1 cup shredded coconut

1. Preheat oven to 350°F.

2. Mix together all the ingredients thoroughly.

3. Grease and lightly flour a 9" × 13" baking pan. Pour the mixture into the pan.

4. Bake for 40 minutes.

Melon Salad

Surprise your breakfast guests by serving this with Easy Huevos Rancheros (see recipe in Chapter 8).

INGREDIENTS | SERVES 6

1 cantaloupe

1 honeydew melon

2–3 jalapeño peppers

1 red bell pepper

1 yellow bell pepper

1 medium Vidalia onion

1 small jicama

4 scallions

1 bunch cilantro

3 tablespoons lime juice

3 tablespoons olive oil

3 tablespoons red cooking sherry

Choosing Ripe Melons

People say there is an art to finding a ripe melon, but it really is as simple as listening. Lightly thump the melon. It should sound hollow inside. An unripe melon is still dense and will make very little sound when thumped.

1. Remove the rind and seeds from the cantaloupe and honeydew melons. Cut the fruit into 1" cubes. Remove the seeds and stems from the jalapeño and bell peppers. Cut into ¼" rounds. Peel the onion and cut into ¼" rounds. Peel the jicama and cut into ¼"-thick strips. Peel the scallions and cut into ¼" pieces. Remove the stems from the cilantro and roughly chop the leaves into ½" pieces.

2. Combine the melons, peppers, onion, jicama, scallions, and cilantro in a large mixing bowl; toss until well mixed.

3. In a small jar, combine the lime juice, olive oil, and cooking sherry. Cover and shake until well blended. Pour the dressing over the fruit and vegetables; toss lightly until evenly coated.

4. Cover and chill in the refrigerator for at least 3 hours before serving.

Flaming Fruit

This makes an elegant ending to a special-occasion meal.

INGREDIENTS | SERVES 6

1 fresh mango
3 ripe bananas
1 cup fresh strawberries
1 cup orange juice
2 tablespoons granulated sugar
1 cup tequila
6 large scoops vanilla ice cream

Browning Fruit

To keep fruit such as bananas and apples from turning brown once they have had their peels removed, sprinkle them with a small amount of lemon juice. The acid in the juice stops the sugars in the fruits from reacting with the air to produce the brown color.

1. Peel the mango and cut into 6 slices. Peel the bananas and slice lengthwise. Remove the stems from the strawberries and cut the berries in half.

2. Put the fruit in a chafing dish or large skillet on medium heat. Pour the orange juice over the fruit and sprinkle with the sugar. Heat to simmering, stirring gently to dissolve the sugar and coat the fruit.

3. Add the tequila. Flame the sauce by pouring a little tequila into a teaspoon and holding it over a flame until it catches on fire. Drop the flame into the fruit mixture. After 5–10 seconds, the flames will disappear or be very small. Gently blow them out if any remain. The alcohol has burned away but occasionally the sugar in the fruit burns slightly.

4. Serve over ice cream.

Fruity Picadillo

Serve over white rice and garnish with fresh orange slices.

INGREDIENTS | SERVES 8

3 bananas

3 nectarines

3 pears

1 cup strawberries

2 green apples

1 medium jicama

1 medium yellow onion

3 medium red tomatoes

3 fresh jalapeño chilies

2 tablespoons olive oil

1 pound ground veal

1 pound ground chicken

½ teaspoon ground cinnamon

½ teaspoon ground cloves

½ cup pistachio meats

1. Peel the bananas and cut into ½" rounds. Peel the nectarines, remove the pits, and cut into 1" pieces. Peel the pears, remove the pits, and cut into 1" pieces. Remove the stems from the strawberries and slice in half. Peel the apples, remove the cores and stems, and cut into 1" pieces. Peel the jicama and cut into 1" pieces. Peel the onion and chop into ¼" pieces. Peel the tomatoes and chop into ¼" pieces. Remove the seeds and stems from the chilies and cut into ¼" pieces.

2. Heat the oil to medium temperature in a large frying pan. Add the veal and chicken. Fry on all sides until the meat is golden. Add the onion, tomatoes, chilies, cinnamon, and cloves; mix well. Lower heat and cover. Simmer, uncovered, for 30 minutes, stirring occasionally.

3. Add the bananas, nectarines, pears, strawberries, apples, jicama, and pistachios; stir gently to blend. Cover and simmer for 15 minutes.

CHAPTER 16

Desserts

Bride's Cookies

To make these cookies extra special, create a mixture of ½ cup confectioners' sugar and 1 tablespoon cinnamon. When the cookies are just cool enough to handle, roll them in the mixture.

INGREDIENTS | MAKES 2 DOZEN

1 cup unsalted, roasted almonds
2 cups all-purpose flour
½ cup confectioners' sugar
¼ teaspoon salt
1 teaspoon ground cinnamon
1 cup softened butter
1 teaspoon vanilla extract

1. Preheat oven to 350°F.

2. Use a food processor or nut grinder to grind the almonds into small pieces. (They should not be ground into a powder.)

3. Mix together the flour, sugar, salt, cinnamon, and almonds in a medium-sized mixing bowl. Add the softened butter and vanilla. Stir until the ingredients are well blended.

4. Make 24 balls about the size of golf balls and place on baking sheets.

5. Bake for 20–30 minutes or until lightly browned.

Coffee Caramel

For a different version, replace the coffee with 1 cup whole milk and use ½ cup ground pistachios instead of the cinnamon.

INGREDIENTS | SERVES 8–12

7 cups whole milk
3 cups granulated sugar
1 teaspoon baking soda
1 cup hot, strong coffee
½ teaspoon ground cinnamon
2 tablespoons butter

1. Combine the milk, sugar, and soda in a large pot on medium heat. Boil, stirring every few minutes, until the mixture turns thick and slightly brown.

2. Add the coffee and cinnamon; stir well. Turn the heat to low and continue cooking until the mixture is thick. When a small drop of the mixture is put in a glass of cold water, it should form a soft ball.

3. Spread the butter onto the bottom and sides of a 9" × 9" cake pan. Pour the mixture into the pan. Chill in the refrigerator at least 2 hours before serving.

Mexican Tea Cakes

Although enjoyed year-round, these are a traditional Christmas holiday treat.

INGREDIENTS | MAKES 5 DOZEN

¼ cup pistachio meats
1 cup butter
2½ cups flour
1¾ cups confectioners' sugar, divided
2 teaspoons vanilla
½ teaspoon salt

1. Grind the pistachio meats. Soften the butter in a medium-sized mixing bowl by stirring with a spoon.

2. Add the pistachio meats, flour, ¾ cup of the sugar, the vanilla, and salt to the butter; mix until a stiff dough is formed.

3. Cover and chill in the refrigerator for 2–4 hours.

4. Preheat oven to 350°F.

5. Form the dough into balls about 1" in diameter. Place on a greased baking sheet and bake for 10–15 minutes. The cookies should be firm but not brown.

6. Remove the cookies from the oven and roll them in the remaining confectioners' sugar. When the cookies are cool, roll them in the sugar again.

Mexican Chocolate Cake

Serve this with Coconut Coffee (see recipe in Chapter 21) or
Mexican Hot Chocolate (see recipe in Chapter 21).

INGREDIENTS | SERVES 8

1¼ cups flour
1 cup granulated sugar
¼ cup cornstarch
5 tablespoons powdered cocoa, divided
1 teaspoon baking soda
2 teaspoons ground cinnamon, divided
½ teaspoon salt
1 tablespoon white wine vinegar
1 teaspoon vanilla
1 tablespoon oil
1 tablespoon corn syrup
1 cup confectioners' sugar

Mexican Chocolate

Mexican chocolate desserts often taste sour and not "chocolatey" enough to those in the United States. If you want a less traditional taste but one you're more familiar with, double the chocolate and sugar, and don't add the vinegar in the dessert recipes calling for chocolate.

1. Preheat oven to 350°F.

2. Combine the flour, granulated sugar, cornstarch, 3 tablespoons of the powdered cocoa, the baking soda, 1 teaspoon of the cinnamon, and the salt; mix well. Add the white wine vinegar, vanilla, and 1 cup cold water; mix with a fork.

3. Pour the mixture into a 9" square greased and floured cake pan. Bake for 30–35 minutes. Cool the cake to room temperature.

4. For the glaze, combine the remaining cocoa and cinnamon, the oil, corn syrup, and 2 tablespoons water in a small saucepan. Cook over low heat until all the ingredients are melded. Add the confectioners' sugar. Continue cooking, stirring constantly, until the sugar is dissolved.

5. Remove the glaze from the heat and beat until it is smooth and shiny. Spread over the top of the cake. Let cool before serving.

Natilla

This light custard is perfect after a spicy, heavy meal of chicken or beef.

INGREDIENTS | SERVES 8

4 large eggs
½ cup flour
1 quart milk
¾ cup granulated sugar
⅛ teaspoon salt
1 teaspoon ground nutmeg
1 teaspoon ground cinnamon

Custards and Puddings

Mexicans enjoy custards and puddings after their meals, perhaps because they are an excellent way to get more milk into the diet. They also are a fun way to use the many spices available in this culture.

1. Separate the eggs.

2. Make a paste of the egg yolks, flour, and 1 cup of the milk.

3. In a medium-sized saucepan, add the sugar and salt to the remaining milk and scald at medium heat. Add the egg yolk mixture to the scalded milk and continue to cook, stirring constantly, at medium temperature until it reaches the consistency of soft custard. Remove from heat and cool to room temperature.

4. Beat the egg whites until stiff. Fold into the custard.

5. Cover and chill for at least 2 hours before serving.

6. Spoon into individual dishes and sprinkle with nutmeg and cinnamon right before serving.

Pistachio-Coconut Flan

For an extra treat, drizzle warm caramel sauce over the individual servings and top with a small slice of bitter chocolate.

INGREDIENTS | SERVES 6

6 large eggs

1 (14-ounce) can sweetened condensed milk

2 teaspoons vanilla extract

2 cups whole milk

2 cups half-and-half

2 tablespoons grated coconut

1 tablespoon ground pistachio meats

1. Preheat the oven to 325°F.

2. In a large mixing bowl, gently stir together the eggs, sweetened condensed milk, and vanilla extract.

3. Pour the milk and half-and-half into a medium saucepan and place on the stove on medium-high heat. Bring to a boil, then remove from heat. Gradually pour the egg mixture into the hot milk, stirring constantly. Make sure no clumps of egg remain.

4. Pass the mixture through a strainer, then pour into a greased 9" cake pan. Sprinkle the coconut and pistachio meats on top. Place the pan into a large roasting pan and fill the roasting pan with warm tap water until it is about halfway up the side of the cake pan.

5. Bake for 60 minutes. The center should feel firm when pressed, but the top should not not be browned. The edges may be slightly browned. Remove from the oven and set aside to cool to room temperature. Cover and refrigerate for at least 4 hours before serving.

Almond Custard

This makes an excellent holiday treat and complements poultry dishes very well.

INGREDIENTS | SERVES 4

2 cups whole milk

6 egg yolks

¼ cup brown sugar

¼ teaspoon salt

1 teaspoon almond extract

½ cup slivered, toasted almonds

Using a Double Boiler

A double boiler consists of two pots, one sitting on top of the other. The food to be cooked goes in the top pot while the boiling water goes in the bottom. The steam from the boiling water cooks the food. Since the food does not have direct contact with the heat source, there is no possibility of burning the food.

1. Heat milk in the top of a double boiler until too hot to touch.

2. Separate the eggs and discard the whites. Add the sugar and salt to the egg yolks and beat until light and fluffy.

3. Gradually add egg mixture to milk, stirring constantly. Heat while stirring until the mixture coats a spoon. Remove from heat and cool to room temperature. Add almond extract. Beat until the mixture is firm.

4. Line individual custard dishes with almonds. Pour mixture on top. Place a few almond slivers atop each custard. Refrigerate 2 hours before serving.

Pecan Pudding

Pistachios and almonds can be substituted for the pecans to complement different dishes.

INGREDIENTS | SERVES 4

½ cup roasted pecans
1 cup water
1 package unflavored gelatin
1 cup white granulated sugar
½ teaspoon vanilla extract
6 large eggs

1. Use a food processor or nut grinder to break the pecans into small pieces. (They should not be ground into a powder.)

2. Put the water in a medium-sized pot on high heat. When boiling, add the gelatin. Stir until the gelatin is dissolved.

3. Add the sugar and stir until it is dissolved. Add the vanilla.

4. Remove from heat and let cool until the mixture begins to thicken.

5. Separate the eggs and discard the yolks. Beat the whites until they form stiff peaks. Fold the egg whites into the gelatin mixture until well blended. Gently stir in the pecans.

6. Pour into individual cups and chill until firm.

Tropical Gelatin

This fun dessert is a special treat on a hot summer day.

INGREDIENTS | SERVES 6

1 cup chopped fresh papaya
1 cup chopped fresh guava
1 cup chopped fresh pineapple
12 lady fingers
2 cups water
3 packages unsweetened gelatin
½ cup granulated sugar

Finding a Fresh Pineapple

Fresh, ripe pineapples have a distinctly yellow hue to their rind and smell only mildly sweet, while those beyond their freshness will have an almost sickly sweet smell and may even be oozing juice. A green pineapple will be just that—its rind will show very little deep yellow color.

1. Mix the pineapple, papaya, and guava together in a small mixing bowl. (Do not drain the juice from the fruit.)

2. Break the lady fingers into 1" pieces and line the bottom of 6 individual custard bowls with the pieces.

3. Bring the water to a boil in a medium-sized pot. Add the gelatin and sugar; stir until both are dissolved. Remove from heat and stir in the fruit. Let cool at room temperature until it begins to thicken.

4. Pour the mixture over the lady fingers. Cool in the refrigerator for at least 2 hours before serving.

Raisin and Pistachio Pudding

Many cultures have a rice pudding, but this is the ultimate recipe. Its subtle flavors instantly transport you to a coastal resort.

INGREDIENTS | SERVES 4

½ cup roasted pistachio meats
½ cup raisins
1 cup dry white wine
1 key lime
1 cup water
½ cup rice
¼ teaspoon salt
4 cups whole milk
1 cup granulated sugar
1 teaspoon ground cinnamon
2 egg yolks

1. Grind the pistachios in a nut grinder or food processor until you have small pieces. (They should not be ground into a powder.) Put the raisins and white wine in a small mixing bowl and set aside. Remove the rind from the key lime and discard the fruit.

2. Bring the water to a boil in a medium-sized pot. Add the lime rind, rice, and salt. Cover and boil for 5 minutes, then reduce heat to low and simmer for 15 minutes.

3. Discard the lime rind. Add the milk, sugar, and cinnamon. Continue cooking, uncovered, on low heat until all the milk has been absorbed.

4. Separate the eggs and discard the whites. Drain off and discard the wine that has not soaked into the raisins. Mix the egg yolks, raisins, and pistachios into the rice mixture; cook for 5 minutes, uncovered.

5. Place the pudding in a serving dish, cover, and refrigerate for at least 2 hours before serving.

Cocoa Pecan Treats

These treats are as easy to make as they are tasty. Even youngsters can make a batch for themselves with little trouble.

INGREDIENTS | SERVES 8–12

½ cup pecans
½ cup whole milk
2 cups white granulated sugar
½ cup shortening
½ teaspoon salt
3 cups quick-cooking oats
½ cup shredded coconut
½ cup cocoa
2 teaspoons vanilla

1. Chop the pecans into ⅛" pieces.

2. Combine the whole milk, sugar, shortening, and salt in saucepan on medium-high heat; boil for 2 minutes.

3. Remove from heat. Stir in the oats, coconut, cocoa, vanilla, and pecans.

4. Drop by rounded teaspoonfuls onto parchment paper. Set in a cool place until the treats reach room temperature.

Wine Cookies

Traditionally, these cookies are made into 3" circles, although you can cut them into any shape you would like.

INGREDIENTS | MAKES 4 DOZEN

1 cup margarine
1 cup white granulated sugar
1 egg
1 teaspoon salt
4 cups flour
¼ cup sweet sherry

1. Preheat oven to 350°F.

2. Mix together the margarine and sugar until creamy. Add the egg and beat until the mixture is light and fluffy.

3. Blend in the salt and 2 cups of the flour. Stir in the sherry. Add the remaining 2 cups of flour and mix well.

4. Chill in the refrigerator for 1 hour or until firm.

5. Roll out the dough on a lightly floured surface until it's about ⅛" thick. Cut with cookie cutters.

6. Place on a lightly greased baking sheet and bake for 10 minutes.

Biscochitos

The fleur-de-lis shape is traditional for these cookies, but you can use any cookie cutter you have on hand.

INGREDIENTS | MAKES 5 DOZEN

6 cups flour
3 teaspoons baking powder
1 teaspoon salt
1 pound softened butter
1¾ cups white granulated sugar, divided
2 teaspoons anise seeds
2 large eggs
½ cup brandy
1 teaspoon ground cinnamon

1. Preheat oven to 350°F.

2. Sift the flour with the baking powder and salt.

3. Cream the butter with 1½ cups of the sugar and the anise seeds using a mixer set on medium speed.

4. Beat the eggs until light and fluffy and add to the butter mixture. Add the flour mixture and the brandy; mix until well blended. The dough should be stiff. If not, add more flour until it is.

5. Knead the dough and roll out to ¼" to ½" thick. Cut with cookie cutters.

6. Mix together the remaining ¼ cup sugar and the cinnamon. Use to dust the top of each cookie.

7. Place on a baking sheet and bake for 10–12 minutes or until lightly browned.

Mexican Carrot Cake

This sweet treat is great for holidays or family get-togethers.

INGREDIENTS | SERVES 4

8 medium carrots
4 teaspoons lemon rind
4 teaspoons lemon juice
1 teaspoon vanilla extract
6 tablespoons granulated sugar
¼ cup vegetable oil
4 medium eggs
4 (8") flour tortillas

Carrots

When using carrots in a dessert dish, be sure to use medium or small carrots. They contain the most flavor and the most juice. Large carrots are fine with meat or vegetable dishes, but they are too acidic and flat-tasting for desserts.

1. Preheat oven to 350°F.

2. Peel the carrots and finely grate.

3. In a small bowl, combine the carrots, lemon rind, lemon juice, and vanilla extract; set aside.

4. Combine the sugar with the vegetable oil. Beat the eggs, then stir them into the sugar and vegetable oil. Tear or cut the tortillas into ¼" pieces. Add the tortillas and carrot mixture to the sugar and egg mixture; mix well.

5. Pour the mixture into a 9" springform pan and bake for 1 hour or until the top is brown.

Pecan Candy

If you're used to pralines from America's southeast, these will taste a little odd at first. However, this authentic candy complements a Mexican meal perfectly.

INGREDIENTS | SERVES 8

2 cups white granulated sugar
½ cup margarine
1 cup canned condensed milk
2 tablespoons white corn syrup
1 teaspoon vanilla extract
¼ teaspoon cayenne pepper
½ teaspoon chili powder
3 cups pecans

1. Combine the sugar, margarine, condensed milk, and corn syrup in a medium-sized pot. Heat on medium-high until the mixture forms a firm, soft ball when a small amount is dropped into cold water.

2. Remove from heat. Stir in the vanilla, cayenne pepper, chili powder, and pecans.

3. Using a tablespoon, drop into patties on parchment paper. Put in a cool place until the clusters reach room temperature.

Mexican Orange

Vary the types of nuts used and add a mixture of lemon and orange rinds for a completely different treat.

INGREDIENTS | SERVES 6

Rind from 2 oranges
1 cup pistachio meats
1½ cups condensed milk
3 cups white granulated sugar
½ cup butter

1. Cut the orange rinds into ¼" pieces. Chop the pistachios into small pieces.

2. Place the milk in the top of a double boiler and heat until scalded—the milk will have a film on top.

3. Melt 1 cup of the sugar in a large pot on medium-high heat until it is a rich yellow color. Add the hot milk to the sugar. Add the remaining sugar, stir, and cook until it reaches 238°F on a candy thermometer.

4. Remove from heat. Stir in the rind, butter, and nuts.

5. Pour into a buttered 7" × 11" pan and place in a cool area until the candy reaches room temperature.

Wine Custard

This makes a perfect ending to a romantic meal.

INGREDIENTS | SERVES 6

6 cups whole milk
2 cups sugar
¼ cup heavy red wine

1. Place the milk in the top of a double boiler and heat over boiling water. Stir in the sugar. Cook for 2 hours, stirring occasionally.

2. Remove from heat and let cool to room temperature.

3. Pour the milk mixture into a saucepan on medium-low heat. Stir in the wine until the wine is completely absorbed.

4. Transfer the mixture to a serving dish. Cover and chill in the refrigerator for 3–4 hours before serving.

Pineapple and Almond Pudding

This sweet and nutty pudding is perfect for a light dessert.

INGREDIENTS | SERVES 6

1 fresh pineapple
4 large eggs
½ cup blanched almonds
1 angel food cake
½ cup, plus 1 tablespoon, granulated sugar
½ cup dry sherry, divided
¼ teaspoon ground cinnamon
½ cup orange marmalade
½ cup sour cream
½ cup toasted, slivered almonds

1. Remove the skin, top, and core from the pineapple. Slice the fruit into ¼" cubes until you have 2 cups. Separate the eggs and discard the whites. Beat the egg yolks. Grind the blanched almonds into small pieces. (Do not grind into a powder.) Cut the angel food cake into twelve 4" × 1" slices.

2. Combine the pineapple, ½ cup of the sugar, ¼ cup sherry, egg yolks, and cinnamon in a medium-sized saucepan. Cook over low heat, stirring constantly, until thickened. Remove from heat and let cool.

3. Spread the cake slices with the marmalade. Arrange half the cake slices in the bottom of a 1-quart serving dish. Sprinkle with 2 tablespoons of the sherry. Spoon half of the pineapple mixture on top. Repeat layers of cake slices, sherry, and pineapple mixture.

4. Cover and refrigerate for 2–3 hours.

5. Mix the remaining 1 tablespoon sugar into the sour cream. Spread over the top of the chilled dessert. Decorate with the toasted, slivered almonds.

Pecan Cake

This is the perfect dessert after a traditional Mexican meal.

INGREDIENTS | SERVES 6

3 large eggs
½ cup pecans
½ cup butter
¾ cup cake flour
1 teaspoon baking powder
⅔ cup, plus ¼ cup granulated sugar
1 tablespoon lemon juice
½ teaspoon salt
½ cup orange marmalade
¼ cup granulated sugar

1. Preheat oven to 350°F.

2. Separate the eggs. Finely grate the pecans. Melt the butter in a small saucepan on low heat.

3. Blend together the flour and baking powder.

4. Beat the egg yolks in a large mixing bowl until they are thick and lemon-colored. Gradually beat in the ⅔ cup sugar. Beat in the lemon juice and grated pecans. Gradually beat in the flour mixture. Slowly beat in the melted butter.

5. Beat the egg whites with the salt until stiff peaks form. Fold the beaten egg whites into the batter.

6. Pour the batter into a greased and floured 9" round cake pan.

7. Bake for 30–35 minutes or until a toothpick inserted in the center comes out clean. Let the cake cool for 10 minutes before removing from the pan.

8. Combine the orange marmalade and the ¼ cup sugar in a small saucepan over medium-low heat. Cook until the sugar is dissolved, stirring constantly. While still warm, use as a glaze for the cake.

Sugared Pumpkin

This is traditionally served as a dessert but makes an excellent vegetable course when served with a beef or pork dish.

INGREDIENTS | SERVES 8

1 medium pumpkin
½ cup butter
2 teaspoons ground cinnamon
2 cups brown sugar

1. Preheat oven to 350°F.

2. Cut the pumpkin into pieces approximately 6" square, removing the seeds and interior fibers.

3. Poke holes in the pumpkin flesh with a fork. Spread a thin layer of butter on each pumpkin piece.

4. Mix together the cinnamon and brown sugar and spread on the pumpkin pieces.

5. Place in a baking dish and bake for 1–2 hours or until a fork slides easily into the flesh.

Molasses Candy

This makes an excellent holiday treat or a nice dessert after an informal meal.

INGREDIENTS | MAKES 1 POUND

1 cup light molasses

1 cup firmly packed brown sugar

2 tablespoons butter

1 teaspoon cider vinegar

¼ teaspoon almond extract

1½ cups toasted, slivered almonds

1. Combine the molasses, brown sugar, butter, and vinegar in a heavy saucepan. Bring to a boil. Boil hard for 7–12 minutes or until the mixture reaches 260°F on a candy thermometer. The mixture should form a firm ball when a small amount is dropped in cold water.

2. Remove from heat. Add the almond extract and almonds; stir well.

3. Pour onto a greased baking sheet. Spread out in as thin a layer as possible. Let cool.

4. Break into 2" pieces.

Pepita Balls

Mexicans love their sweets and will serve these as appetizers or dessert.

INGREDIENTS | MAKES 6 DOZEN

1 pound unsalted hulled pepitas
(pumpkin seeds)

1 cup sweetened condensed milk

3½ cups confectioners' sugar, divided

1. Grind the pepitas finely.

2. Mix the pepitas with the condensed milk and 3 cups of the confectioners' sugar.

3. Shape into 1" balls and roll in the remaining sugar. Place on parchment paper on a baking sheet.

4. Refrigerate for 2–3 hours or until set.

Orange Liqueur Mousse

Serve as a light dessert after Mexican Pot Roast (see recipe in Chapter 12).

INGREDIENTS | SERVES 4

1 (3-ounce) package orange-
flavored gelatin
1 cup boiling water
¼ cup cold water
¼ cup orange liqueur
1 cup whipping cream
½ teaspoon ground cinnamon
½ cup shredded coconut

Making It Nonalcoholic

If you want to make uncooked foods calling for liqueur nonalcoholic, simply substitute 1 tablespoon of the flavored extract mixed with half water and half corn syrup. You will get a very similar flavor without the alcohol.

1. Dissolve the gelatin in the boiling water. Add the cold water and cool the mixture to room temperature. Stir in the orange liqueur. Chill in the refrigerator until the mixture starts to thicken, about 30 minutes.

2. Whip the cream until it piles softly. Gradually add the gelatin mixture and cinnamon, stirring gently until evenly blended. Pour into a mold. Chill until set, about 1 hour.

3. Turn the mold onto a serving plate and top with the shredded coconut.

CHAPTER 17

Traditional Favorites

Gazpacho

*Gazpacho makes an excellent first course to a heavier beef or chicken meal.
However, it also makes a good lunch served with white bread and cheese.*

INGREDIENTS | SERVES 8

4 large tomatoes

1 small yellow onion

1 green bell pepper

2 celery ribs

4 cups canned condensed tomato soup

2 tablespoons olive oil

2 tablespoons white wine vinegar

2 teaspoons salt

1 teaspoon ground black pepper

1 medium cucumber

Bell Peppers

Bell peppers have different flavors depending on their color. Green is the most acidic and sour-tasting. Red has the most peppery flavor. Yellow and orange have a gentle flavor. Combine them to create unique flavors and a beautiful dish.

1. Peel the tomatoes and cut into quarters. Remove the skin from the onion and cut into quarters. Remove the stem and seeds from the green pepper and cut into quarters. Remove the leaves from the celery and cut the ribs into quarters.

2. Combine 2 cups of the tomato soup, the olive oil, wine vinegar, salt, pepper, and half of the quartered vegetables in a blender. Blend until liquefied, about 1 minute. Pour into a bowl. Repeat with the remaining tomato soup and quartered vegetables. Combine with the previous mixture.

3. Cover and chill in the refrigerator for at least 2 hours before serving.

4. Chop the cucumber and place on top right before serving.

Black Bean Soup

Garnish with grated Cheddar cheese and sour cream.

INGREDIENTS | SERVES 4

2 cups dried black beans

2½ quarts water, divided

2 garlic cloves

2 medium yellow onions

½ cup vegetable oil

½ teaspoon salt

½ teaspoon ground black pepper

¼ teaspoon whole fennel seeds

¼ teaspoon dried basil

1 teaspoon granulated sugar

1 teaspoon dried mustard

1 teaspoon grated lemon rind

¼ teaspoon ground allspice

1 teaspoon dried cilantro

1 cup canned condensed tomato soup

3 tablespoons lemon juice

1. Soak the beans overnight in ½ quart of the water.

2. Remove the skin from the garlic and mince. Remove the skin from the onions and cut into ¼" pieces. Put oil, onions, and garlic in a medium frying pan on medium heat. Sauté until the onions are limp, not brown. Drain the oil.

3. Combine all the ingredients except the lemon juice in a large soup pot. Stir until well blended. Bring to a boil, then lower temperature to medium-low. Simmer, uncovered, for 2 hours or until the beans are soft.

4. Add the lemon juice and stir right before serving.

Beans Galore

Although we think of only a couple types of beans, there are many, many varieties that Mexicans routinely use. Traditional grocery stores are beginning to carry more of these varieties, but you also might try a local food co-op. Virtually any bean can be substituted in these recipes, depending on your taste.

Churros

These traditional treats also can be formed into small patties and served with jam.

INGREDIENTS | SERVES 12

3 cups vegetable oil
1 cup water
½ cup butter
1 cup flour
¼ teaspoon salt
3 large eggs
1 cup sugar

Frying Food

Although it seems easy, frying food is a great art. The oil must be hot enough to cook the food without soaking into the food. At the same time, if the oil is too hot, it will cook the outside of the food before the inside is completely cooked.

1. Pour oil into a medium-sized frying pan (the oil should be 1"–2" deep). Heat to 375°F.

2. Heat the water to a rolling boil in a medium-sized saucepan. Add the butter and continue to boil.

3. Quickly stir in the flour and salt. Reduce heat to low and stir vigorously until the mixture forms a ball.

4. Remove from heat and beat in the eggs 1 at a time, until the mixture is smooth and glossy.

5. Spoon the dough into a pastry bag fitted with a large star tip. Squeeze out sticks about 10" long and 1" thick.

6. Fry the sticks 2 or 3 at a time until light brown.

7. Remove the sticks and cool on paper towels.

8. Pour the sugar onto a large plate. As soon as the churros are cool, roll them in the sugar. Set aside until completely cool.

Chicken Chalupas

Serve with spinach salad and fresh fruit compote.

INGREDIENTS | SERVES 6

12 (6") corn tortillas

1¼ cups chicken broth

1 pound Monterey jack cheese

1 cup sour cream

2 cups Spicy Chicken (see recipe in Chapter 2)

1 teaspoon paprika

1. Soak the tortillas in 1 cup of the broth. Grate the cheese.

2. Combine the remaining ¼ cup broth with the sour cream.

3. Layer the ingredients in a casserole dish as follows: single layer of soaked tortillas, Spicy Chicken, sour cream mixture, cheese. Repeat until all the ingredients are used. Sprinkle with paprika.

4. Cover and refrigerate at least 8 hours.

5. Preheat oven to 350°F. Bake the dish, uncovered, for 1 hour.

Traditional Pollo Verde

Serve with Zesty Cheese Salad (see recipe in Chapter 7).

INGREDIENTS | SERVES 4

1 medium white onion

1 garlic clove

2 tomatillos

1 bunch fresh parsley

1 cup Green Chili Sauce (see recipe in Chapter 2)

1 teaspoon salt

1 teaspoon ground white pepper

1 fryer chicken

1. Peel the onion and cut into quarters. Peel the garlic. Remove the stems and skins from the tomatillos, then cut in half. Remove the stems from the parsley and roughly chop the leaves.

2. Combine the onion, garlic, tomatillos, parsley, chili sauce, salt, and white pepper in a blender or food processor; blend until liquefied.

3. Rinse the chicken and arrange in a large frying pan. Pour the sauce over the top. Cover and bring to a boil. Reduce heat to low and simmer for about 1 hour or until chicken is tender.

Traditional Flan

This traditional dessert makes a fabulous end to any Mexican meal.

INGREDIENTS | SERVES 4

8 large eggs
⅔ cup white granulated sugar
¼ teaspoon salt
3½ cups evaporated milk
2 teaspoons vanilla extract
½ cup, plus 2 tablespoons light brown sugar

Different Sugars

Brown sugar is actually white sugar with molasses added. White sugar usually comes from either beets or sugarcane. Cane sugar actually tastes slightly sweeter. Confectioners' sugar is finely ground white sugar.

1. Preheat oven to 350°F.

2. In a medium-sized mixing bowl, beat the eggs until the yolks and whites are well blended. Add the granulated sugar and salt. Beat in the evaporated milk and vanilla extract.

3. Sprinkle ½ cup of the brown sugar onto the bottom of a loaf pan. Gently pour the custard mixture over the brown sugar.

4. Place the loaf pan in a shallow baking pan containing hot water. Place in oven and bake for 1 hour or until a knife inserted into the center comes out clean.

5. Refrigerate for 8–12 hours. Before serving, turn the loaf onto a platter, then sprinkle the top with remaining brown sugar. Place it under the broiler and lightly brown the top immediately before serving.

Polenta with Tomatoes and Cheese

Serve with Cactus Salad (see recipe in Chapter 7).

INGREDIENTS | SERVES 6

4½ cups cold water
1½ cups masa harina or yellow cornmeal
1 small yellow onion
1 garlic clove
2 pounds canned tomatoes
½ pound fontina cheese
½ pound Gorgonzola cheese
1 tablespoon olive oil
1 bay leaf
½ teaspoon dried basil
1 teaspoon salt
½ teaspoon ground black pepper
1 teaspoon white granulated sugar
1 bunch fresh parsley

1. Preheat oven to 400°F.

2. Put the cold water in a medium saucepan over medium-high heat. Add the cornmeal or masa harina. Whisk the cornmeal or masa harina into the cold water. Continue whisking while bringing to a boil. Cook for 15 minutes, stirring frequently to prevent lumping.

3. Pour into a 9" × 12" pan and spread out evenly. Let sit until firm. Cut into 3" × 3" squares and remove from the pan.

4. Peel and mince the onion and garlic. Drain the tomatoes and chop coarsely. Grate the cheeses and mix together.

5. In a large frying pan heat the olive oil to medium temperature; sauté the onion and garlic in the oil for 3–5 minutes or until the onion is limp and clear. Set aside.

6. Combine the tomatoes, bay leaf, basil, salt, pepper, and sugar in a saucepan on medium heat. Bring to a boil, then reduce heat to low and simmer for 15 minutes.

7. Add the onion and garlic to the tomato mixture. Mash with a potato masher or blend in a food processor or blender.

8. Spread 1 cup sauce in the bottom of the 9" × 12" pan. Lean the polenta squares at an angle in the pan. Between each square, add about ½ cup of grated cheeses. Pour the remaining sauce over the polenta and cheese.

9. Bake for 25–35 minutes. Roughly chop the parsley leaves and use as a garnish.

Empanaditas de Carne

These are just as good cold as they are hot. They go great in a sack lunch, too.

INGREDIENTS | SERVES 8

1 (1-pound) beef roast

1 (1-pound) pork roast

3 cups flour

1 teaspoon baking powder

2 teaspoons salt, divided

1 cup, plus 1 tablespoon, granulated sugar

3 tablespoons shortening

1 egg

1 cup water

1 cup raisins

2 cups applesauce

1 teaspoon ground cinnamon

½ teaspoon crushed cloves

½ cup chopped pecans

4 cups vegetable oil

1. Put the beef roast and pork roast in a pot and add just enough water to cover the meat. Cover the pot and turn heat to medium. Simmer until the meat is completely cooked, at least 1 hour. Do not discard the cooking liquid.

2. Combine the flour, baking powder, 1 teaspoon salt, and 1 tablespoon sugar. Blend in the shortening.

3. Beat the egg in a separate bowl and slowly add to the flour mixture. Add the water and mix to form a dough. Roll out the dough to about ⅛" thick and cut with a biscuit cutter.

4. Remove the meat from the bones. Discard the bones and grind the meat with a meat grinder or food processor. Place the meat in a large pot. Add the raisins, applesauce, 1 cup sugar, cinnamon, cloves, 1 teaspoon salt, and the chopped pecans. Mix to combine, adding enough of the cooking liquid from the meat to thoroughly moisten the mixture.

5. Simmer, uncovered, for 15 minutes, adding more water if the mixture seems dry. Make sure the mixture holds together, though; it should not be runny.

6. Put about 3 tablespoons of meat mixture in the center of each of the biscuits. Fold over and pinch the edges shut.

7. Heat the oil in a large frying pan until medium-hot. Add several empanaditas. Fry on both sides until golden brown. Place on paper towels to cool.

Enchiladas

Experiment until you find your own favorite ingredients. Try mixing beans and meat or adding Spicy Chicken (see recipe in Chapter 2). Or, for a cheesy enchilada, mix 3 different cheeses and don't include meat or beans.

INGREDIENTS | SERVES 4

1 cup salsa

12 (8") corn tortillas

3 cups cooked shredded beef or refried beans

2 cups grated Monterey jack cheese

2 cups red or green chili sauce

¼ cup chopped cilantro

1. Preheat oven to 375°F.

2. Ladle ½ cup of the salsa into a 9" × 12" baking pan.

3. Put ¼ cup of the beef or beans in the center of each tortilla. Add 2 tablespoons shredded cheese. Roll up and place in baking pan.

4. When all the enchiladas are in the baking pan, cover with the remaining sauce and cheese. Bake for 15–20 minutes. Remove from the oven and garnish with cilantro.

Burritos

Burritos are the "poor boy" sandwich of Mexico. They contain whatever is leftover from yesterday. Don't hesitate to add olives, lettuce, or even yesterday's ham.

INGREDIENTS | SERVES 4

1 cup refried beans

1 cup red rice

1 cup cooked shredded beef

½ pound Cheddar cheese

1 cup salsa

8 (8") flour tortillas

½ cup red chili sauce

½ cup sour cream

½ cup guacamole

1. Heat the beans, rice, and beef separately on low heat. Shred the cheese.

2. Add ¼ cup of the beans, ¼ cup beef, ¼ cup rice, and 1 tablespoon salsa to the middle of each tortilla. Drizzle 1 teaspoon of chili sauce on top. Roll up.

3. Top each burrito with a dollop of sour cream and a dollop of guacamole.

Chiles Rellenos

Serve as an appetizer or a vegetable dish to accompany any meat or bean dish.

INGREDIENTS | SERVES 6

6 large Anaheim chilies
½ pound Monterey jack cheese
1 small white onion
¼ cup canned jalapeño peppers, or 2 fresh jalapeños
2 cups canned tomatoes, with juice
½ tablespoon olive oil
2 cups chicken broth
2 tablespoons cornstarch
3 large eggs
2 cups masa harina or cornmeal

1. Preheat oven to 350°F.

2. Place the Anaheim peppers on a pan in the oven. Turn them when the tops are white. When both sides are white, remove the peppers and put them in a paper bag. Close the bag tightly, and let the peppers cool. (This makes it easier to peel off the skin.) Peel the skin from the peppers.

3. Cut the cheese into wedges about ½" wide. Stuff the wedges into the chilies.

4. Peel the onion and chop into ¼" pieces. Drain the jalapeño peppers (if using canned) and cut into ¼" pieces. Chop the tomatoes into ¼" pieces, reserving the juice.

5. In a medium-sized saucepan, heat the olive oil to medium temperature. Add the onion and sauté until brown. Add the chopped chilies and tomatoes with their juice. Add the broth and cornstarch; sauté on medium heat, stirring constantly until the sauce is the consistency of gravy.

6. Beat eggs, then combine with the cornmeal or masa harina; mix well. If the mixture is not sticky, add water until it is about the consistency of thick pancake batter.

7. Dip the peppers into the egg and cornmeal batter.

8. Put the peppers into a lightly greased frying pan on medium heat. Brown the peppers on all sides.

9. Cover with sauce before serving.

Beef Flautas

Flautas can be made with spicy chicken meat, ground beef, or pork.

INGREDIENTS | SERVES 4

16 (6") corn tortilla

3 cups Shredded Beef (see recipe in Chapter 2)

1½ cups shredded Colby cheese

1 cup vegetable oil

1. Place a tortilla on a flat surface; lay out another tortilla so that it overlaps the first tortilla about halfway. Spoon about ⅓ cup of the Shredded Beef down the center length, where the tortillas overlap. Sprinkle about 2 tablespoons of cheese on top of the meat. Roll up, starting with 1 long side and rolling toward the other. Pin closed with wooden toothpicks or small skewers. Repeat with the remaining tortillas, beef, and cheese to make 8 flautas.

2. Heat the oil to medium-high in a large frying pan. Fry each flauta until golden brown on both sides. Sprinkle the remaining cheese on top before serving.

CHAPTER 18

Tex-Mex

Texas Chili

Serve with Jalapeño Corn Bread (see recipe in Chapter 6).

INGREDIENTS | SERVES 8

3 garlic cloves
2 large white onions
2 pounds lean ground beef
2 cups canned tomatoes, with juice
3 cups canned tomato sauce
4 cups canned kidney beans
1 tablespoon salt
½ teaspoon ground black pepper
3 teaspoons chili powder
1 teaspoon dried oregano
3 tablespoons granulated sugar

1. Peel and mince the garlic. Peel the onions and cut into ¼" pieces.

2. In a large skillet on medium heat, cook the ground beef until it is browned. Drain off the grease.

3. Combine all the ingredients in a large pot and simmer on medium heat until heated through.

White Chili

Top the chili with shredded Monterey jack cheese, crushed tortilla chips, and a dollop of sour cream.

INGREDIENTS | SERVES 8

1 pound dry navy beans
12 cups Chicken Stock (see recipe in Chapter 2)
2 garlic cloves
1 medium onion
4 cups cubed cooked chicken, light and dark meat
2 (4-ounce) cans green chilies
2 teaspoons ground cumin
1½ teaspoons dried oregano
½ teaspoon ground cloves
¼ teaspoon cayenne pepper

1. Soak the beans in 4 cups water for 2–10 hours.

2. Place the stock in a large pot on low heat. Add the beans.

3. Remove the skin from the garlic and onion. Chop into ¼" pieces and add to the pot.

4. Add the remaining ingredients; stir well. Simmer for 3 hours.

Pork and Potatoes

Serve with Pineapple and Coconut Salad (see recipe in Chapter 15) for a blending of sweet and spicy.

INGREDIENTS | SERVES 6

1 (3-pound) pork roast
3 large white onions
4 garlic cloves
10 assorted whole chili peppers
5 medium potatoes
10 whole cloves
1 cinnamon stick
10 black peppercorns
1 teaspoon whole cumin seeds
2 tablespoons white vinegar

Mushy Potatoes

Have your raw potatoes gone mushy? They're still good if you use them right away. Remove the peels and slice the potatoes thickly. Put them in a soup or stew and no one will know they were past their prime.

1. Preheat oven to 350°F.

2. Trim the fat from the pork roast. Peel the onions and cut into quarters. Peel and mince the garlic. Remove the stems from the chili peppers and cut in half lengthwise. (Do not remove the seeds.) Peel the potatoes and cut in half.

3. Place the pork in a large baking pan. Cover with the onions, garlic, chili peppers, cloves, cinnamon stick, peppercorns, and cumin seeds. Add just enough water to cover the ingredients. Cover and cook for 1 hour.

4. Stir the mixture. Add the potatoes, cover, and cook for 1 hour or until the potatoes are soft. Ten minutes before serving, remove the spices and add the vinegar. Leave uncovered for the last 10 minutes of cooking time.

Mexican Popcorn

While not as common a treat in Mexico as in the United States, corn is a common crop and it is frequently popped and served at parties.

INGREDIENTS | SERVES 8

1 pound bacon
½ cup butter
1 teaspoon chili powder
¼ teaspoon garlic salt
¼ teaspoon onion salt
½ teaspoon paprika
4 quarts popped popcorn
1 cup canned french-fried onions

1. Preheat oven to 250°F.

2. Cook the bacon in a large frying pan until very crisp. Drain off the grease and transfer the bacon to paper towels to cool. When cool, crumble the bacon into small pieces.

3. Melt the butter in a small saucepan. Add the chili powder, garlic salt, onion salt, and paprika; stir until well blended.

4. Pour the butter mixture over the popcorn and toss until well covered.

5. Add the bacon and onions to the popcorn and toss lightly.

6. Pour the mixture onto a baking sheet. Bake for 10 minutes.

Lonches

There are no serious rules with this recipe. You can substitute meats and cheeses, and add onions or olive slices.

INGREDIENTS | SERVES 6

6 slices bacon
6 large hard rolls
½ pound Monterey jack cheese
1½ cups Red Chili Sauce (see recipe in Chapter 2)

1. Preheat oven to 350°F.

2. Fry the bacon until crisp. Drain off the grease.

3. Thinly slice the cheese. Split the rolls in half horizontally. Fill each generously with cheese and top with a bacon strip. Close the rolls to form sandwiches and place on a baking sheet.

4. Put in the oven for 5–10 minutes or until the rolls are hot and the cheese is melted.

5. While the rolls are baking, heat the sauce to bubbling.

6. Place each filled roll in a soup bowl and ladle ¼ cup sauce over the top.

Taco Soup

Serve this satisfying, warming soup on the next cool day.

INGREDIENTS | SERVES 8

1 large white onion

1 green bell pepper

2 pounds lean ground beef

1 tablespoon paprika

1 tablespoon chili powder

1 tablespoon salt

1 tablespoon ground black pepper

3 (15-ounce) cans stewed tomatoes, with juice

2 cups canned pinto beans, undrained

1 cup canned kidney beans, undrained

1 cup canned golden hominy, undrained

1 cup canned whole-kernel corn, undrained

6 cups water

4 Tostadas (see recipe in Chapter 2)

Hominy

Hominy is actually dried white field corn that has been cooked with powdered lime until the skin falls off. The kernel opens up until it resembles a piece of wet popcorn.

1. Peel the onion and chop into ¼" pieces. Remove the stem and seeds from the green pepper and chop into ¼" pieces.

2. Combine the onion, green pepper, ground beef, paprika, chili powder, salt, and ground black pepper in a large frying pan on medium heat. Cook until the ground beef is browned.

3. Add the ground beef mixture to a large stockpot. Add the stewed tomatoes, pinto beans, kidney beans, hominy, and whole-kernel corn, along with all their liquids.

4. Stir, add the water, and bring to a boil. Turn the temperature to medium-low, cover, and simmer for 2 hours.

5. Top with crumbled tostadas right before serving.

Layered Mexican Dip

Serve with freshly fried and salted corn tortillas.

INGREDIENTS | SERVES 8

3 medium avocados
2 tablespoons lemon juice
1 teaspoon salt
1 teaspoon garlic powder
½ cup mayonnaise
1 teaspoon chili powder
1 teaspoon onion salt
1 bunch green onions
3 medium red tomatoes
1 cup pitted black olives
½ pound Cheddar cheese
2 cups canned bean dip

1. Peel the avocados and remove the pits. Mash together with the lemon juice, salt, and garlic powder. Set aside.

2. Mix together the mayonnaise, chili powder, and onion salt. Set aside.

3. Remove the roots from the green onions and chop into ½" pieces. Remove the stems from the tomatoes and cut into ½" pieces. Chop the black olives into ½" pieces. Grate the cheese.

4. Layer on a large plate or platter in the following order: bean dip, avocado mix, mayonnaise mixture, onions, tomatoes, olives, cheese.

5. Cover and chill in the refrigerator for 4 hours before serving.

Enchiladas Rancheras

Garnish with sour cream, guacamole, and chopped green onions.

2 garlic cloves

2 medium yellow onions

2 fresh jalapeño peppers

4 large red tomatoes

2 tablespoons vegetable oil

1 teaspoon dried oregano

1 pound Monterey jack cheese

¾ pound fresh button mushrooms

1 cup pitted black olives

4 cups cubed cooked chicken

4 cups sour cream

30 (8") flour tortillas

Mushrooms

Different mushrooms have very different tastes. Don't hesitate to substitute exotic dried mushrooms such as wood ear, enoki, and porcini even if the recipe calls for fresh mushrooms.

1. Preheat oven to 350°F.

2. Peel and mince the garlic and onions. Remove the stems and seeds from the jalapeños and cut into ¼" pieces. Peel the tomatoes and chop into ½" pieces.

3. Heat the vegetable oil to medium temperature in a medium-sized frying pan. Add the garlic, onions, and jalapeño peppers; sauté until the onions are transparent. Add the tomatoes and oregano; cook for about 5 minutes, stirring frequently.

4. Grate the cheese. Clean the mushrooms and slice thinly. Cut the black olives into ¼" rounds.

5. Mix together the chicken, cheese, mushrooms, and black olives. Stir in the sour cream.

6. Put 3–4 tablespoons of filling on each tortilla. Roll up and place in a 9" × 13" baking dish. Pour the sauce over the top.

7. Bake for 30 minutes or until heated through.

Chimichangas

Serve with sour cream, guacamole, and your favorite salsa.

INGREDIENTS | SERVES 4

1 medium white onion

1 medium red tomato

½ cup canned jalapeño peppers, or 4 fresh jalapeños

½ pound Colby cheese

1 pound lean ground beef

1½ teaspoons chili powder

½ teaspoon ground black pepper

1 teaspoon garlic salt

¼ teaspoon cayenne pepper

½ teaspoon dried oregano

8 (8") flour tortillas

2 cups vegetable oil

A Word about Cheese

Like virtually every culture in the world, the various regions of Mexico have their own types of cheese. Unfortunately very few of these are available outside of Mexico, even in authentic Mexican restaurants. At the same time, because Mexican cuisine was influenced by Spanish cuisine centuries ago, the entire world of European cheeses is used in their recipes.

1. Peel the onion and cut into ¼" pieces. Remove the stem from the tomato and cut into ¼" pieces. Chop the jalapeño peppers into ¼" pieces. Grate the cheese.

2. In a medium-sized frying pan, fry the ground beef and onion on medium heat until the meat is brown and the onion is translucent. Drain off the grease.

3. Add the tomatoes, jalapeños, chili powder, black pepper, garlic salt, cayenne pepper, and oregano; simmer for 10 minutes.

4. Put 2–3 tablespoons of the mixture in the middle of each tortilla. Add 1 tablespoon of cheese on top. Fold the tortillas and secure with toothpicks.

5. Heat the vegetable oil to medium-high in a large skillet. Add 2 or 3 tortillas at a time. Fry quickly until golden brown on each side.

Fajitas

Serve with guacamole, sour cream, and salsa.

INGREDIENTS | SERVES 2

1 pound beef, deboned and skinned chicken, and/or shrimp

1 garlic clove

1 tablespoon vegetable oil

¼ cup soy sauce

1 teaspoon ground black pepper

1 tablespoon Worcestershire sauce

½ tablespoon lemon juice

1 medium yellow onion

1 green or red bell pepper

8 (8") flour tortillas

How to Marinate Meat

Never marinate meat for longer than 24 hours. The meat begins to break down and the texture becomes mushy. The flavors should penetrate after about 2 hours. Always marinate in the refrigerator so that bacteria doesn't begin to grow.

1. If using beef or chicken, cut the meat into ½"-wide strips. If using shrimp, boil for 10 minutes, let cool, and remove the shells and veins. Peel and mince the garlic.

2. Combine the garlic, vegetable oil, soy sauce, black pepper, Worcestershire sauce, and lemon juice. Place the meat in a medium-sized mixing bowl. Pour the sauce on top. Cover and refrigerate for 4–8 hours.

3. Drain the meat. Peel the onion and cut into 1" pieces. Remove the seeds and stem from the bell pepper and cut into 1" pieces. Add the onion and bell pepper to the bowl with the meat; mix well.

4. Sauté the mixture on medium heat in a large frying pan until the meat is thoroughly cooked. Serve with flour tortillas.

Southwestern Fried Chicken

Fried chicken is an easy-to-make staple in Tex-Mex cuisine. Give it a try!

INGREDIENTS | SERVES 4

3 pieces white bread
1 bunch fresh cilantro
2 garlic cloves
2 large eggs
2 tablespoons masa harina or cornmeal
2 tablespoons pine nuts
½ teaspoon ground cumin
1½ teaspoons dried oregano
½ teaspoon salt, divided
¼ teaspoon cayenne pepper
⅛ teaspoon ground cloves
2 tablespoons prepared yellow mustard
1 tablespoon water
2 teaspoons honey
4 chicken breasts
¼ teaspoon ground black pepper
2 tablespoons butter

Masa Harina

Masa harina is flour made from dried corn dough that is then ground into a powder. Although similar to cornmeal, it does have a subtly different texture and taste because of the double-grinding process. You can usually substitute cornmeal in most recipes, although masa harina will give a more authentic flavor and texture.

1. Preheat oven to 400°F.

2. Tear the bread into 1" pieces. Remove the stems from the cilantro. Peel the garlic. Separate the eggs and discard the yolks.

3. Blend the bread, cilantro, garlic, cornmeal, pine nuts, cumin, oregano, ¼ teaspoon of the salt, cayenne pepper, and cloves in a blender until you have fine crumbs. Add the egg whites and mix until the crumbs are moist. Spread out the crumb mixture on a large plate.

4. Mix together the mustard, water, and honey in a small bowl. Brush over the chicken with a pastry brush. Sprinkle the chicken with the pepper and remaining ¼ teaspoon salt. Dip the chicken 1 piece at a time in the bread mixture, pressing slightly so the mixture sticks.

5. Melt the butter in a 9" × 11" baking dish. Place the chicken breasts skin-side down in the butter; bake for 20 minutes. Flip the chicken and bake for an additional 20 minutes.

Taco Skillet Casserole

Add a side of Extra-Special Frijoles Refritos (see recipe in Chapter 14).

INGREDIENTS | SERVES 6

1 small yellow onion
1 garlic clove
¼ head lettuce
8 (6") corn tortillas
1½ pounds ground beef
1 teaspoon salt
½ teaspoon ground black pepper
1 teaspoon chili powder
2 cups canned tomato sauce
½ cup vegetable oil
½ cup grated Cheddar cheese

1. Peel the onion and chop into ¼" pieces. Peel and mince the garlic. Shred the lettuce. Cut the tortillas into ½"-wide strips.

2. Crumble the ground beef into a large frying pan and brown on medium heat. Pour off excess fat.

3. Add the onion and garlic and cook for about 5 minutes longer, until the onion is soft; stir frequently.

4. Stir in the salt, pepper, chili powder, and tomato sauce, and continue cooking over low heat for about 15 minutes longer; stir frequently.

5. In a separate frying pan, heat the vegetable oil to medium-high. Fry the tortilla strips until crisp. Transfer to paper towels to absorb excess grease.

6. Stir the tortilla strips into the meat mixture and cook for about 5 minutes, stirring frequently.

7. Sprinkle with cheese. As soon as the cheese melts, remove from heat. Top with shredded lettuce and serve immediately.

Key Lime Pie

This makes a perfect dessert for Southwestern Fried Chicken (see recipe in this chapter).

INGREDIENTS | SERVES 8

3 cups flour

1 teaspoon baking powder

1 tablespoon granulated sugar

3 tablespoons shortening

3 large eggs

1 (14-ounce) can sweetened condensed milk

½ cup fresh-squeezed key lime juice

3 teaspoons grated key lime peel, divided

¾ cup whipping cream

2 tablespoons confectioners' sugar

1. Preheat oven to 350°F.

2. Combine the flour, baking powder, sugar, and shortening; mix well. Spread on a floured surface and roll out to about ⅛" thick. Put into a 9" pie pan. Cut off and discard any extra dough. Place in the oven for 10 minutes.

3. Beat the eggs, milk, lime juice, and 2 teaspoons of the grated lime peel on medium speed in a medium-sized mixing bowl. Pour the mixture into the pie crust.

4. Bake for 30–35 minutes or until the center is set. Cool on a wire rack for 15 minutes. Cover and refrigerate for 2–8 hours before serving.

5. No more than 4 hours before serving, combine the whipping cream, remaining 1 teaspoon grated lime peel, and confectioners' sugar in a well-chilled bowl and whip until it doubles in size. Spread on top of the pie.

Bean Nachos

The combination of smooth refried beans along with chunky whole beans is really nice in these nachos. They can be topped with just about anything you like; chopped cooked chicken or turkey works well.

INGREDIENTS | SERVES 6–8

4 cups tortilla chips
1 (15-ounce) can refried beans
1 cup canned pinto beans
1 tablespoon chili powder
1 cup chunky salsa
1 tomato, seeded and chopped
1 serrano chili, seeded and chopped
2 cups shredded Cheddar cheese
1 cup shredded Muenster cheese
¼ cup chopped cilantro
1 cup sour cream
1 cup guacamole

1. Preheat oven to 400°F. Place tortilla chips on a large rimmed baking sheet and set aside. In medium saucepan, combine refried beans, pinto beans, chili powder, and salsa. Heat over medium heat until mixture just begins to bubble, stirring frequently.

2. Pour bean mixture evenly over chips. Sprinkle with tomato, chili, and cheeses. Bake for 15–20 minutes until cheeses melt and begin to bubble.

3. Sprinkle with cilantro and serve with sour cream and guacamole.

CHAPTER 19

Occasions

Mexican Wedding Cake

This traditional celebration cake keeps well and actually tastes better after sitting for a day or so. It's even good without the frosting!

INGREDIENTS | SERVES 12

2 cups flour
2 teaspoons baking soda
1 (20-ounce) can crushed pineapple, with juice
1 cup chopped pecans, plus extra for garnish
2 cups granulated sugar
2 large eggs
8 ounces cream cheese
2 cups confectioners' sugar
½ cup butter
1 teaspoon vanilla

1. Preheat oven to 350°F. Grease and flour a 9" × 13" pan.

2. Combine the flour, baking soda, pineapple and juice, chopped pecans, granulated sugar, and eggs in a medium-sized mixing bowl; stir until well mixed. Pour into the prepared pan and bake, uncovered, for 30–35 minutes.

3. For the frosting, mix together the cream cheese, confectioners' sugar, butter, and vanilla until well blended. Let the cake cool thoroughly before frosting. Sprinkle with more chopped pecans.

Candlemas Drink

Although you might be tempted to strain this drink before serving, the solid ingredients actually are eaten as a sort of wet salad after the drink is gone.

INGREDIENTS | MAKES 2 QUARTS

1 pound canned beets
½ cup pitted prunes
¼ head lettuce
1 green apple
¼ cup blanched almonds
1½ quarts water
½ cup sugar
¼ cup seedless raisins
¼ cup unsalted peanuts

1. Chop the beets and prunes into ¼" pieces. Shred the lettuce. Peel and remove the core from the apple; chop into ¼" pieces. Chop the almonds into small pieces.

2. Pour the water into a glass or ceramic container. Dissolve the sugar in the water. Add all the ingredients and stir gently. Refrigerate for 3–4 hours before serving.

Grilled Shrimp in Prickly Pear Cactus Vinaigrette

This is a favorite meal to celebrate a special event such as a wedding anniversary or birthday.

INGREDIENTS | SERVES 4

28 large fresh shrimp
1 gallon water
2 prickly pear cactus fruits
1 bunch cilantro
2 tablespoons garlic paste
½ cup red wine vinegar
1 tablespoon peanut oil
1 tablespoon olive oil
½ tablespoon balsamic vinegar
1 ounce hearts of palm
1 teaspoon salt
1 teaspoon ground black pepper
6 ounces arugula

Arugula

Arugula is a leaf that serves double-duty as both a spice and an eating green. It has a very peppery flavor that complements seafood and poultry very well. Discard the discolored leaves because they will be bitter. Its small leaves are usually added whole to salads.

1. Boil the shrimp in the water for 10 minutes. Drain, and run cold water over the shrimp. Peel the shrimp and use a fork tine to remove the back vein.

2. Peel the prickly pear cactus by cutting off both ends and slitting both sides. If ripe, the peel will easily come off. Cut into 1" pieces. Cut the stems off the cilantro.

3. In a blender, combine the prickly pear, cilantro, garlic paste, red wine vinegar, and peanut oil; blend at medium speed until smooth.

4. Place the shrimp in a glass or plastic container and pour the sauce over the top. Cover and refrigerate for 8–12 hours. Discard the sauce.

5. Preheat the grill to medium temperature. Grill the shrimp for 2–3 minutes on each side or until slightly browned.

6. While the shrimp are cooking, combine the olive oil and balsamic vinegar. Cut the hearts of palm into ½" pieces. Combine olive oil and balsamic vinegar mixture with the salt, pepper, hearts of palm, and arugula; toss gently.

7. Spread the hearts of palm and arugula onto a serving platter and top with the freshly grilled shrimp.

Chiles Rellenos en Croute with Tomato-Cilantro Sauce

This is often served for special events such as birthdays or anniversaries.

INGREDIENTS | SERVES 4

4 fresh poblano chili peppers
¾ pound Monterey jack cheese
½ pound goat cheese
2 sticks butter
4 sheets whole-wheat phyllo pastry
1 large yellow onion
16 roma tomatoes
4 bunches fresh cilantro
1 tablespoon olive oil
1 teaspoon salt

1. Preheat oven to 350°F.

2. Put the peppers on a baking sheet and roast for about 20 minutes or until well browned. (Leave the oven at 350°F.) Remove the peppers from the oven and place them in a paper bag; close tightly and let the peppers cool. (This makes it easier to peel the peppers.) Remove the skin, stems, and seeds when cool. Do not cut the peppers open other than at the top.

3. Grate the Monterey jack cheese. Crumble the goat cheese. Combine the cheeses.

4. Fill each pepper with ¼ of the cheese mixture.

5. Melt the butter in a small saucepan on low heat. Remove the phyllo and lay it out flat on a work surface. Take 1 sheet of phyllo at a time and brush with butter, using a pastry brush. Put 1 chili in the corner of 1 sheet of phyllo dough and roll up, brushing all unbuttered surfaces with butter.

6. Place the chiles rellenos on a baking sheet and bake for 20–25 minutes or until the dough is well browned.

7. Peel the onion and cut into ¼" pieces. Cut the tomatoes into ¼" pieces. Remove the stems from the cilantro and chop into ¼" pieces.

8. Sauté the onion in the olive oil at medium heat until the onion is clear and limp. Add the tomatoes and cook for 5–10 minutes or until the liquid has evaporated. Add the salt and chopped cilantro. Stir well.

9. To serve, pour the sauce on a plate and top with the chiles rellenos.

Capirotada

This bread pudding is a Christmas tradition in most Mexican households.

INGREDIENTS | SERVES 8

8 slices white bread
2 large tart apples
½ pound mild Cheddar cheese
2 cups water
1 cup white granulated sugar
1 cup firmly packed brown sugar
1 teaspoon ground cinnamon
½ teaspoon ground nutmeg
½ teaspoon ground cloves
½ teaspoon salt
2 tablespoons butter
2 cups raisins

Cheese and Fruit

Many Mexican desserts feature milk and fruit products, taking advantage of the two sweetest, unprocessed items in their diet. When combined with their wide array of spices, the result is an unusual blending of flavors that at first seems odd but gradually grows to be a pleasant culinary treat.

1. Preheat oven to 350°F.

2. Toast the bread and tear into 1" cubes. Peel the apples, remove the cores, and slice the apples into ½" pieces. Grate the cheese.

3. Combine the water, white sugar, brown sugar, cinnamon, nutmeg, cloves, and salt in a medium-sized saucepan and bring the mixture to a boil. Lower the heat and simmer for 10 minutes or until the mixture becomes syrupy.

4. Butter the bottom and sides of a rectangular baking. Place the bread cubes on the bottom. Sprinkle the apples and raisins on top. Then sprinkle the cheese on top of that. Pour the syrup over the top.

5. Bake for 30 minutes.

Mexican Christmas Salad

This is perfect for a buffet dinner because guests can make their own salads, choosing the ingredients they like best.

INGREDIENTS | SERVES 6

2–6 key limes

1 cup mayonnaise

3 tablespoons granulated sugar

2 tablespoons whole milk

1 small head iceberg lettuce

1 medium pineapple or 1 (20-ounce) can sliced pineapple

3 medium oranges

3 small bananas

2 large sweet apples

2 cups canned sliced beets

½ cup salted, skinless peanuts

Lettuce

Different lettuces have very different flavors. Iceberg lettuce tends to be the most mild. Leaf lettuces can be slightly more bitter. Experiment with different types of lettuce or the prepackaged lettuce mixes to find your favorites.

1. Grate 1 tablespoon of peel from the key limes. Squeeze ¼ cup juice from the limes. In a small bowl, mix the lime juice, lime peel, mayonnaise, sugar, and milk.

2. Slice the lettuce into ½"-wide strips. If using a fresh pineapple, remove the stem, rind, and core; cut the fruit into ½"-thick pieces. If using canned pineapple, drain and discard the juice. Peel the oranges and slice thinly. Peel the bananas and slice into ¼" rounds. Core the apples and cut into ½"-thick wedges. Drain the beets.

3. Place the bowl of dressing in the middle of a large platter. Arrange the lettuce around the platter. On the lettuce, arrange separate piles of pineapple, oranges, bananas, apples, and beets. Sprinkle peanuts over the fruit.

Mexican Trifle

This is often served as dessert for special holidays such as Cinco de Mayo or to celebrate an event such as a work promotion or getting a good report card.

INGREDIENTS | SERVES 6

¼ cup granulated sugar
1 tablespoon cornstarch
¼ teaspoon salt
2 cups whole milk
2 large eggs
1 teaspoon vanilla
4 cups cubed pound cake
4 tablespoons brandy, divided
4 tablespoons apricot preserves
½ cup whipping cream
1 tablespoon confectioners' sugar
4 ounces semisweet baker's chocolate
½ cup toasted, slivered almonds

1. Combine the sugar, cornstarch, and salt in a medium-sized saucepan. Stir in the milk until well blended. Cook over medium heat, stirring constantly, until the mixture boils.

2. Break the eggs into a medium-sized mixing bowl. Add about ¼ cup of the sugar mixture to the eggs and beat slightly. Add the egg mixture to the sugar mixture in the saucepan and cook on medium heat, stirring constantly, until the mixture starts to bubble. Stir in the vanilla. Remove from heat, cover with waxed paper, and let cool to room temperature.

3. Place pound cake cubes in a glass bowl. Sprinkle with 3 tablespoons brandy. Drizzle with preserves. Pour the sugar and egg mixture (which should be like a custard when cooled) over the pound cake.

4. Whip the cream with the confectioners' sugar until stiff. Fold in the remaining 1 tablespoon brandy. Top the cake and custard with whipped cream.

5. Grate the chocolate. Sprinkle the chocolate and almonds on top of the cake.

6. Cover and chill for at least 4 hours before serving.

Christmas Candy Balls

These traditional Christmas treats are a favorite with young children.

INGREDIENTS | MAKES 2 DOZEN

2 medium white potatoes
2 cups pecans
1 cup red candied cherries
1 cup confectioners' sugar
1 teaspoon ground cinnamon
1 cup granulated sugar
1 teaspoon vanilla extract

1. Scrub the potatoes but do not peel. Cut into 1" cubes. Chop the pecans into small pieces. Cut the candied cherries in half. Mix the confectioners' sugar and cinnamon in a small bowl.

2. Put the potatoes in a medium-sized pot. Add water to cover. Bring to a boil and continue boiling until the potatoes are soft. Drain off the water.

3. Press the potatoes through a ricer or put through a food mill. Mix in the granulated sugar, vanilla extract, and nuts.

4. Form balls about the size of marbles. Coat them with the confectioners' sugar and cinnamon mixture.

5. Store in the refrigerator until ready to serve. Put into small fluted paper cups and garnish with cherry halves.

Christmas Codfish

This is traditionally served on a platter garnished with pimiento-stuffed green olives and parsley. Plain white rice is the traditional accompaniment.

INGREDIENTS | SERVES 4

1 (1-pound) piece salted codfish
2 small yellow onions
2 garlic cloves
3 medium-sized red tomatoes
5 pickled jalapeño chili peppers
3 canned pimientos
1 teaspoon salt
1 teaspoon ground black pepper
3 tablespoons vegetable oil

Peppers or Peppercorns?

Chili peppers are not related at all to the plant that produces peppercorns. It's likely that they received the same name when the Spanish conquistadors arrived in Mexico during the 1500s and found that the chilies had a similar "bite" to the more familiar peppercorns.

1. Soak the codfish for 6–8 hours in cold water. Change the water several times.

2. Peel the onions and garlic cloves and chop into ¼" pieces. Peel the tomatoes and cut into quarters. Remove stems and seeds from the jalapeños and cut into ¼" pieces. Slice the pimientos into ¼" strips.

3. Drain the codfish and put into a saucepan. Add 1 onion and water to cover. Bring to a simmer. Cover and cook gently for about 15 minutes or until the fish flakes easily when tested with a fork. Drain. Sprinkle salt and pepper on top.

4. While the fish is cooking, put the tomatoes, remaining onion, and garlic in an electric blender or food processor; blend until puréed.

5. Heat the oil to medium temperature in a skillet. Add the tomato sauce. Cook until thickened, stirring occasionally. Mix in the chilies and pimiento strips. Pour over fish and serve.

Cream-Filled Chestnut Cake

This is frequently used as a birthday or anniversary cake.

INGREDIENTS | SERVES 6

1¾ pounds fresh chestnuts in the shells
6 large eggs
¾ cup butter
1 cup granulated sugar
1 teaspoon vanilla extract, divided
1¼ cups flour
1 teaspoon baking powder
½ cup whole milk
1 cup whipping cream
⅔ cup confectioners' sugar

1. To prepare the chestnuts, rinse the chestnuts and make a slit on 2 sides of each shell. Put into a saucepan. Cover with boiling water and boil about 20 minutes. Remove the shells and skins. Return the chestnuts to the saucepan and cover with boiling salted water. Cover and simmer until the chestnuts are tender, about 10–20 minutes. Drain and finely chop.

2. Preheat oven to 325°F.

3. Separate the eggs. Cream the butter with the sugar and ½ teaspoon of the vanilla extract until fluffy. Add 1¼ cups of the chopped chestnuts, then the egg yolks 1 at a time. Mix well after each egg yolk is added.

4. Mix the flour with the baking powder and add to the chestnut mixture; mix well. Add the milk and mix well.

5. Beat the egg whites until stiff but not dry. Fold into the batter.

6. Divide the mixture among 2 greased and floured 9" round cake pans. Bake for 25 minutes.

7. Whip the whipping cream until thickened. Mix in the confectioners' sugar and the remaining ½ teaspoon vanilla extract. Blend in the remaining chopped chestnuts. Place a generous portion on the top of the bottom layer of the cake. Add the top layer of the cake and use the remaining frosting to frost the entire cake.

CHAPTER 20

Regional Favorites

Yucatán Tamale Pie

For a stronger flavor, remove the vegetables from the stockpot and drain the liquid. Mix the vegetables with the chicken pieces when placing them in the casserole dish.

INGREDIENTS | SERVES 6

½ cup lard
3 cups masa harina or cornmeal
1 large white onion
2 garlic cloves
4 jalapeño chilies
4 medium ripe tomatoes
1 (3–4-pound) whole chicken
4 cups chicken broth
1 teaspoon dried oregano
¼ teaspoon dried cilantro
½ teaspoon brown sugar

Try Turkey

For a lean alternative in your next chicken recipe, substitute turkey. It has much less fat and much more protein than chicken while often being a better per-pound buy at the grocery store.

1. Preheat oven to 350°F.

2. Combine the lard and cornmeal, adding small amounts of water until the dough is soft enough to work with. Grease an ovenproof casserole dish and line the bottom and sides with the dough.

3. Remove the skin from the onion and garlic cloves; chop into ¼" pieces. Remove the stems and seeds from chilies and chop into ¼" pieces. Cut the tomatoes into 1" pieces.

4. Place the chicken, onion, garlic, chilies, tomatoes, broth, oregano, cilantro, and brown sugar in a large stockpot. Bring to a boil. Reduce heat to medium and simmer, covered, for 1 hour.

5. Remove the chicken and let cool. Reserve the broth. Remove the bones and skin from the chicken and tear the meat into strips about 1" wide. Layer the chicken on the dough in the casserole dish.

6. Bake, covered, for 1 hour. Pour 1 cup of the broth over the pie before serving.

Pumpkin Blossom Soup from Morelos

This is a wonderful first course for any chicken or red-meat dish.

INGREDIENTS | SERVES 8

1 pound pumpkin blossoms

1 small white onion

3 sprigs fresh parsley (for a more authentic flavor, use epazote)

¼ cup butter

8 cups chicken broth

1 teaspoon salt

1 teaspoon ground white pepper

1. Remove the stems from the blossoms and roughly chop into 2" pieces. Chop the onion into ¼" pieces. Chop the parsley. Melt the butter in a small frying pan at medium heat and sauté the onion until limp but not brown. Add the blossoms and sauté for 5 minutes.

2. Put the broth and parsley in a medium-sized stockpot. Bring to a boil and reduce heat to medium. Add the onion and blossoms, draining off and discarding any excess butter. Stir gently, add the salt and pepper, and simmer for 10 minutes.

Northern Border Chili con Carne

This is just as traditional if made with beef, but it never contains tomatoes.

INGREDIENTS | SERVES 4

1 pound pork steak

1 pound veal steak

2 tablespoons olive oil

1 medium yellow onion

2 garlic cloves

6 jalapeño chilies

1 teaspoon dried oregano

1 teaspoon salt

2 cups canned kidney beans

1. Cut the pork and veal steaks into 1" cubes. Place the meat in a large frying pan along with the olive oil. Cook on medium heat until the meat is lightly browned.

2. Peel the onion and cut into quarters. Remove the stems and seeds from the chilies and cut into ¼" pieces. Place the onion, garlic, chilies, oregano, and salt in blender and blend on medium setting until you have a purée. Add the purée to the meat. Stir and cook, uncovered, for 10 minutes.

3. Add the kidney beans to frying pan. Reduce heat, cover, and cook for 1–2 hours.

Mayan Lamb

Serve with Red Rice (see recipe in Chapter 2).

INGREDIENTS | SERVES 4

2 pounds boneless lamb

1 medium yellow onion

1 garlic clove

1 cup canned red tomatoes

1 teaspoon salt

¼ teaspoon ground black pepper

1 cup hulled pepitas (pumpkin seeds)

1 tablespoon annatto seeds

2 tablespoons vegetable oil

1 tablespoon lemon juice

When to Use a Slow Cooker

Slow cookers are excellent appliances if you want to make a meal while you aren't at home or if you want to keep an appetizer warm for several hours. Soups and stews work well, as does any dish that doesn't require the food to brown and doesn't need to be quick-cooked, such as fried foods.

1. Cut the lamb into 2" chunks. Peel the onion and chop into ¼" pieces. Peel and mince the garlic. Drain the tomatoes and chop into ¼" pieces.

2. Combine the lamb, onion, garlic, tomatoes, salt, and pepper in a heavy saucepan; stir well. Add water to cover. Bring to a boil. Reduce heat, cover, and simmer until the meat is tender, about 2 hours.

3. Combine the pepitas and annatto seeds in an electric blender or food processor; blend until pulverized.

4. In a small frying pan, heat the oil to medium temperature. Add the pepitas and annatto seeds and fry for 2–3 minutes, stirring constantly. Stir in the lemon juice.

5. Right before serving, stir the seed mixture into the meat sauce.

Coliflor Acapulco

Serve on a buffet with traditional Mexican favorites.

INGREDIENTS | SERVES 4

1 large head fresh cauliflower
1½ cups vegetable oil
½ cup lemon juice
1½ teaspoons salt
1 teaspoon chili powder
¼ cup canned pimientos
2 cups canned pickled beets
1 large cucumber
2 cups canned garbanzo beans
8 red radishes
1 cup pimiento-stuffed olives
1 cup chopped lettuce
1 bunch parsley sprigs
1 cup guacamole

1. Add water to a large saucepan to the depth of 1". Bring to a boil. Add the cauliflower, cover, and cook for about 20 minutes or until tender. Drain off the water.

2. Combine the vegetable oil, lemon juice, salt, and chili powder in a container with a lid. Cover and shake until well mixed to create a marinade.

3. Place the cauliflower, head down, in a deep bowl and pour the marinade over it. Cover and chill for at least 8 hours in the refrigerator.

4. Slice the pimientos lengthwise into ¼"-wide strips. Slice the pickled beets into ¼"-thick rounds. Slice the cucumber into ¼" rounds. Chill these vegetables separately for at least 2 hours, covered, in the refrigerator.

5. Drain off the water from the garbanzo beans. Cut the tops and bottoms off the radishes and slice slightly down the sides to create roses.

6. Thread the garbanzos, olives, and pimiento strips onto wooden skewers to create decorative kabobs.

7. Drain the cauliflower. Line a chilled serving plate with the lettuce and place the cauliflower, head up, in the center. Arrange the pickled beets and cucumber slices around the base. Tuck in the parsley sprigs and radish roses.

8. Spread guacamole over the cauliflower. Decorate the cauliflower with kabobs. Serve cold.

Tostadas from Guadalajara

These make a wonderful replacement for a salad, or they can be a light lunch all by themselves. You can also make petite tostadas and use these as appetizers.

INGREDIENTS | SERVES 8

1 cup lettuce

1 tablespoon olive oil

2 tablespoons vinegar

1 teaspoon salt

½ teaspoon ground white pepper

4 spicy sausage patties

2 cups refried beans

1 medium yellow onion

2 cups guacamole

¼ pound mozzarella cheese

8 freshly made (still warm) Tostadas (see recipe in Chapter 2)

1. Put the lettuce in a small bowl. Combine the olive oil, vinegar, salt, and white pepper in a small container with a lid. Cover and shake until well mixed, then pour over the lettuce and set aside.

2. Crumble the sausage patties and heat on medium in a small frying pan. Sauté until browned. Heat the beans in a small saucepan.

3. Peel the onion and chop into ¼" pieces. Drain the lettuce. Grate the cheese.

4. Put the ingredients in layers on the tostadas in the following order: refried beans, sausage, onion, guacamole, lettuce, cheese.

Puerto Vallarta's Catfish Soup

For fishier flavor, cook the fish with the head and skin on. After 15 minutes of simmering, remove the head, skin, and bones and return the meat to the pot. Cook for another 5 minutes.

INGREDIENTS | SERVES 8

1 large white onion

3 garlic cloves

4 fresh jalapeño peppers

6 medium carrots

2 quarts water

4 cups canned whole tomatoes

1 teaspoon dried oregano

1 teaspoon salt

½ teaspoon ground black pepper

½ teaspoon paprika, plus some for garnish

2 pounds catfish fillets

1. Peel the onion and chop into ¼" pieces. Peel and mince the garlic. Remove the stems and seeds from the jalapeños and chop into ¼" pieces. Peel the carrots and cut into ¼" rounds.

2. Fill a large pot with the water. Add the onion, garlic, jalapeños, carrots, tomatoes, oregano, salt, black pepper, and paprika to the pot; stir gently. Heat on high until boiling. Reduce heat to medium and simmer, uncovered, until the tomatoes have disintegrated and the carrots are tender (about 2 hours).

3. Cut the catfish fillets into 1" cubes. Add the cubes to the broth and simmer for 15 minutes.

4. Sprinkle with paprika before serving.

Sea Bass from Veracruz

If you can't find largo chilies, substitute 12 jalapeños.

INGREDIENTS | SERVES 4

4 large sea bass fillets

½ cup flour

1 teaspoon salt

½ teaspoon ground white pepper

½ cup olive oil, divided

½ cup black olives

1 medium yellow onion

2 garlic cloves

3 fresh largo chilies

2 cups canned tomato paste

¼ teaspoon ground cinnamon

¼ teaspoon ground cloves

1 tablespoon lime juice

½ teaspoon ground black pepper

1 teaspoon granulated sugar

1. Coat the sea bass fillets with the flour. Sprinkle both sides with the salt and white pepper.

2. Heat ¼ cup of the olive oil in a large frying pan. Add the fish fillets and fry on each side until thoroughly cooked and golden brown. The flesh should be opaque and flake easily with a fork. Remove from heat and set aside.

3. Chop the black olives into ¼" pieces. Peel the onion and chop into ¼" pieces. Peel and mince the garlic. Remove the seeds and stems from the chilies and chop into ¼" pieces.

4. Add the remaining ¼ cup olive oil to the frying pan and heat to medium. Add the onion, garlic, and chilies; sauté until the onion is limp. Add the tomato paste, cinnamon, black olives, and ground cloves. Cook until heated through. Add the lime juice, ground pepper, and sugar; gently stir in.

5. Reduce heat to low. Add the fish fillets. Cover and cook for 5 minutes.

Cozumel Chicken

Serve with grilled corn on the cob and a green salad.

INGREDIENTS | SERVES 8

1 tablespoon butter
8 large boneless chicken breasts
8 key limes
2 lemons
1 cup orange juice
1 cup Red Chili Sauce (see recipe in Chapter 2)

Key Limes

Mexicans love key lime juice in almost everything. They squirt fresh key lime juice into soups, onto salty tostadas, and into their drinking water. The secret is that key limes—golf ball–sized fruits—are actually very sweet and mild-tasting as compared to the Florida and California limes that people in the United States are used to.

1. Preheat oven to 325°F.

2. Melt the butter on medium heat in a large skillet. Add the chicken breasts and cook until brown on 1 side. Flip and brown the other side.

3. Wash the limes and lemons but do not peel. Slice as thinly as possible.

4. Transfer the chicken to an ovenproof baking dish. Top with the lime and lemon slices. Pour the orange juice over the top.

5. Cover with foil and bake for about 1 hour or until the chicken is tender.

6. Remove the lime and lemon slices and pour the chili sauce over the chicken. Heat for 5 more minutes.

Green Mountain Stew

Serve with red rice and refried beans.

INGREDIENTS | SERVES 6

1 pound mutton

1 pound chicken

6 tomatillos

3 garlic cloves

2 large white onions

2 chayote squash

12 fresh serrano chilies

1 tablespoon vegetable oil

1 teaspoon salt

1 teaspoon ground black pepper

1. Cut the mutton into 1" cubes. Remove the skin and bones from the chicken and cut into 1" cubes. Remove the skins and stems from the tomatillos and quarter. Peel and mince the garlic. Peel and quarter the onions. Remove the rinds and seeds from the squash and cut into 1" pieces. Remove the stems from the chilies and split in half lengthwise.

2. Heat the vegetable oil to medium heat in a large frying pan. Add the mutton and chicken, and fry until golden. Add all the other ingredients and mix lightly. Fry for 5 minutes. Reduce heat to medium-low. Cover and simmer for 1½ hours.

Mexico City's Chicken with Mushrooms

Serve with Pineapple and Coconut Salad (see recipe in Chapter 15) and refried beans.

INGREDIENTS | SERVES 8

2 fryer chickens
1 pound fresh button mushrooms
1 medium yellow onion
1 garlic clove
6 fresh jalapeños
¼ cup olive oil
2 cups canned tomatoes, with juice
1 cup chicken broth
1½ teaspoons salt
1 cup sour cream

1. Cut each of the chickens into 8 serving pieces (legs, wings, breasts, etc.). Wash the mushrooms and slice thinly. Peel the onion and chop into ¼" pieces. Peel the garlic and cut into quarters. Remove the stems and seeds from the chili peppers.

2. Heat the oil to medium temperature in a large frying pan. Fry the chicken pieces until golden brown. Transfer the chicken to a large saucepan.

3. Sauté the mushrooms in the oil remaining in the frying pan. Spoon the mushrooms over the chicken. Do not drain the oil from the pan.

4. Combine the tomatoes with their juice, the chili peppers, onion, and garlic in an electric blender or food processor; blend until puréed. Pour the purée into the skillet with the oil. Bring to a boil and cook for about 5 minutes. Stir in the broth and salt.

5. Pour the sauce over the chicken and mushrooms. Cover and cook over low heat until the chicken is tender, about 1 hour. Just before serving, stir in the sour cream and heat through, but do not boil.

Caribbean Coast Pickled Tuna

This makes an excellent summer luncheon when served with Fruit Compote (see recipe in Chapter 15).

INGREDIENTS | SERVES 6

1 pound fresh tuna steak
¼ cup lime juice
1 medium yellow onion
1 garlic clove
2 canned jalapeño chilies
½ cup pimiento-stuffed olives
¼ cup vegetable oil
½ teaspoon dried oregano
½ teaspoon ground cumin
¾ cup white wine vinegar

1. Put the tuna in a medium-sized stockpot. Add ½" of water. Cover and heat on low until the fish is cooked through. The fish should flake easily with a fork. When cool, flake the fish and put in a small bowl.

2. Pour the lime juice over the fish and let stand for about 10 minutes (while preparing the rest of the meal).

3. Peel the onion and slice into ⅛" rounds. Peel and mince the garlic. Cut the jalapeños into thin strips. Slice the olives into ¼" rounds.

4. Heat the oil to medium temperature in a medium-sized frying pan. Add the onion, garlic, and chilies. Cook for about 5 minutes, until the onion is limp but not brown. Stir in the oregano and cumin. Stir in the vinegar. Bring to a boil.

5. Pour the sauce over the fish and stir until well coated.

6. Cover and refrigerate for at least 8 hours before serving. Garnish with olive slices.

Aztec Potatoes

Add onions, hot peppers, pimientos, minced garlic, or even peas and carrots to the dough to create interesting alternatives.

INGREDIENTS | SERVES 8

1 cup masa harina or cornmeal
¼ cup warm water
1½ cups leftover mashed potatoes
1 egg
½ cup grated Monterey jack cheese
1 teaspoon salt
1 cup vegetable oil

1. Combine the masa harina with the warm water and mashed potatoes; mix well.

2. Beat the egg and add it to the potato mixture, along with the cheese and salt. Mix well and form into patties about ¾" thick.

3. Heat the vegetable oil to medium temperature in a large frying pan. Fry the patties until golden brown on both sides.

Flounder from Ixtapa

Serve with red rice and a spinach salad.

INGREDIENTS | SERVES 4

2 (1-pound) fresh flounder fillets
½ cup orange juice, divided
1 small yellow onion
1 cup canned tomato paste
1 teaspoon chili powder
1 teaspoon salt
½ teaspoon ground pepper

1. Place the fish fillets in a medium-sized frying pan and add water to cover. Add ¼ cup of the orange juice. Bring to a boil, reduce heat, and simmer for about 10 minutes or until the fish flakes when tested with a fork. Drain and skin, if necessary.

2. Cut the fish into finger-sized pieces and return to the frying pan. Peel the onion and chop into ¼" pieces.

3. In a small saucepan, combine the remaining ¼ cup orange juice, the onion, tomato paste, 1 cup water, and chili powder. Bring to a boil. Add the salt and pepper. Pour the sauce over the fish fingers. Simmer the fish, uncovered, until the sauce thickens and the fish is well coated.

Baja-Style Crab

Try this dish with Pineapple, Mango, and Cucumber Salsa (see recipe in Chapter 2).

INGREDIENTS | SERVES 4

1 cup dry white rice
1 pound crabmeat
1 medium white onion
2 garlic cloves
2 fresh pimientos
2 medium tomatoes
2 medium carrots
¼ cup olive oil
1 teaspoon ground annatto seeds
2½ cups chicken broth
1 teaspoon salt
½ teaspoon ground white pepper
¼ cup dry sherry

1. Soak the rice in hot water for 30 minutes. Break the crabmeat into 1" pieces. Peel the onion and garlic, and chop into quarters. Chop the pimientos into quarters. Remove the stems and skins from the tomatoes; chop into quarters. Peel the carrots and slice into ¼" rounds.

2. Preheat oven to 350°F.

3. Drain the rice and place on paper towels to dry. Heat the olive oil to medium temperature in a medium-sized frying pan; sauté the rice until it is golden brown.

4. Put the onion, garlic, tomatoes, annatto seeds, and ½ cup of the chicken broth in a blender or food processor; blend on medium setting until smooth. Pour the mixture into a mixing bowl.

5. Add the remaining broth, salt, pepper, crabmeat, pimientos, and carrots. Mix well and pour into an ovenproof casserole dish. Cover and bake for 30 minutes. Gently stir in the sherry and heat, covered, in the oven for an additional 5 minutes.

Stuffed Chayote Squash from Morelos

While most Europeans tend to keep their fruit and vegetables separate, Mexicans make no distinction. This dessert offers a unique blend of flavors to complement any Mexican meal.

INGREDIENTS | SERVES 6

3 chayote squash
3 large eggs
½ vanilla pound cake
1 cup golden raisins
1 cup granulated sugar
1 teaspoon ground nutmeg
1 teaspoon ground cinnamon
½ cup crushed saltine crackers
1 cup dry white wine
½ cup toasted whole almonds

What's a Chayote?

Chayote is actually a fruit but is most often used as a vegetable. It is a member of the squash family that is very popular in warm climates. It has a single seed that is edible and considered a delicacy.

1. Preheat oven to 350°F.

2. Cut the chayotes in half and place in a large stockpot. Cover with water and bring to a boil. Reduce heat to medium and simmer for 15–20 minutes or until they are tender. Remove from water to cool.

3. When cool, remove the seeds and discard. Remove the pulp, leaving the shell intact. Mash the pulp.

4. Beat the eggs well. Combine with the pulp and mix well. Crumble the pound cake and add it to the mixture, along with the raisins, sugar, nutmeg, cinnamon, white wine, and crackers.

5. Stuff the chayote shells with the mixture. Press the almonds into the top. Place in a greased, ovenproof casserole dish. Bake for 15 minutes.

CHAPTER 21

Beverages

Mexican Hot Chocolate

Serve as an after-dinner drink with Capirotada (see recipe in Chapter 19).

INGREDIENTS | SERVES 6

3 ounces unsweetened chocolate
½ cup white granulated sugar
2 tablespoons brewed instant coffee
2 teaspoons ground cinnamon
1 teaspoon ground nutmeg
¼ teaspoon salt
2 cups water
4 cups whole milk
Whipped cream

1. Place the chocolate, sugar, coffee, cinnamon, nutmeg, salt, and water in a large saucepan and heat over low heat until the chocolate melts and the mixture is smooth.

2. Bring to a boil. Turn heat to low and simmer for 5 minutes, stirring constantly. Stir in the milk. Beat with a hand beater until foamy.

3. Top with a dollop of whipped cream.

Fruit Smoothies

Substitute your favorite in-season fruits for a different treat each time.

INGREDIENTS | SERVES 2

1 banana
⅔ cup milk
⅓ cup cubed fresh mango
⅓ cup cubed fresh papaya
⅓ cup cubed fresh strawberries
⅓ cup cubed fresh peaches
1 teaspoon honey
¼ cup crushed ice

1. Peel and slice the banana.

2. Combine all the ingredients in a blender. Blend on high speed until smooth and frothy.

Substituting Frozen Fruits

The act of freezing fruit changes the natural sugars. As a result, many frozen fruits have sugar added. Those that don't often taste bitter. If you must use frozen fruit, especially berries, add extra sugar or honey to the drink.

Pumpkin Seed Tea

Although it's traditionally served over ice, this tea is also excellent served warm with your favorite cookie.

INGREDIENTS | SERVES 8

2 cups pumpkin seeds
1 key lime
8 cups water
½ cup honey

1. Put the pumpkin seeds in a food processor or blender and grind until you have a coarse powder.

2. Cut the lime into ¼" rounds.

3. Put the water, lime, and pumpkin seeds in a covered glass jar and store in a warm place for 6–12 hours.

4. Strain the tea and discard the pumpkin seed mash as well as the lime pieces. Stir in the honey.

Jasmine and Rose Hips Tea

Instead of using sugar, add a teaspoon of honey to each glass before serving.

INGREDIENTS | SERVES 8

8 cups cold water
¼ pound jasmine flowers
¼ pound rose hips
½ cup granulated sugar

1. Place all the ingredients in a glass container. Stir until the sugar is dissolved.

2. Cover and set in a warm place for 6–8 hours.

3. Remove the jasmine flowers and rose hips. Stir before serving.

Edible Flowers

Most flowers are edible, although it is best to consult a horticulture book before gorging on your garden. Pansies, for example, are a delightful addition to a salad. Rose petals give a soft, rosy taste to water, unlike rose hips, which provide a tangy, almost bitter flavoring.

Coconut Coffee

The coconut adds a creaminess to the coffee that you'll just love.

INGREDIENTS | SERVES 8

¼ cup shredded coconut
16 tablespoons ground coffee
8 cups water
½ cup coconut milk

Coffee Notes

As a general rule, the darker the color of the coffee, the stronger the flavor. Most of today's flavored coffees simply have a liquid flavoring poured over them, something you can do just as well at home. If you like full-bodied coffees, avoid commercial varieties that likely have fillers and are roasted to a lesser degree.

1. Using a percolator or drip coffee maker, add the shredded coconut to the ground coffee.

2. Fill the coffee maker with 8 cups of water and brew as you normally would.

3. Stir in the coconut milk before serving. Top with a few strands of grated coconut.

Angelina and Jose

In the United States we have Shirley Temples. In Mexico, kids get these fruity drinks while their elders are drinking, well, fruity drinks mixed with other things.

INGREDIENTS | SERVES 1

6 ounces sparkling water
1 tablespoon grenadine
2 ounces orange juice
1 key lime

1. Combine the sparkling water, grenadine, and orange juice.

2. Cut the lime in half, squeeze the juice from half the key lime into the drink, and stir.

3. Use the other half of the lime as a garnish.

4. Serve over ice.

Mock Sangria

This is a great drink to serve when you don't feel like drinking any alcohol.

INGREDIENTS | SERVES 8–12

1 orange
1 lemon
4 key limes
6 cups purple grape juice
6 cups white grape juice
1 cup orange juice
½ cup lemon juice

1. Cut the orange, lemon, and limes into ¼" rounds, retaining the rinds.

2. Combine all the ingredients in a large pitcher. Refrigerate for at least 4 hours before serving.

Tamarind-ade

Tamarind drinks are as popular in Mexico as lemonade is in the rest of North America. After trying this, you might make the switch.

INGREDIENTS | SERVES 4

2 cups frozen or fresh tamarind pulp
½ cup brown sugar
2 cups water

1. Combine all the ingredients. Stir until the sugar is dissolved.

2. Chill before serving.

Tamarind

Tamarind is more commonly known as the main ingredient in Worcestershire sauce. In its original form, however, it is a dried brown seed pod. It produces a distinctive, sour taste, and many herbologists believe it can help the body break down fatty acids.

Raspberry Atole

This traditional Mexican drink doesn't usually appeal to other North Americans,
but it can be a fun addition if you're having a totally Mexican meal.

INGREDIENTS | SERVES 8

½ cup masa harina or cornmeal

4 cups water

3 cups skim milk

1 cup whipping cream

2 cups fresh raspberries

2 cups white granulated sugar

1. Place the cornmeal, water, milk, and whipping cream in a large saucepan. Heat at medium temperature, stirring constantly. Do not boil.

2. Crush the raspberries with a potato masher.

3. When the mixture thickens, add the sugar and raspberries, as well as the juice from the raspberries. Continue heating, stirring constantly. When the mixture produces small bubbles, it is ready to serve.

Chocolate Horchata

This hearty drink is a good start to a cold morning.

INGREDIENTS | SERVES 8

½ cup uncooked white rice

4 cups water

4 cups whole milk

4 ounces unsweetened chocolate

2 cups brown sugar

1 teaspoon cayenne pepper

1. Grind the rice to a fine powder in a food processor or blender.

2. Place the rice, water, and milk in a large saucepan. Heat at medium temperature, stirring constantly. Do not boil.

3. Grate the chocolate with a vegetable grater.

4. When the mixture thickens, add the brown sugar, cayenne pepper, and chocolate. Continue heating, stirring constantly. When the mixture produces small bubbles, remove from the stove and whip with a hand mixer until it is frothy.

Mexican Coffee

This is a great drink to serve with breakfast or a sweet treat.

INGREDIENTS | SERVES 6

6 cups water
¼ cup packed brown sugar
1 (3") cinnamon stick
6 whole cloves
¾ cup brewed regular grind,
roasted coffee

1. In a medium-sized saucepan, combine the water, brown sugar, cinnamon, and cloves. Heat at medium temperature, stirring periodically, until the sugar is dissolved.

2. Add the coffee. Bring to a boil. Reduce heat and simmer, uncovered, for 1–2 minutes. Remove from heat.

3. Cover and let stand for 15 minutes. Strain before serving.

Hibiscus and Lime Water

This makes the perfect drink for the hottest summer days. It is light and refreshing yet flavorful.

INGREDIENTS | SERVES 8

8 cups cold water
1 cup dried hibiscus flowers
½ cup white granulated sugar
4 key limes

1. Combine the water, hibiscus flowers, and sugar in a glass container. Stir until the sugar dissolves.

2. Cut 3 of the limes in half and squeeze the juice into the water. Discard the rinds.

3. Cut the remaining lime into ¼" rounds and put in the water.

4. Cover the container and store in a warm place for 6–12 hours.

5. Strain to remove the hibiscus flowers and lime rounds before serving.

Sparkling Fruit Drink

This festive drink is often served at parties where children are present.
Everyone loves snacking on the fruit once the liquid is gone.

INGREDIENTS | SERVES 12–24

1 mango
1 papaya
1 pineapple
1 guava
2 cups fresh strawberries
1 cup white granulated sugar
2 gallons sparkling water
4 cups cubed watermelon
2 pounds ice cubes

1. Remove the rinds, stems, seeds, and cores from the fruits. Cut the fruit into ½" pieces. Reserve all the juices.

2. Stir the sugar into the water until it dissolves.

3. Add the fruit and the juices, including the watermelon, to the water; stir well.

4. Add the ice cubes and serve immediately.

Lime Margaritas

Beer adds smoothness and a bit of carbonation to these classic margaritas.

INGREDIENTS | SERVES 6

1 (6-ounce) can frozen limeade concentrate
2 tablespoons lemon juice
1 cup tequila
¼ cup beer
½ cup triple sec
¼ cup sugar
1 cup ice water
1 lime, sliced

Combine all ingredients in a blender and mix until thoroughly blended. Serve in margarita glasses and garnish with lime slices.

Consider Your Equipment

If you serve a lot of cocktails and drinks at your parties, it makes sense to invest in a good cocktail shaker, a few shot glasses, and a heavy-duty blender, along with an assortment of wine glasses, highball glasses, margarita glasses, and swizzle sticks.

Cucumber Margaritas

Cucumbers offer a mild and cooling contrast in these pretty, light-green drinks. Garnish each with a cucumber wheel: Peel stripes from a cucumber, then slice the cucumber into rounds with a slit cut in the side.

INGREDIENTS | SERVES 6

2 cucumbers
1/3 cup lime juice
2 tablespoons superfine sugar
1/2 cup tequila
1/2 teaspoon salt
1/8 teaspoon cayenne pepper
1 cup crushed ice

1. Peel cucumbers, cut in half lengthwise, and remove seeds with a spoon. Cut into chunks and place in blender container or food processor with remaining ingredients. Cover and blend or process until mixture is smooth and thick.

2. Serve immediately, garnished with small chili peppers and cucumber slices.

Red Sangria

Red wine sweetened with sugar and honey and spiked with lots of citrus juice makes a wonderfully refreshing drink.

INGREDIENTS | SERVES 8–10

2 oranges
1 grapefruit
2 limes
1 (750-ml) bottle red wine
1/3 cup sugar
1/3 cup honey
1 (5-ounce) can crushed pineapple
1 (16-ounce) bottle club soda, chilled

1. Juice 1 orange and cut the other into thin slices. Juice the grapefruit and 1 lime. Cut the other lime into thin slices. In large container, combine juices, fruit slices, red wine, sugar, honey, and undrained pineapple and mix well until sugar dissolves. Cover and chill for 2–4 hours.

2. When ready to serve, pour wine mixture into large pitcher or punch bowl. Slowly pour in the club soda and mix gently; serve immediately.

Strawberry Margaritas

Cantaloupe is the secret ingredient in this fabulous margarita recipe. It adds a smoothness, richness, and slight taste of honey to this delicious drink.

INGREDIENTS | SERVES 4

½ cup tequila

⅓ cup triple sec

1 (8-ounce) package frozen strawberries

½ cup chopped cantaloupe

1 cup crushed ice

½ cup simple syrup (see sidebar)

2 tablespoons lime juice

2 tablespoons lemon juice

Combine all ingredients in a blender or food processor and blend or process until mixture is smooth and thick. Pour into margarita glasses that have their rims dipped in water and sugar to coat.

How to Make Simple Syrup

To make simple syrup, combine 1 part water with 2 parts sugar in a heavy saucepan, stir well, and bring to a boil. Simmer mixture, stirring frequently, until sugar is completely dissolved. Store the syrup, covered, in the refrigerator for up to 2 weeks and use in beverages such as lemonade or margaritas.

Tequila Sunrise

This cocktail is called a "sunrise" because the grenadine, tequila, and orange juice layer in the glass so the drink looks like a bright sky at sunrise.

INGREDIENTS | SERVES 4

2 cups orange juice

1 tablespoon lemon juice

½ cup tequila

Ice cubes

Cracked ice

2 tablespoons grenadine

In a cocktail shaker, combine orange juice, lemon juice, and tequila. Add ice cubes and shake well. Strain into 4 cocktail glasses over cracked ice. Quickly pour grenadine syrup over each glass. Serve immediately.

Glossary of Mexican Food and Cooking Terms

achiote paste
a seasoning paste made from the seed of the achiote tree

adobado or adobo
Mexican barbecue sauce

agua fresca
literally "fresh water"; refers to nonalcoholic teas and juices

ajo
garlic

ancho
a dried poblano chili

añejo
aged, as in cheese or liquor

arroz
rice

asado
roasted or grilled

blanco
white

brazo de reina
literally "queen's arm"; a type of large tamale

cajeta
caramel

caldo
broth

canela
cinnamon

carne
meat, usually beef

carnitas
meat chunks

cascabel
a small, red dried chili pepper

ceviche
a dish of small fish pieces marinated in lime juice

chayote
a small, green squash

chilaca
a long, thin, dark-brown chili pepper

chili negro
a dried chilaca pepper

chipotle
a smoked and dried jalapeño chili pepper

comal
a round, flat, cast-iron griddle (used for cooking tortillas)

comino
cumin

crema
Mexican sour cream

enchilada
stuffed and rolled tortillas with chili sauce

enfrijolada
stuffed and rolled tortillas in bean sauce

enmolada
stuffed and rolled tortillas in mole sauce

epazote
a wild herb used as a seasoning

escabèche
a sweet and sour marinade

fresco
fresh

frijoles
beans

frijoles refritos
refried beans

fuerte
a type of avocado

habanero
a type of chili pepper

huevos
eggs

jalapeño
a type of chili pepper

jicama
a white root vegetable usually eaten raw

lima
lime

limón
lemon

maiz
corn

manzanilla
a small green olive

masa
dough (usually corn)

mesa
table

molcajete y tejolote
a mortar and pestle; used to grind spices

mole
a traditional stew or sauce made with a variation of spices, nuts, chili peppers, and Mexican chocolate

morita
a small dried chili

naranja agria
a type of orange from the Yucatán

nopale
cactus paddle

nopalitos
"baby" cactus paddles

pasilla
a dried chilaca chili pepper

pepita
pumpkin seed

pescado
fish

picadillo
ground meat seasoned with spices, nuts, peppers, and sometimes fruit

picholines
large, green olives

pico de gallo
a salsa made of fresh tomatoes

poblano
a type of green chili pepper

pollo
chicken

posole
a traditional stew with meat and hominy

raja
a roasted chili pepper strip

ranchero
ranch or country-style

salsa
sauce or dip

sandía
watermelon

seco
dry

serrano
a small, green chili

sopa
soup

tomatillo
a small, green fruit that looks like a tomato

torta
sandwich

verde
green

Index

Note: Page numbers in **bold** indicate recipe category lists.